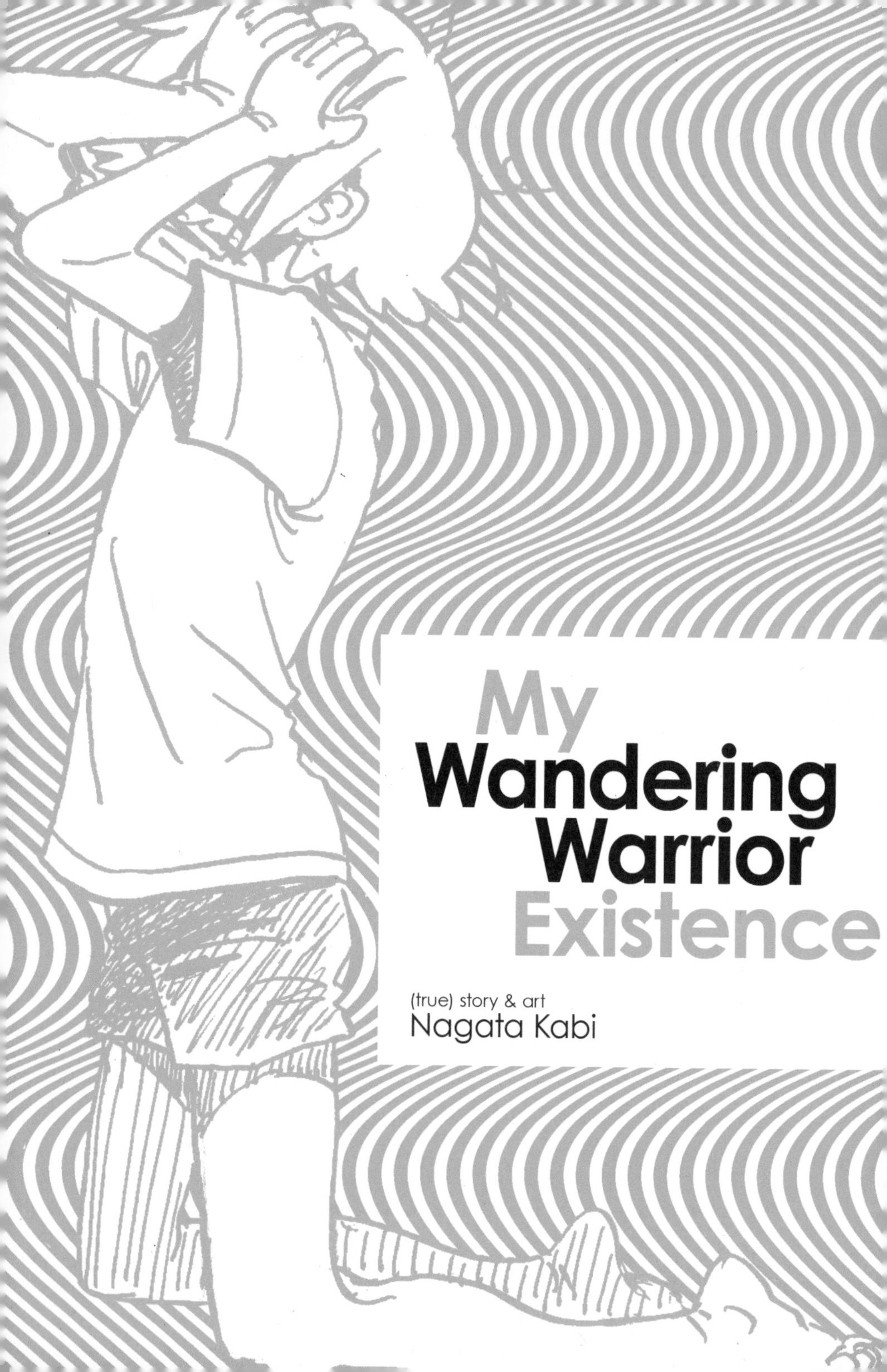

My Wandering Warrior Existence

(true) story & art
Nagata Kabi

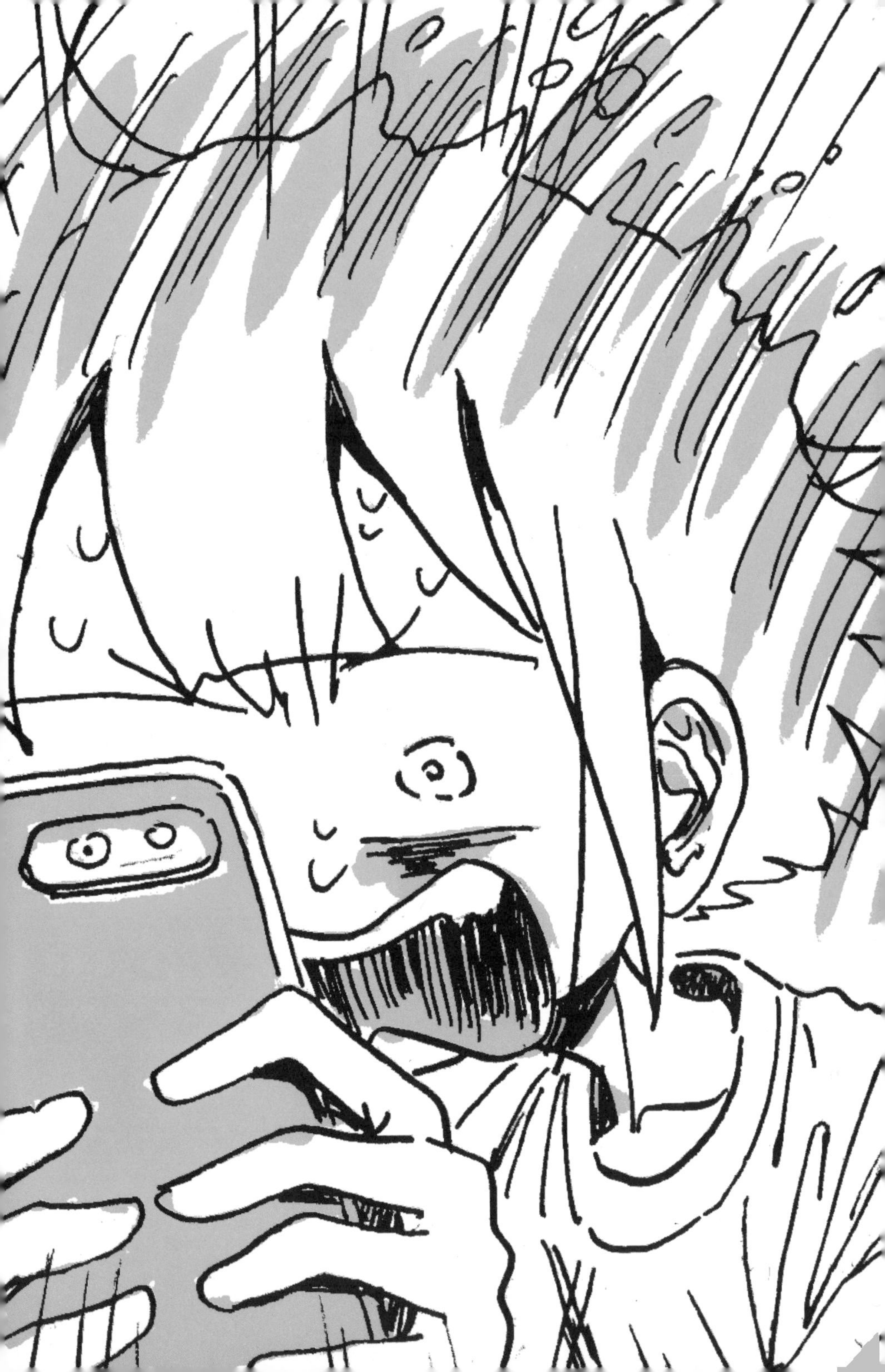

CONTENTS

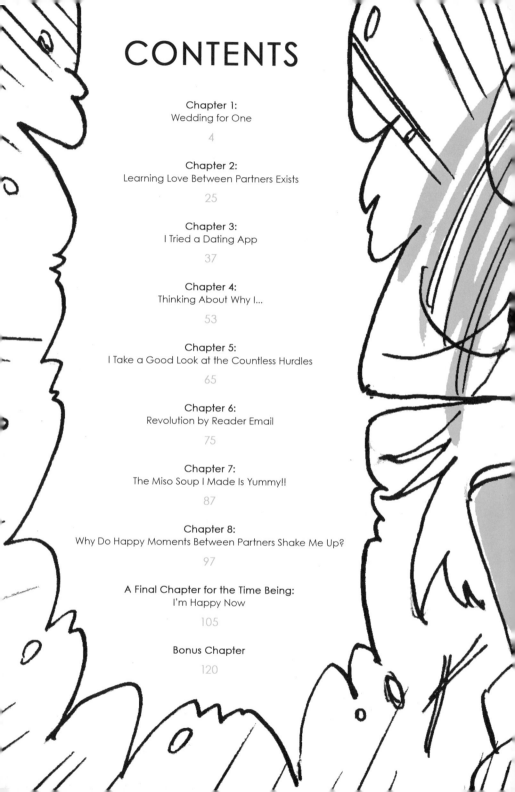

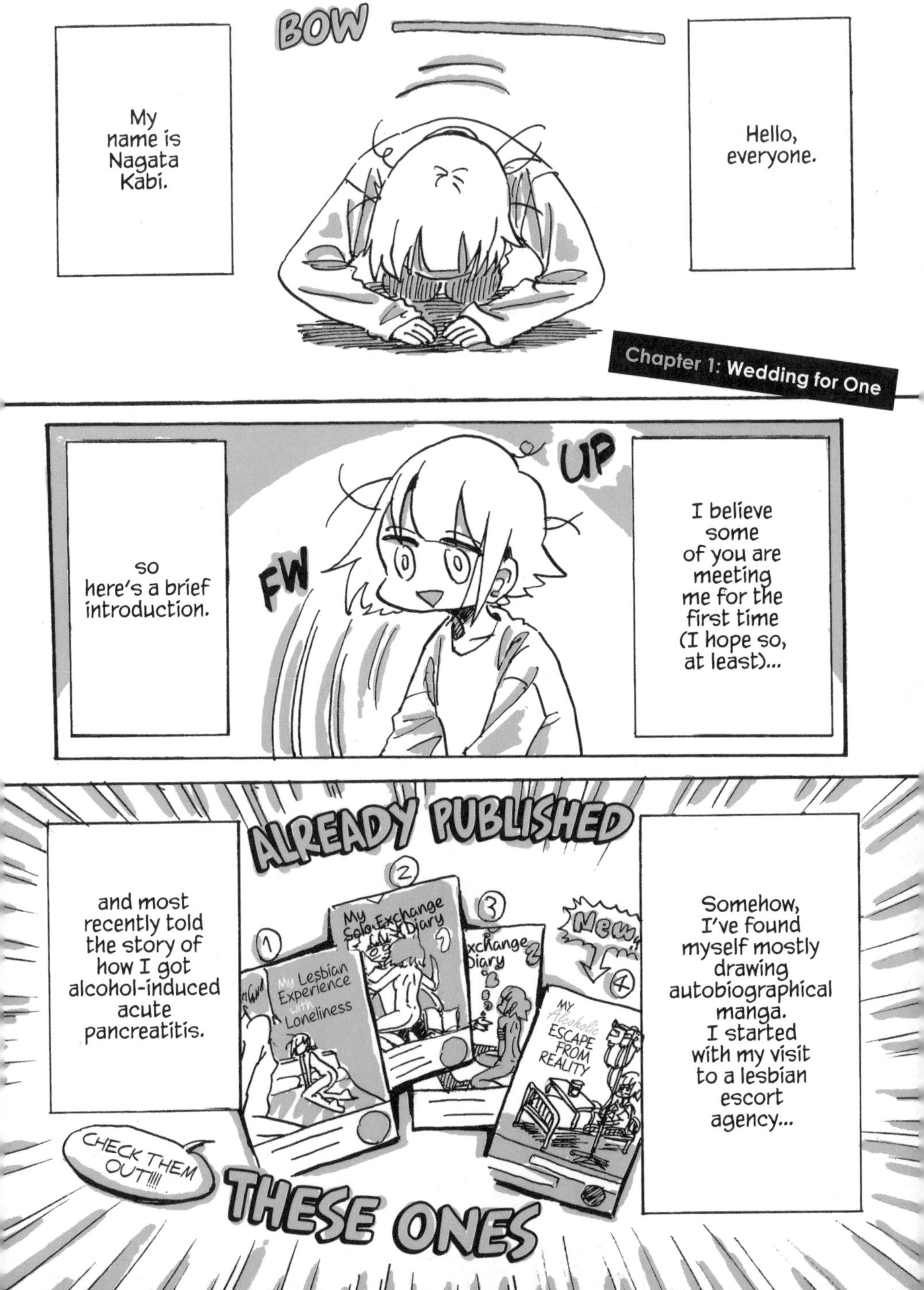

Hello, everyone.
BOW
My name is Nagata Kabi.
Chapter 1: Wedding for One
I believe some of you are meeting me for the first time (I hope so, at least)...
UP
FW
so here's a brief introduction.
Somehow, I've found myself mostly drawing autobiographical manga. I started with my visit to a lesbian escort agency...
ALREADY PUBLISHED
New
1
My Lesbian Experience with Loneliness
2
My Solo Exchange Diary
3
Exchange Diary 2
4
My Alcoholic Escape from Reality
and most recently told the story of how I got alcohol-induced acute pancreatitis.
CHECK THEM OUT!!!!
THESE ONES

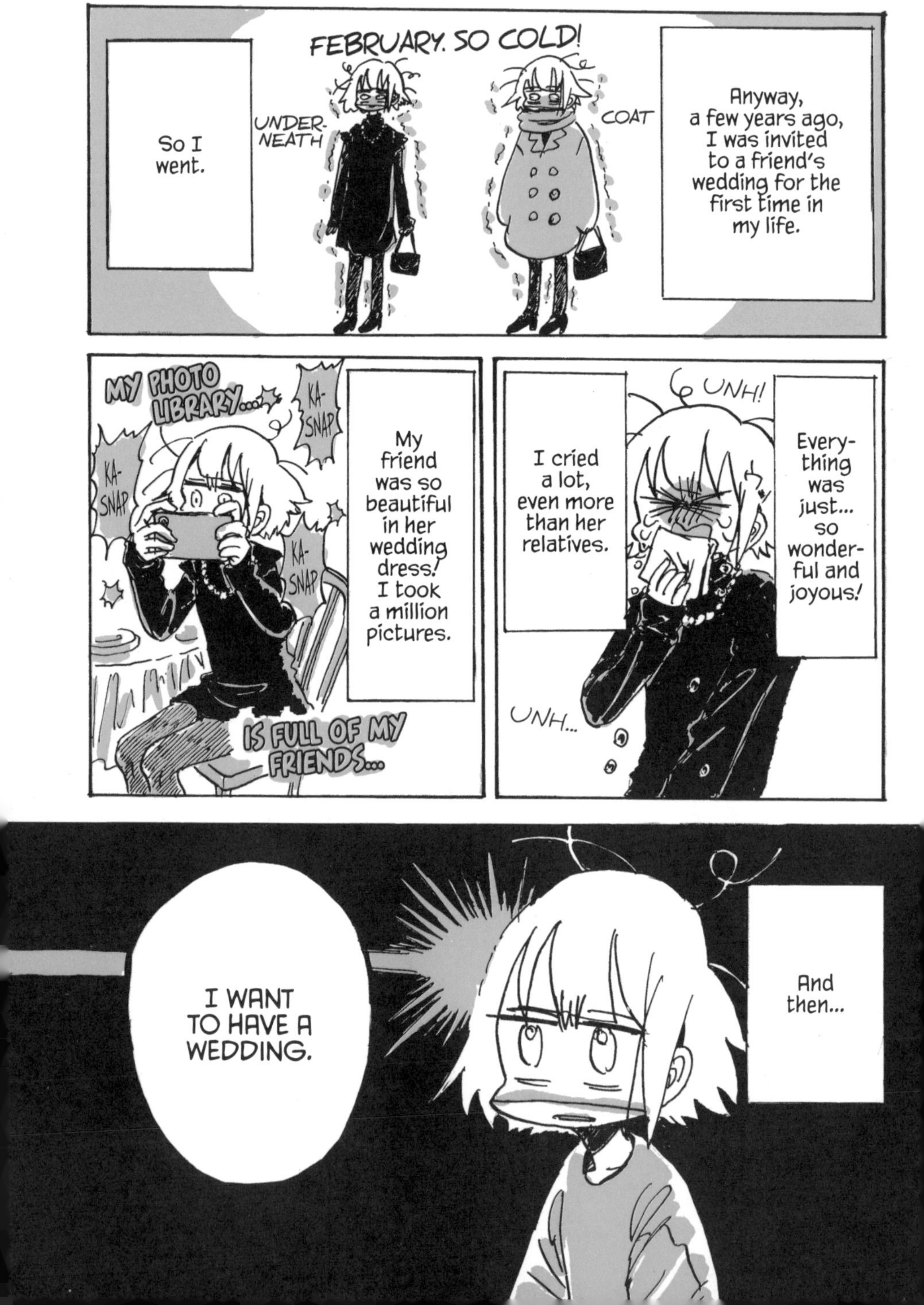
Anyway, a few years ago, I was invited to a friend's wedding for the first time in my life.
FEBRUARY. SO COLD!
COAT
UNDER-NEATH
So I went.
Every-thing was just... so wonder-ful and joyous!
UNH!
I cried a lot, even more than her relatives.
UNH...
My friend was so beautiful in her wedding dress! I took a million pictures.
KA-SNAP
MY PHOTO LIBRARY...
KA-SNAP
KA-SNAP
IS FULL OF MY FRIENDS...
And then...
I WANT TO HAVE A WEDDING.

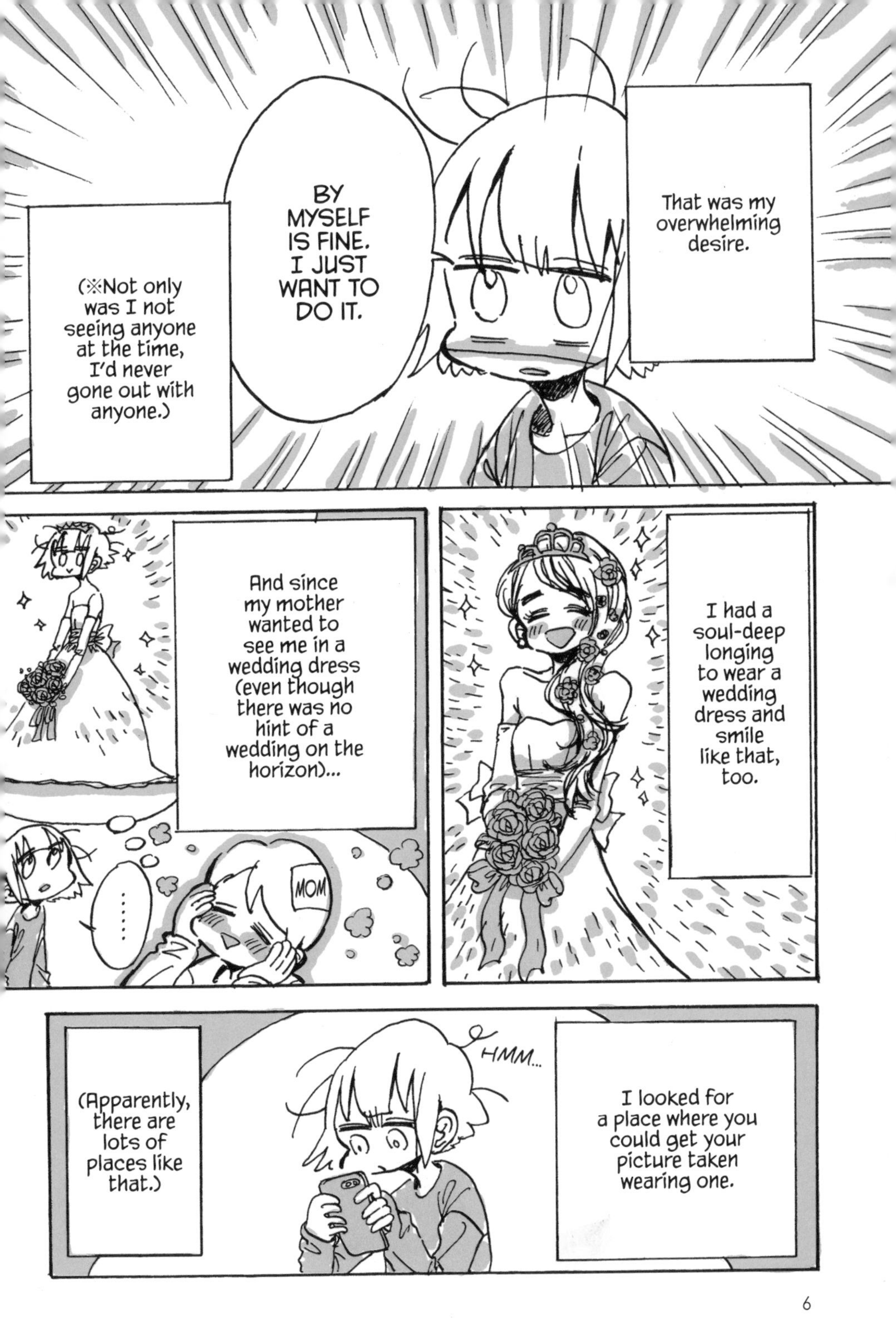

That was my overwhelming desire.
BY MYSELF IS FINE. I JUST WANT TO DO IT.
(※Not only was I not seeing anyone at the time, I'd never gone out with anyone.)
I had a soul-deep longing to wear a wedding dress and smile like that, too.
And since my mother wanted to see me in a wedding dress (even though there was no hint of a wedding on the horizon)...
MOM
......
I looked for a place where you could get your picture taken wearing one.
HMM...
(Apparently, there are lots of places like that.)

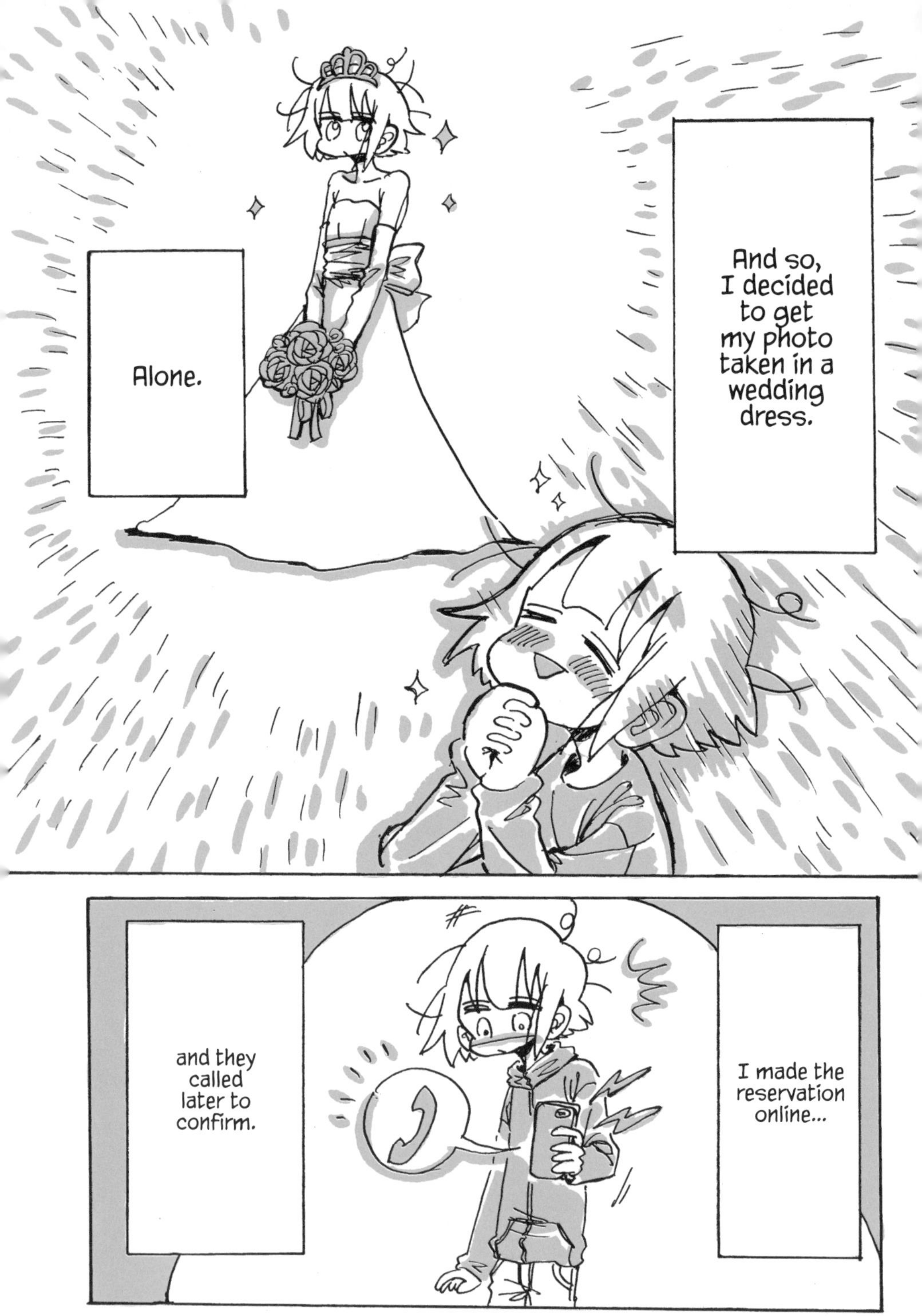
And so, I decided to get my photo taken in a wedding dress.
Alone.
I made the reservation online...
and they called later to confirm.

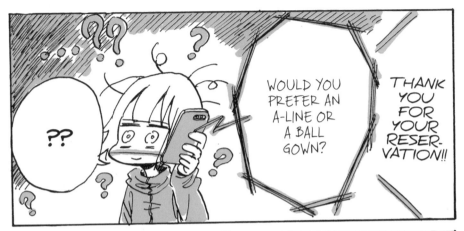

??

WOULD YOU PREFER AN A-LINE OR A BALL GOWN?

THANK YOU FOR YOUR RESERVATION!!

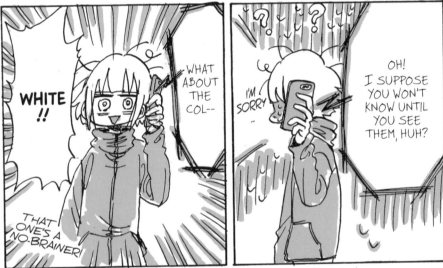

WHITE!!

·WHAT ABOUT THE COL--

THAT ONE'S A NO-BRAINER!

I'M SORRY...

OH! I SUPPOSE YOU WON'T KNOW UNTIL YOU SEE THEM, HUH?

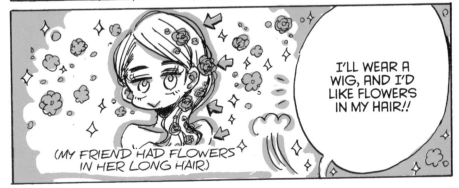

I'LL WEAR A WIG, AND I'D LIKE FLOWERS IN MY HAIR!!

(MY FRIEND HAD FLOWERS IN HER LONG HAIR.)

8

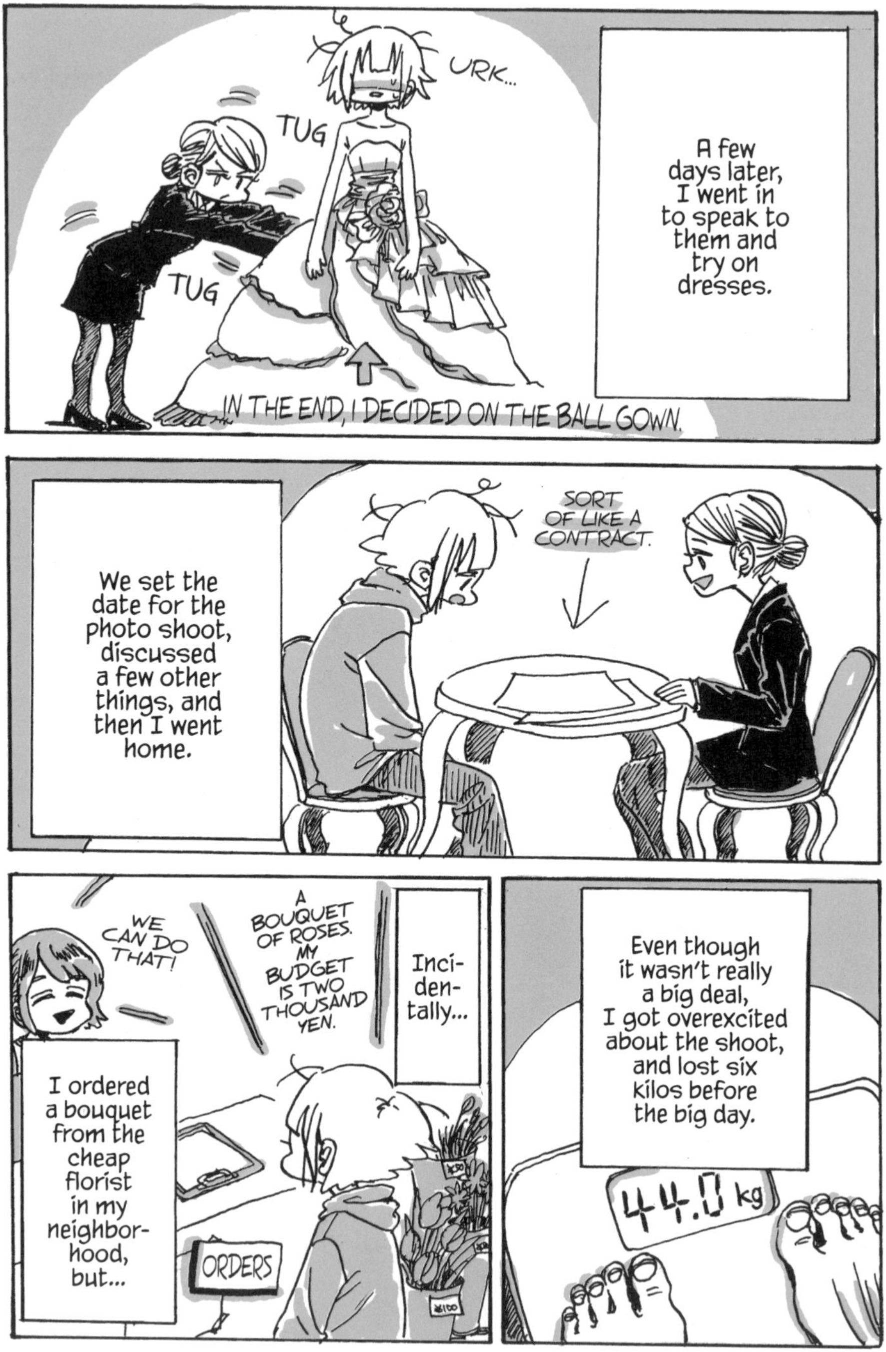
A few days later, I went in to speak to them and try on dresses.
URK...
TUG
TUG
IN THE END, I DECIDED ON THE BALL GOWN.
SORT OF LIKE A CONTRACT.
We set the date for the photo shoot, discussed a few other things, and then I went home.
Even though it wasn't really a big deal, I got overexcited about the shoot, and lost six kilos before the big day.
44.0 kg
Inci-den-tally...
A BOUQUET OF ROSES. MY BUDGET IS TWO THOUSAND YEN.
WE CAN DO THAT!
I ordered a bouquet from the cheap florist in my neighbor-hood, but...
ORDERS

※Note: 44kg = 97lbs.

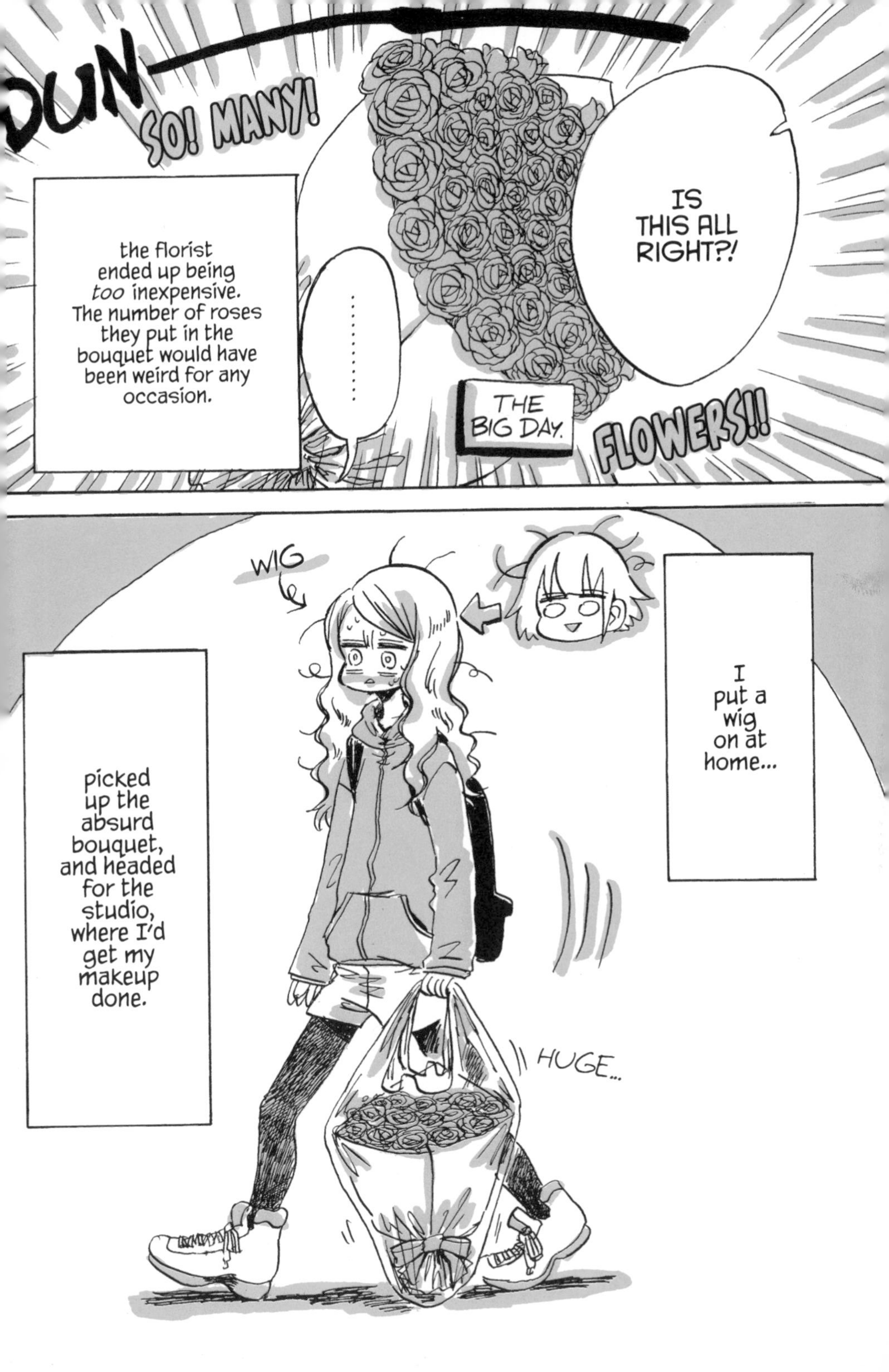
IS THIS ALL RIGHT?!
FLOWERS!!
THE BIG DAY.
SO! MANY!
DUN
......
the florist ended up being *too* inexpensive. The number of roses they put in the bouquet would have been weird for any occasion.
I put a wig on at home...
WIG
HUGE...
picked up the absurd bouquet, and headed for the studio, where I'd get my makeup done.

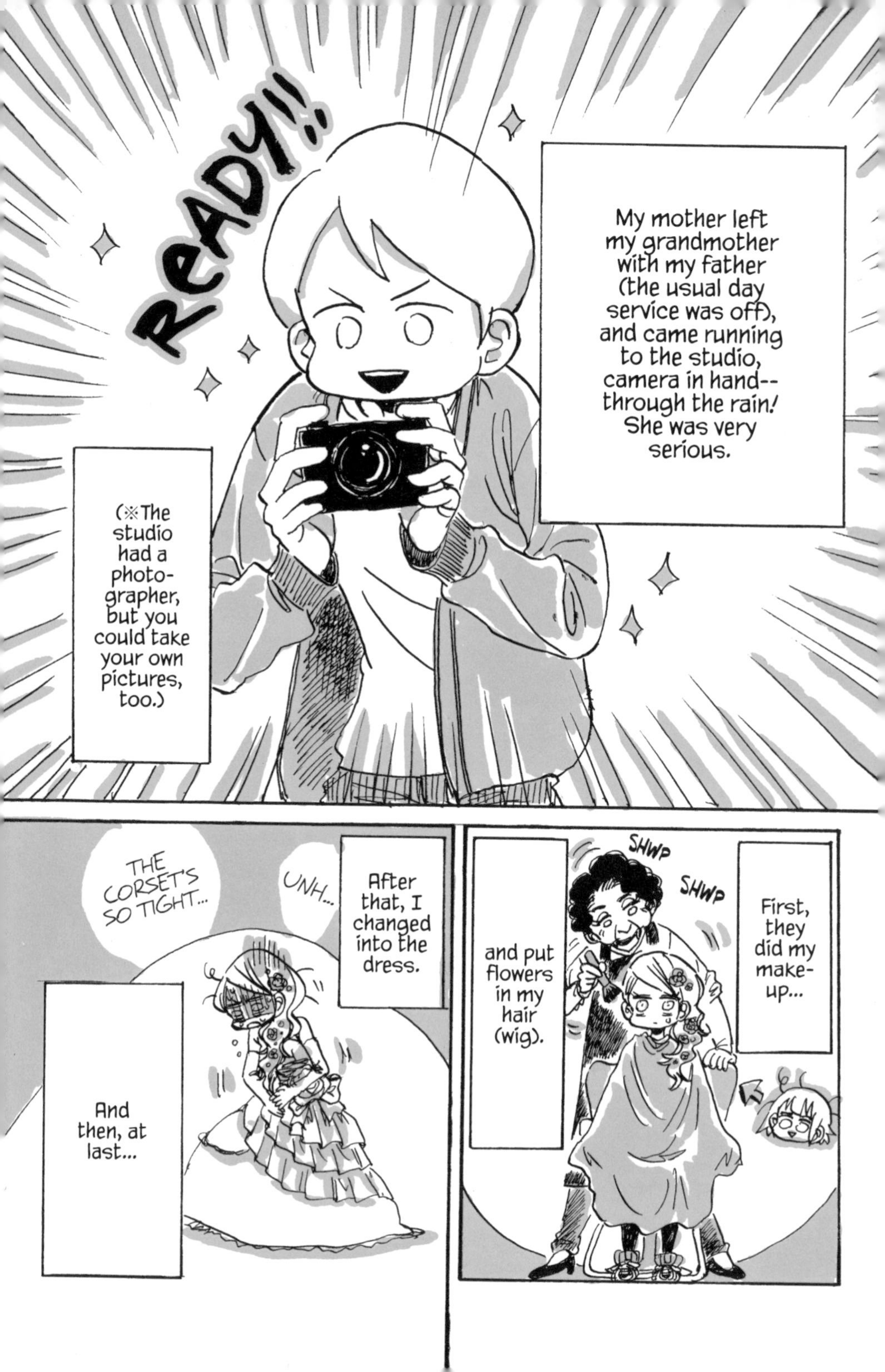
My mother left my grandmother with my father (the usual day service was off), and came running to the studio, camera in hand-- through the rain! She was very serious.
READY!!
(※The studio had a photo-grapher, but you could take your own pictures, too.)
First, they did my make-up...
SHWP
SHWP
and put flowers in my hair (wig).
After that, I changed into the dress.
UNH...
THE CORSET'S SO TIGHT...
And then, at last...

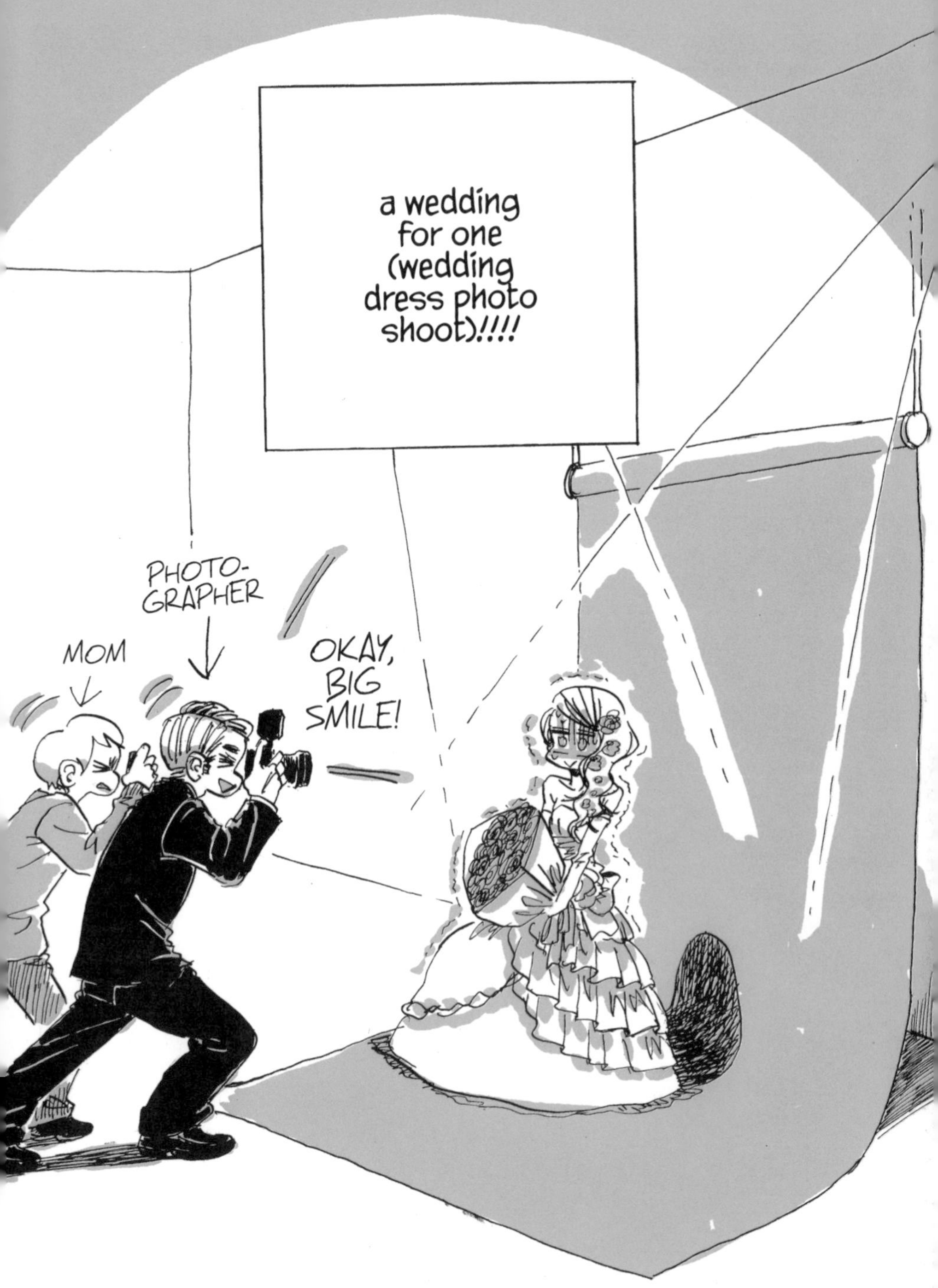
a wedding for one (wedding dress photo shoot)!!!!
OKAY, BIG SMILE!
PHOTO-GRAPHER
MOM

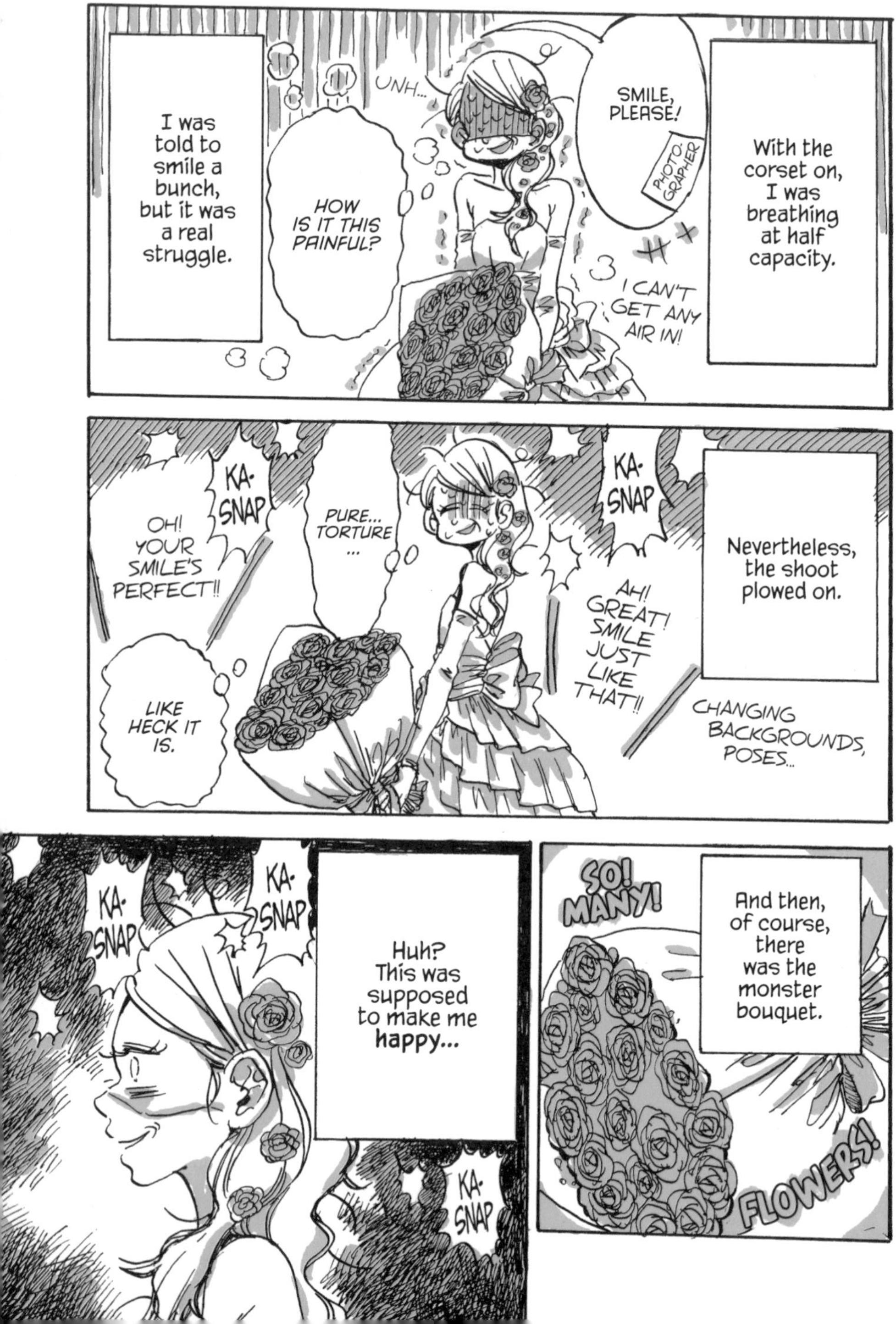
With the corset on, I was breathing at half capacity.
SMILE, PLEASE!
PHOTOGRAPHER
I CAN'T GET ANY AIR IN!
UNH...
HOW IS IT THIS PAINFUL?
I was told to smile a bunch, but it was a real struggle.
Nevertheless, the shoot plowed on.
CHANGING BACKGROUNDS, POSES...
KA-SNAP
AH! GREAT! SMILE JUST LIKE THAT!!
PURE... TORTURE ...
KA-SNAP
OH! YOUR SMILE'S PERFECT!!
LIKE HECK IT IS.
And then, of course, there was the monster bouquet.
SO! MANY!
FLOWERS!
KA-SNAP
Huh? This was supposed to make me **happy**...
KA-SNAP
KA-SNAP
KA-SNAP

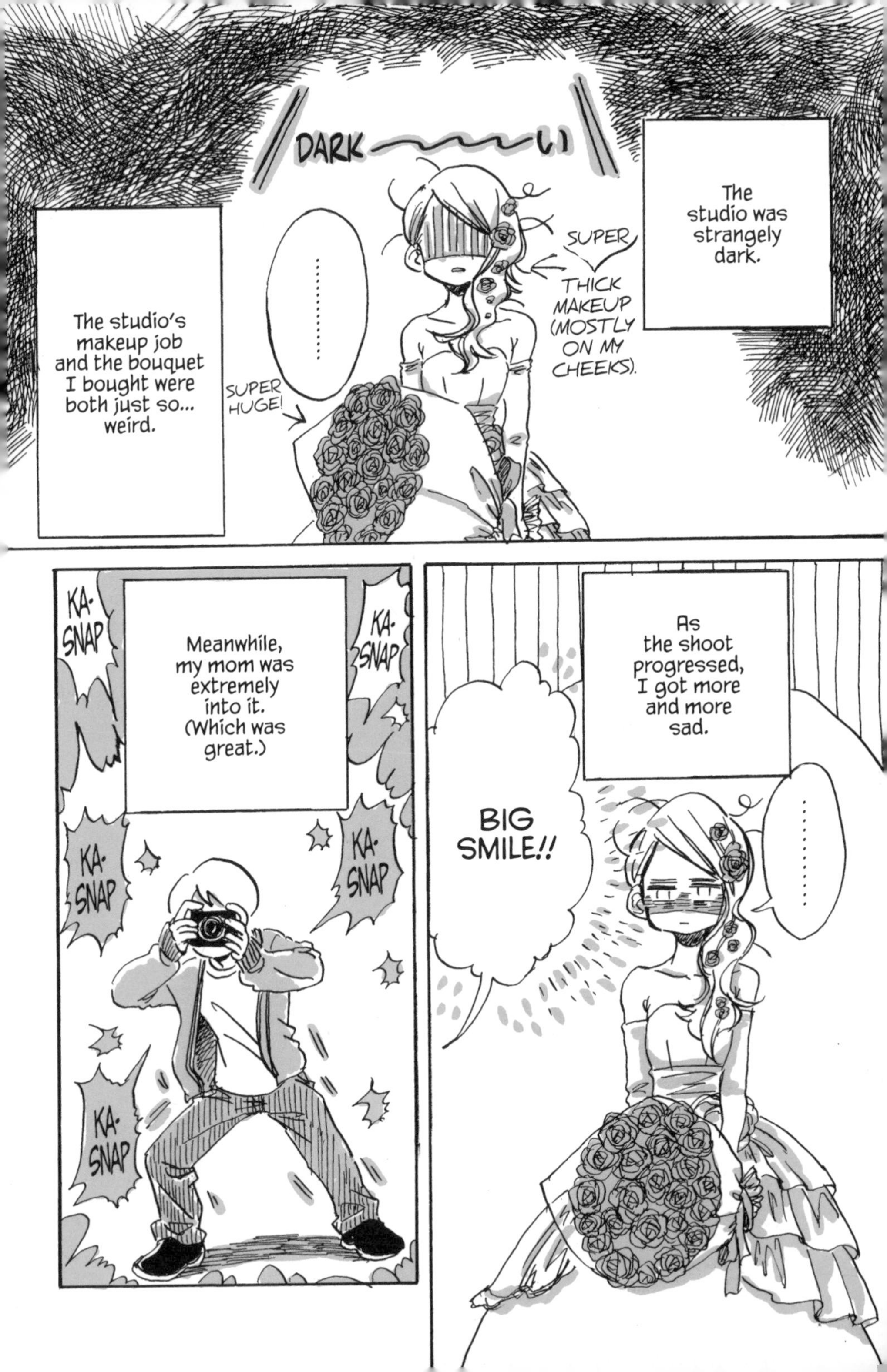
The studio was strangely dark.
DARK~~~
SUPER THICK MAKEUP (MOSTLY ON MY CHEEKS).
......
SUPER HUGE!
The studio's makeup job and the bouquet I bought were both just so... weird.
As the shoot progressed, I got more and more sad.
......
BIG SMILE!!
KA-SNAP
Meanwhile, my mom was extremely into it. (Which was great.)
KA-SNAP
KA-SNAP
KA-SNAP
KA-SNAP

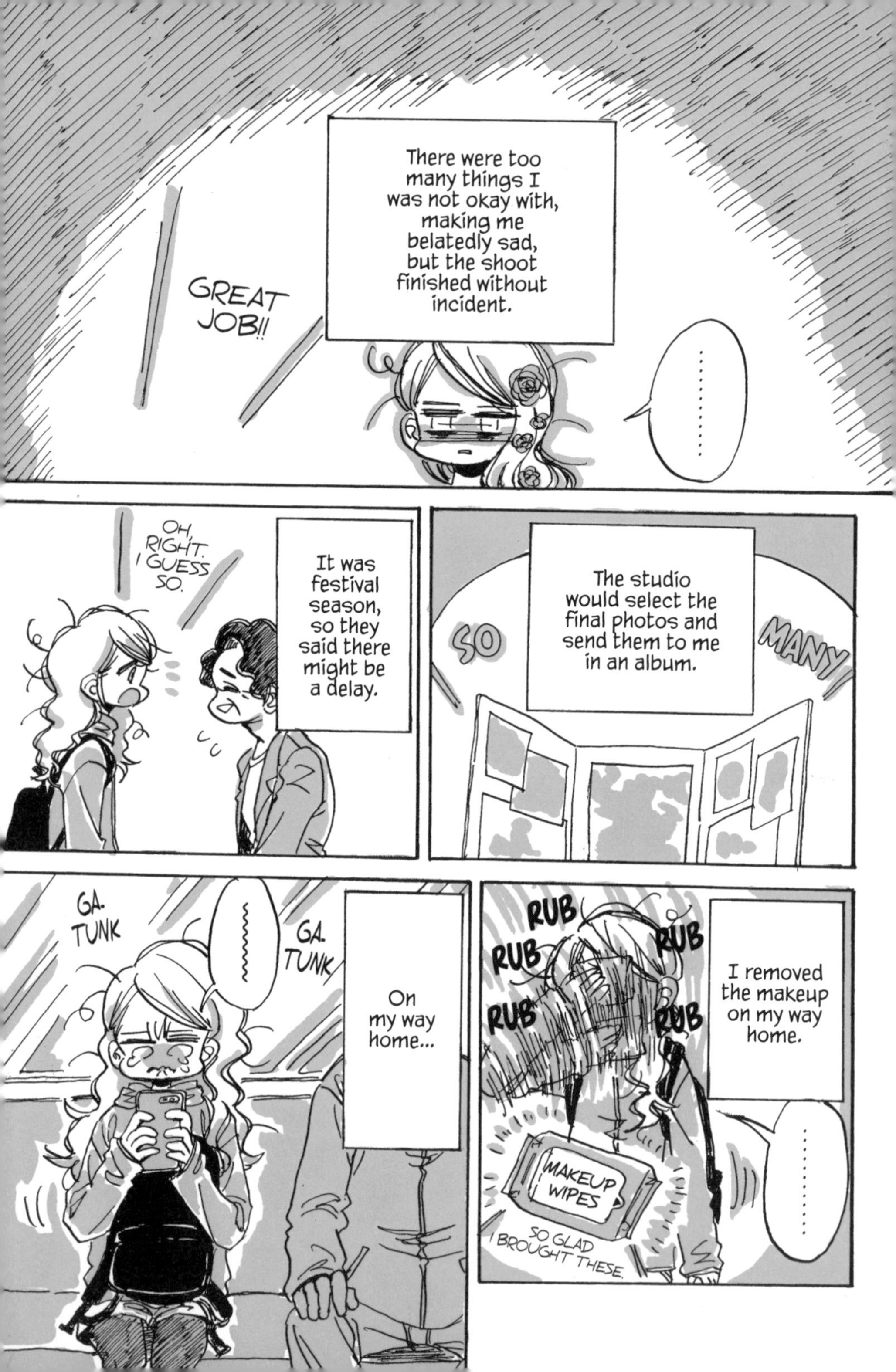
There were too many things I was not okay with, making me belatedly sad, but the shoot finished without incident.
......
GREAT JOB!!
The studio would select the final photos and send them to me in an album.
MANY
SO
It was festival season, so they said there might be a delay.
OH, RIGHT. I GUESS SO.
I removed the makeup on my way home.
RUB
RUB
RUB
RUB
RUB
......
MAKEUP WIPES
SO GLAD I BROUGHT THESE.
On my way home...
GA. TUNK
GA. TUNK

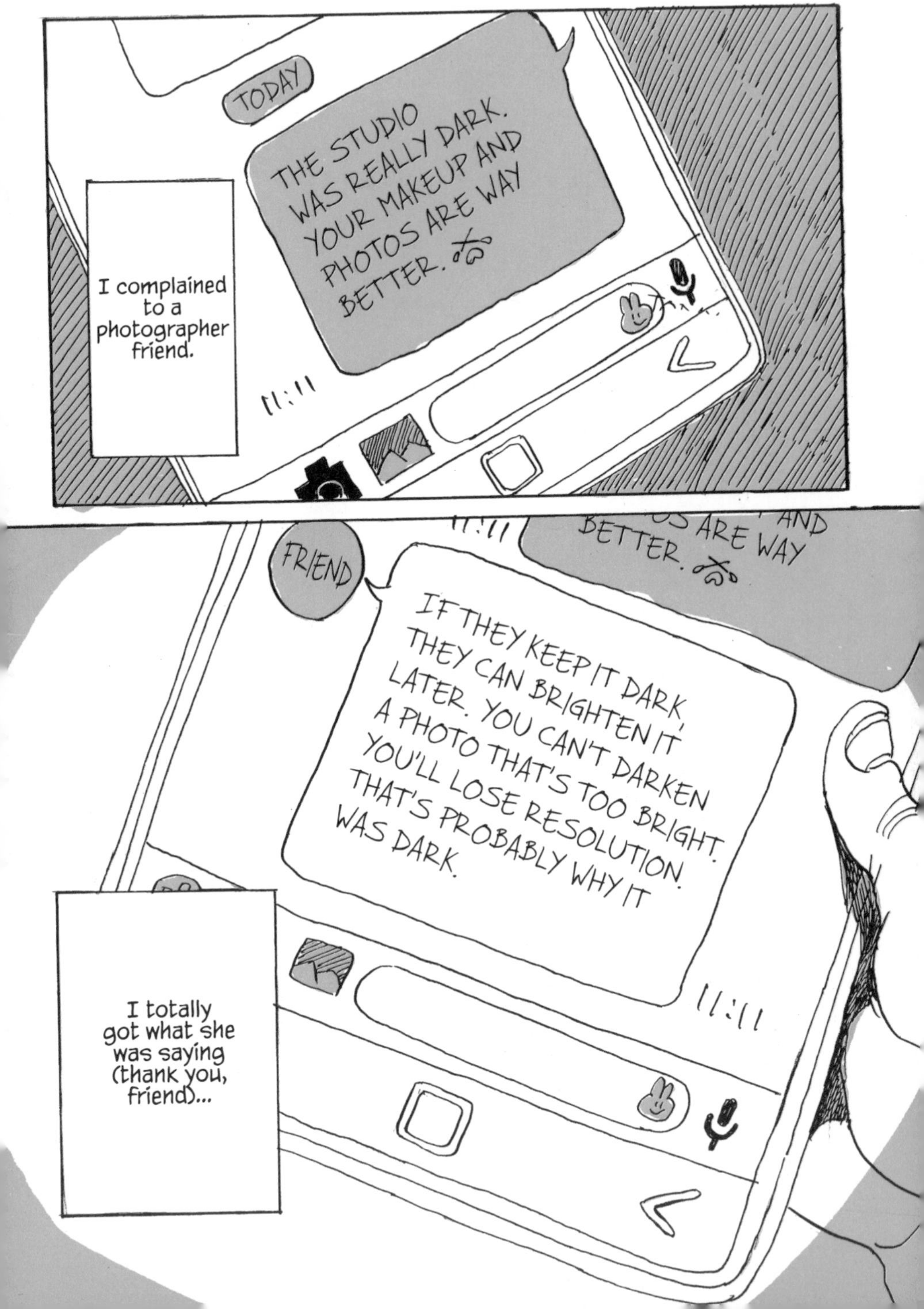
TODAY
THE STUDIO WAS REALLY DARK. YOUR MAKEUP AND PHOTOS ARE WAY BETTER.
I complained to a photographer friend.
FRIEND
IF THEY KEEP IT DARK, THEY CAN BRIGHTEN IT LATER. YOU CAN'T DARKEN A PHOTO THAT'S TOO BRIGHT. YOU'LL LOSE RESOLUTION. THAT'S PROBABLY WHY IT WAS DARK.
I totally got what she was saying (thank you, friend)...

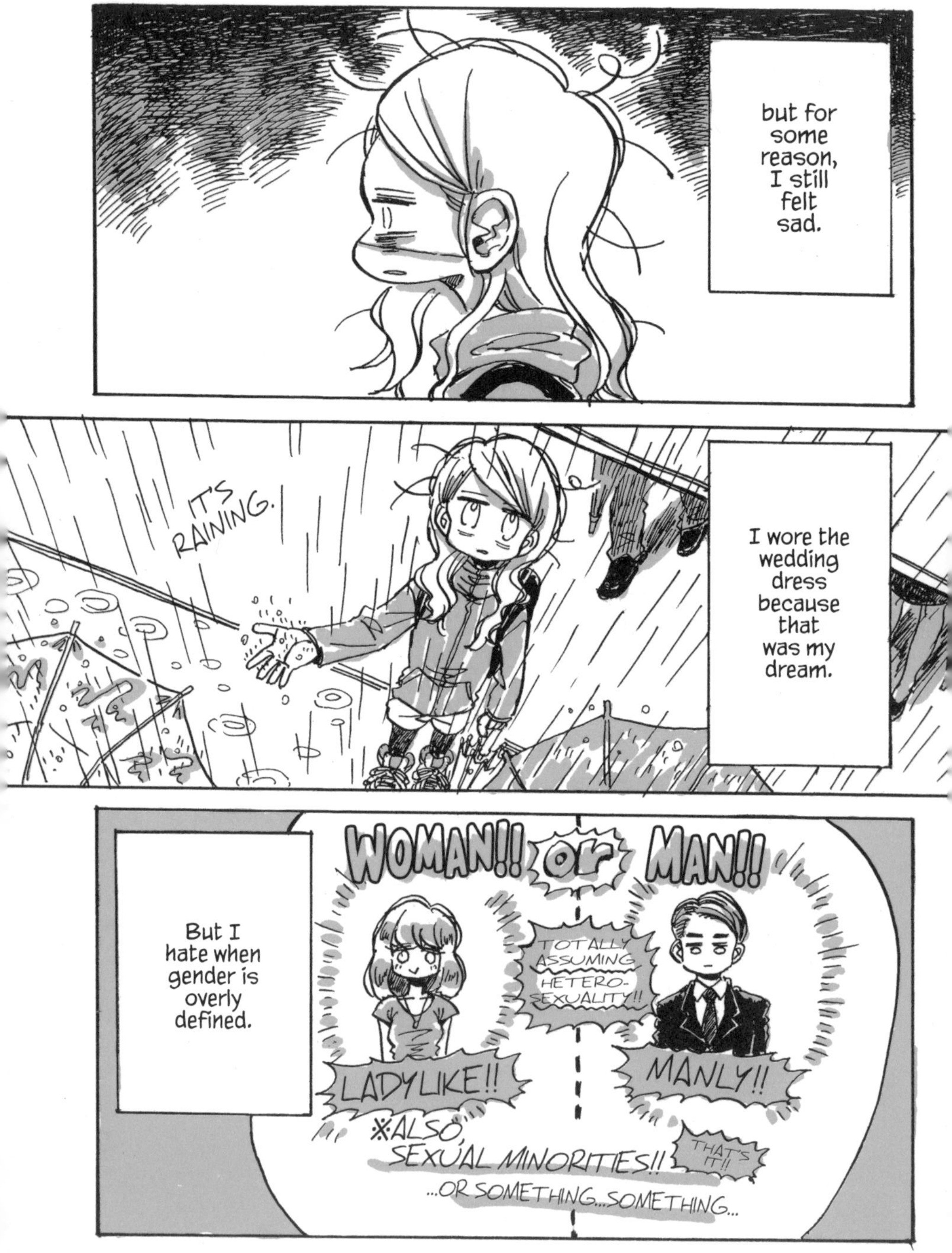
but for some reason, I still felt sad.
I wore the wedding dress because that was my dream.
IT'S RAINING.
WOMAN!! or MAN!!
TOTALLY ASSUMING HETERO-SEXUALITY!!
MANLY!!
LADYLIKE!!
But I hate when gender is overly defined.
THAT'S IT!!
※ALSO, SEXUAL MINORITIES!!
...OR SOMETHING...SOMETHING...

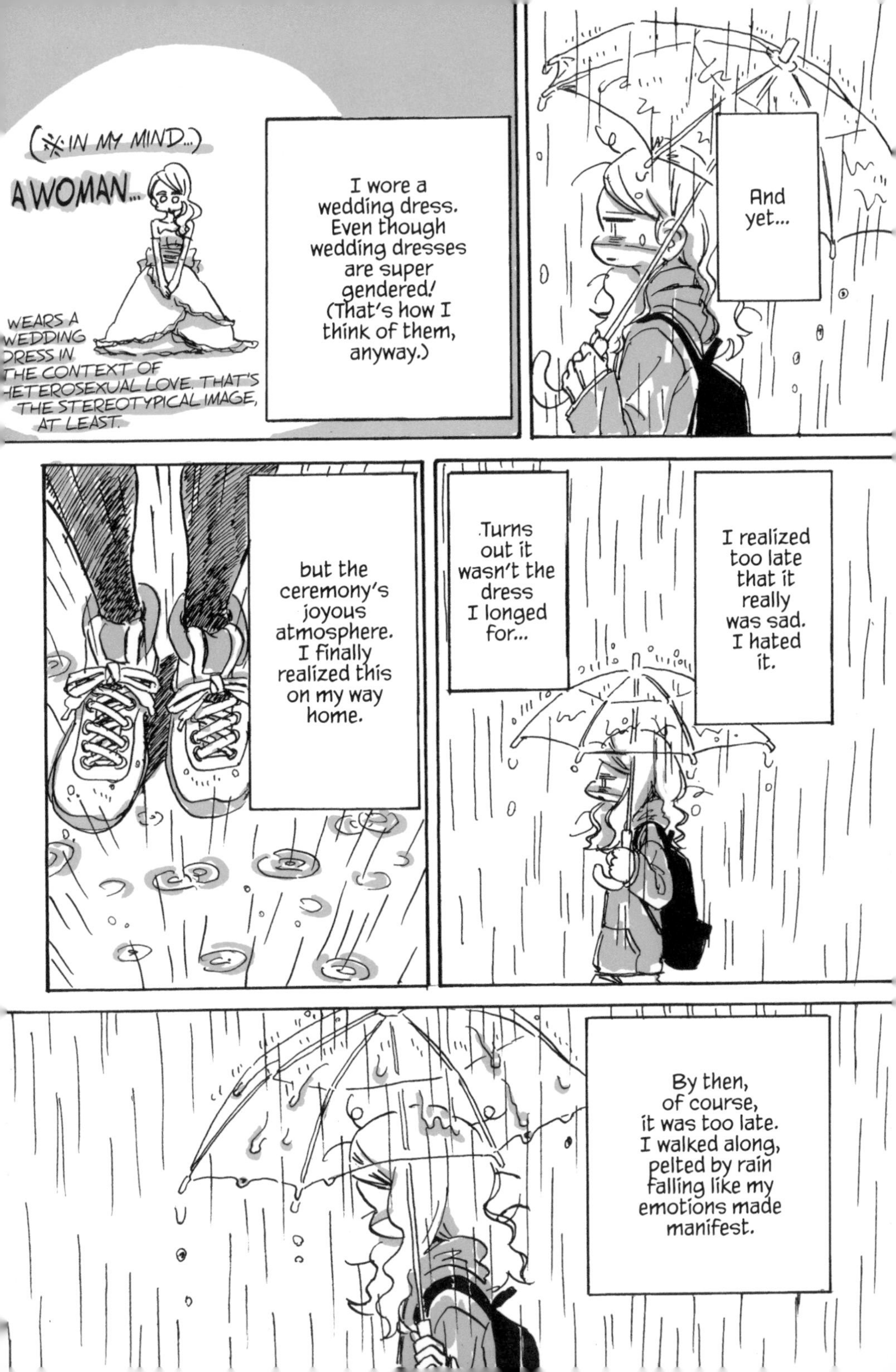

And yet...
I wore a wedding dress. Even though wedding dresses are super gendered! (That's how I think of them, anyway.)
(※IN MY MIND...)
A WOMAN...
WEARS A WEDDING DRESS IN THE CONTEXT OF HETEROSEXUAL LOVE. THAT'S THE STEREOTYPICAL IMAGE, AT LEAST.
I realized too late that it really was sad. I hated it.
Turns out it wasn't the dress I longed for...
but the ceremony's joyous atmosphere. I finally realized this on my way home.
By then, of course, it was too late. I walked along, pelted by rain falling like my emotions made manifest.

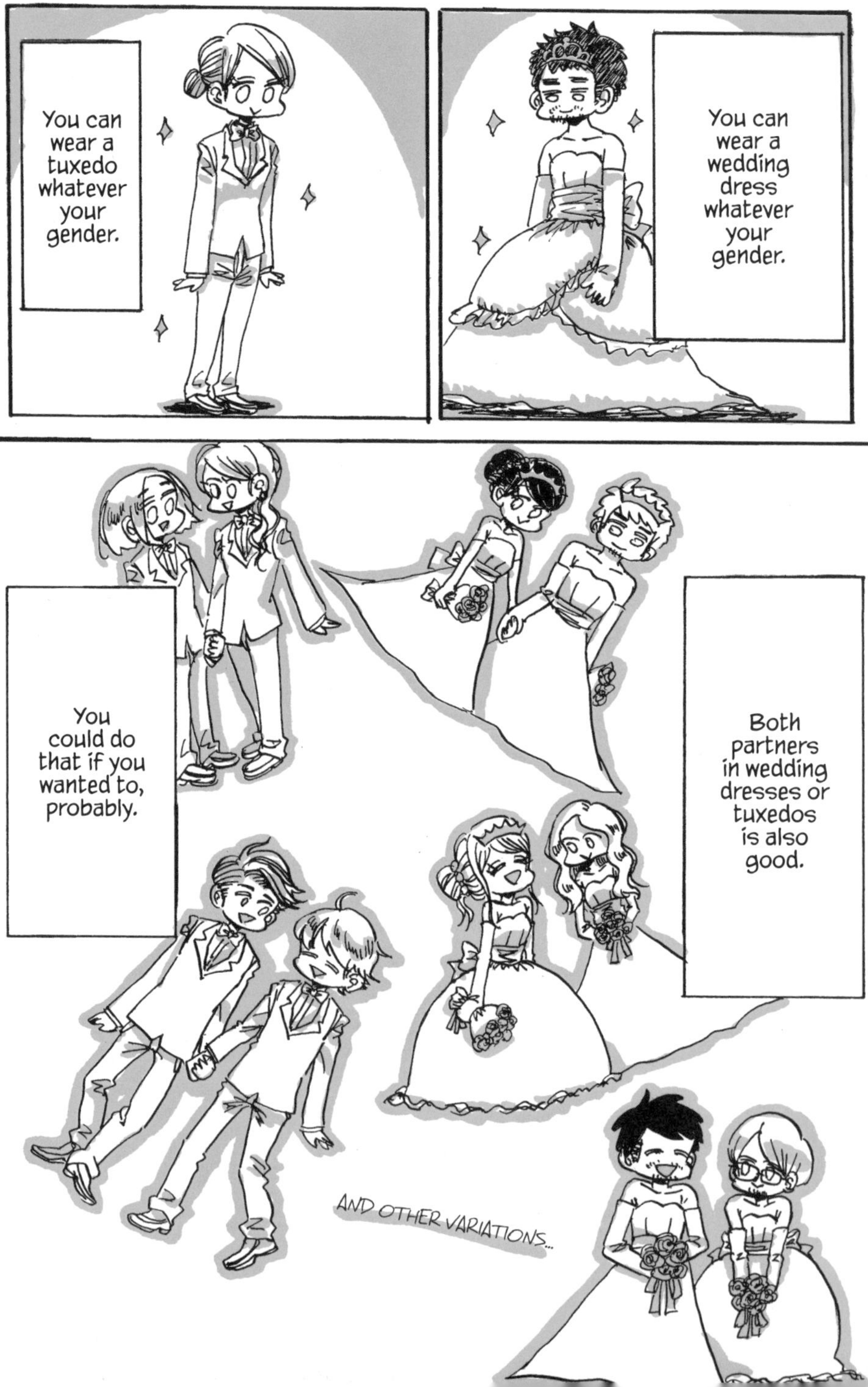
You can wear a wedding dress whatever your gender.
You can wear a tuxedo whatever your gender.
Both partners in wedding dresses or tuxedos is also good.
You could do that if you wanted to, probably.
AND OTHER VARIATIONS...

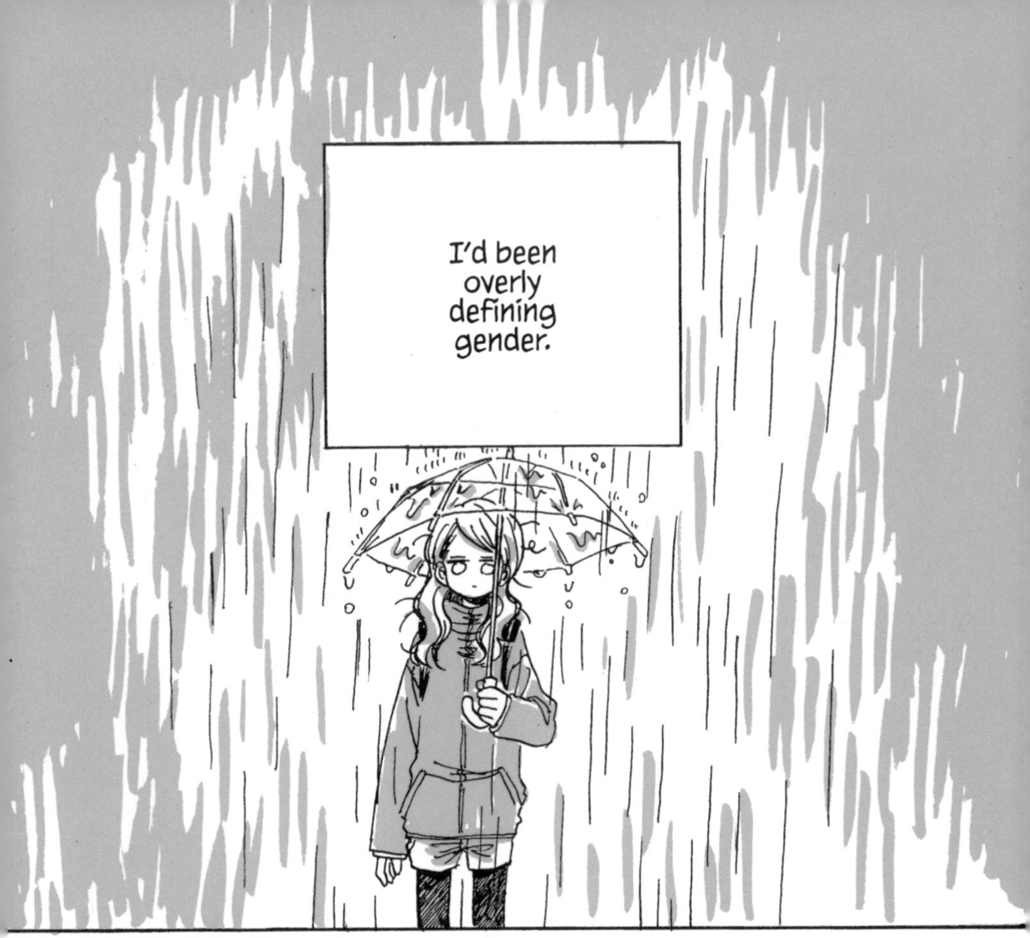
I'd been overly defining gender.

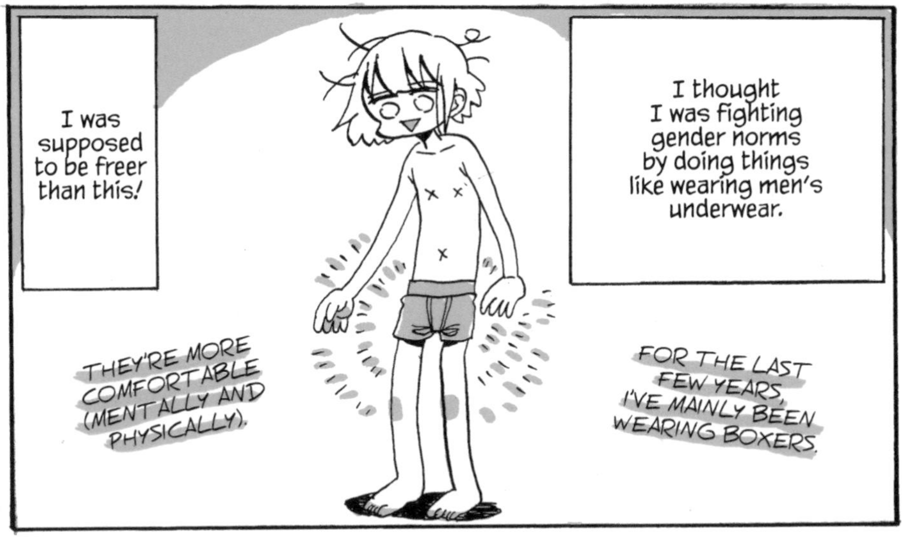
I thought I was fighting gender norms by doing things like wearing men's underwear.
I was supposed to be freer than this!
FOR THE LAST FEW YEARS, I'VE MAINLY BEEN WEARING BOXERS.
THEY'RE MORE COMFORTABLE (MENTALLY AND PHYSICALLY).

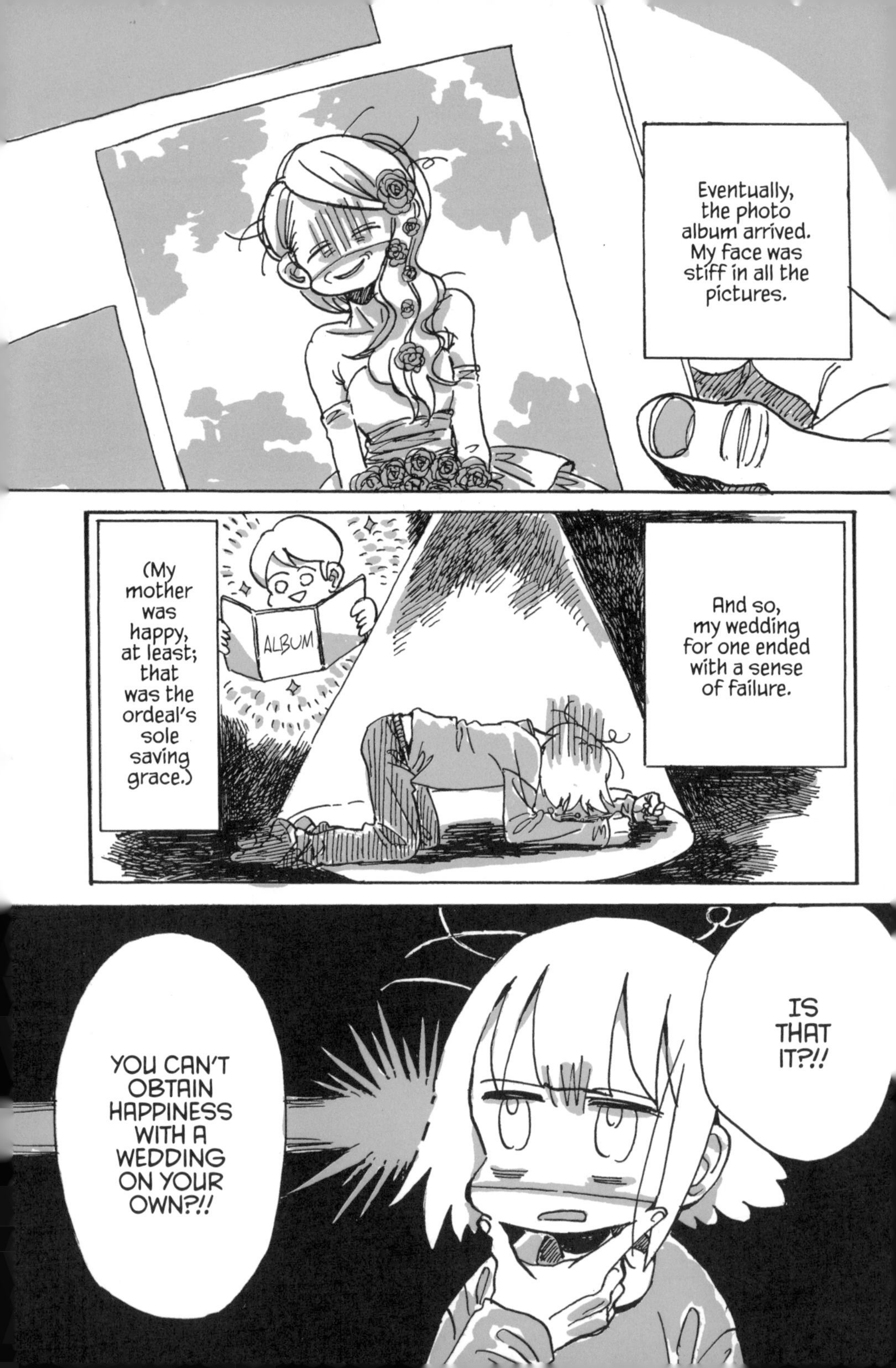
Eventually, the photo album arrived. My face was stiff in all the pictures.
And so, my wedding for one ended with a sense of failure.
(My mother was happy, at least; that was the ordeal's sole saving grace.)
ALBUM
IS THAT IT?!!
YOU CAN'T OBTAIN HAPPINESS WITH A WEDDING ON YOUR OWN?!!

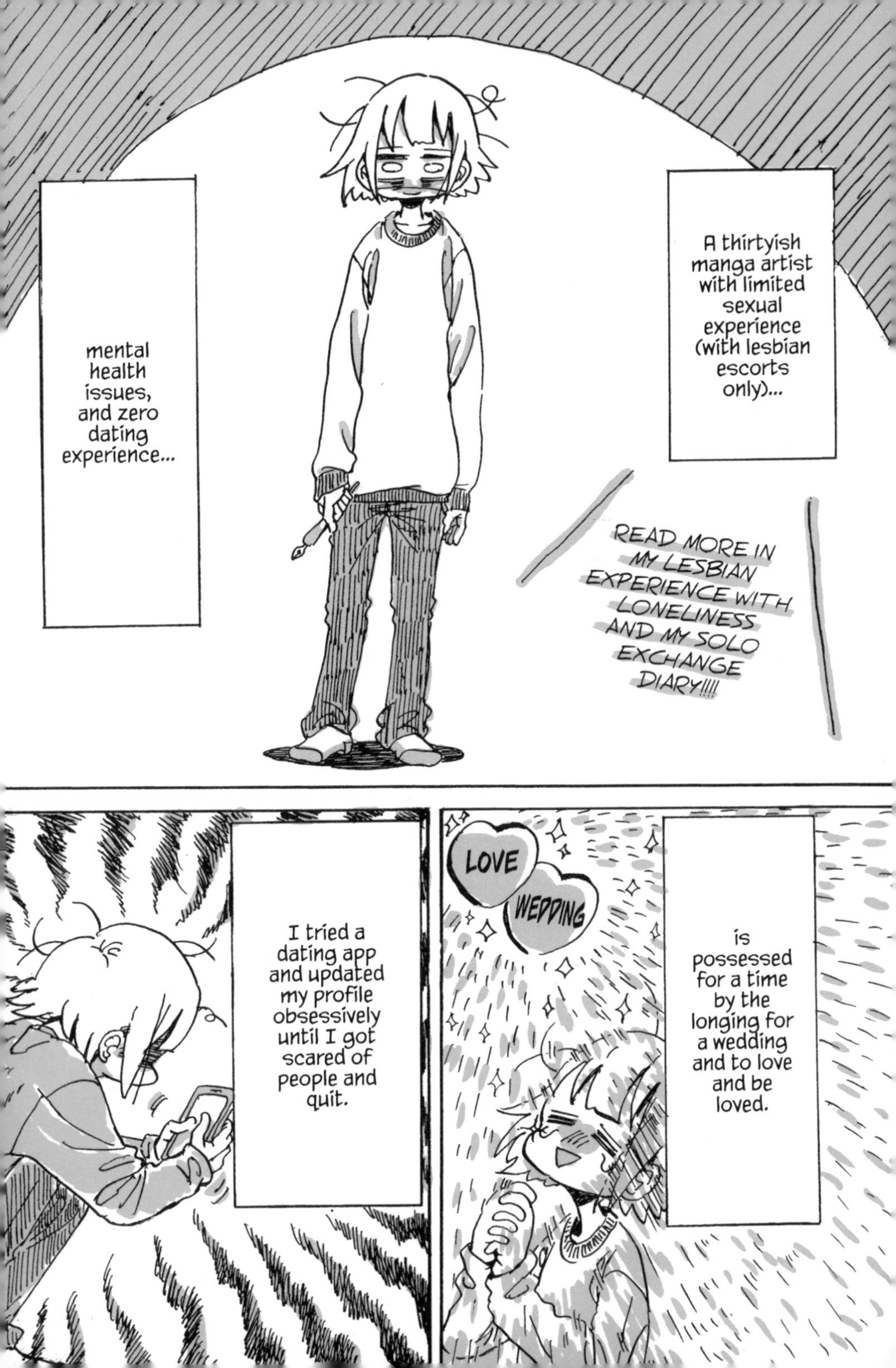
A thirtyish manga artist with limited sexual experience (with lesbian escorts only)...
mental health issues, and zero dating experience...
READ MORE IN MY LESBIAN EXPERIENCE WITH LONELINESS AND MY SOLO EXCHANGE DIARY!!!!
LOVE
WEDDING
is possessed for a time by the longing for a wedding and to love and be loved.
I tried a dating app and updated my profile obsessively until I got scared of people and quit.

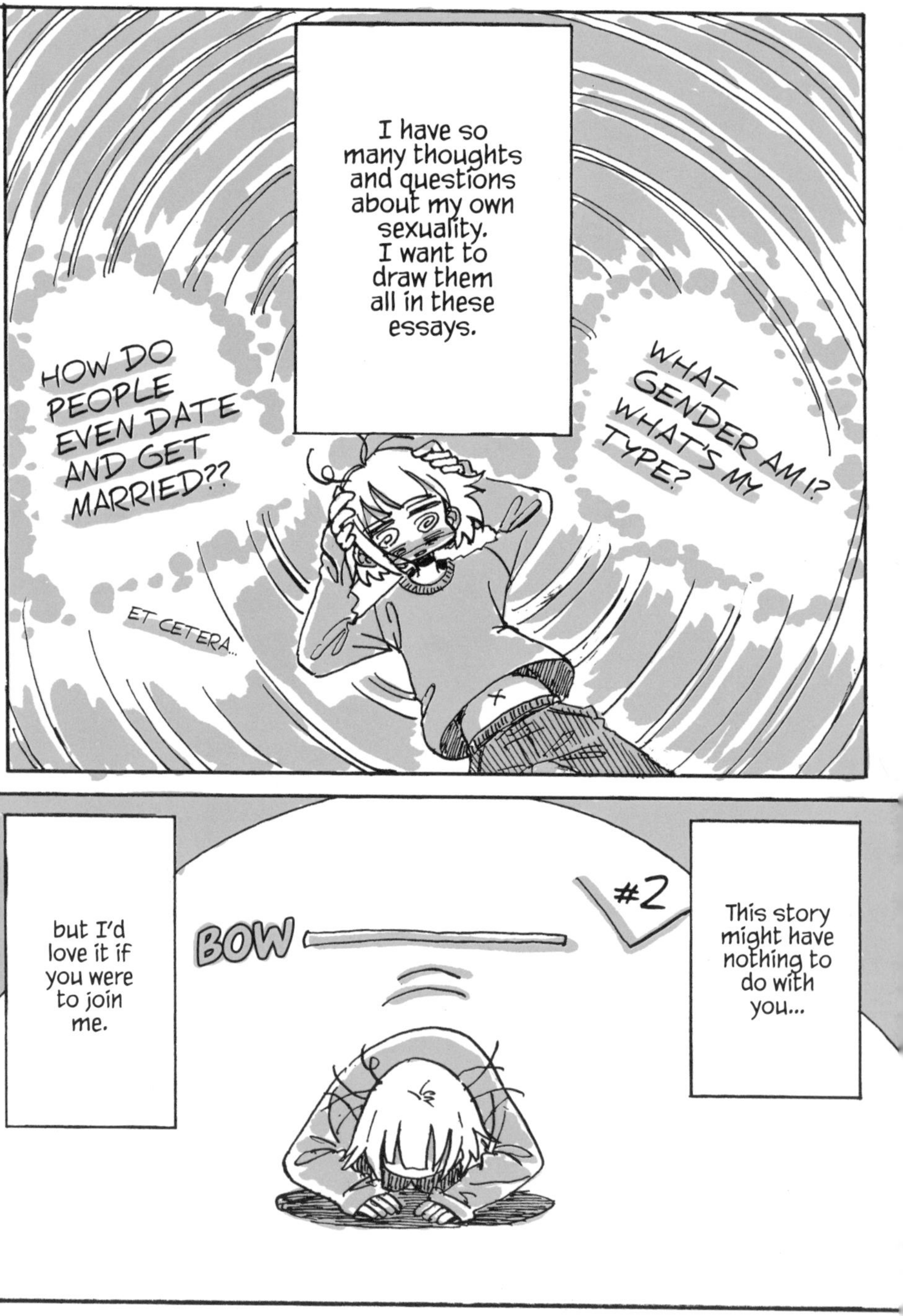
I have so many thoughts and questions about my own sexuality. I want to draw them all in these essays.
WHAT GENDER AM I? WHAT'S MY TYPE?
HOW DO PEOPLE EVEN DATE AND GET MARRIED??
ET CETERA...
This story might have nothing to do with you...
#2
BOW
but I'd love it if you were to join me.

Chapter 1/END

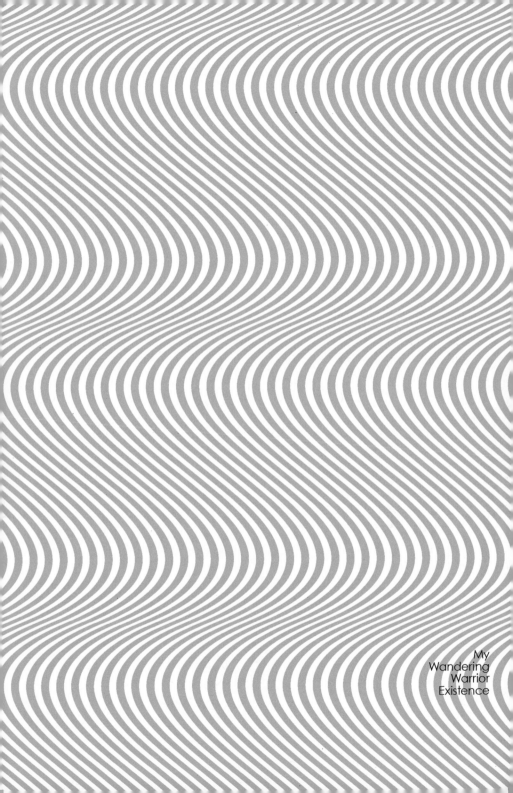

My
Wandering
Warrior
Existence

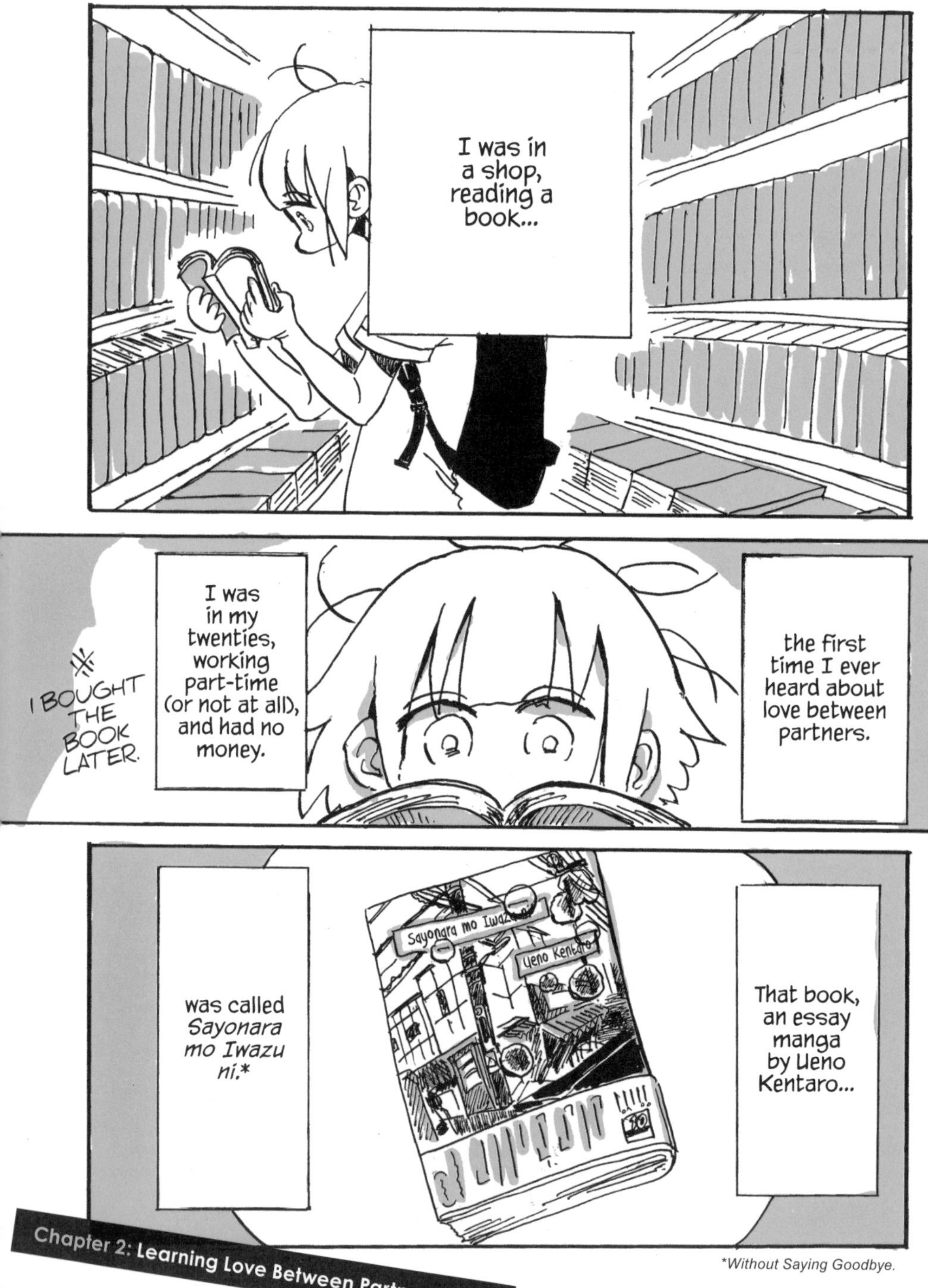
I was in a shop, reading a book...
the first time I ever heard about love between partners.
I was in my twenties, working part-time (or not at all), and had no money.
※ I BOUGHT THE BOOK LATER.
That book, an essay manga by Ueno Kentaro...
Sayonara mo Iwazu ni
Ueno Kentaro
was called *Sayonara mo Iwazu ni.**

Chapter 2: Learning Love Between Partners Exists

*Without Saying Goodbye.

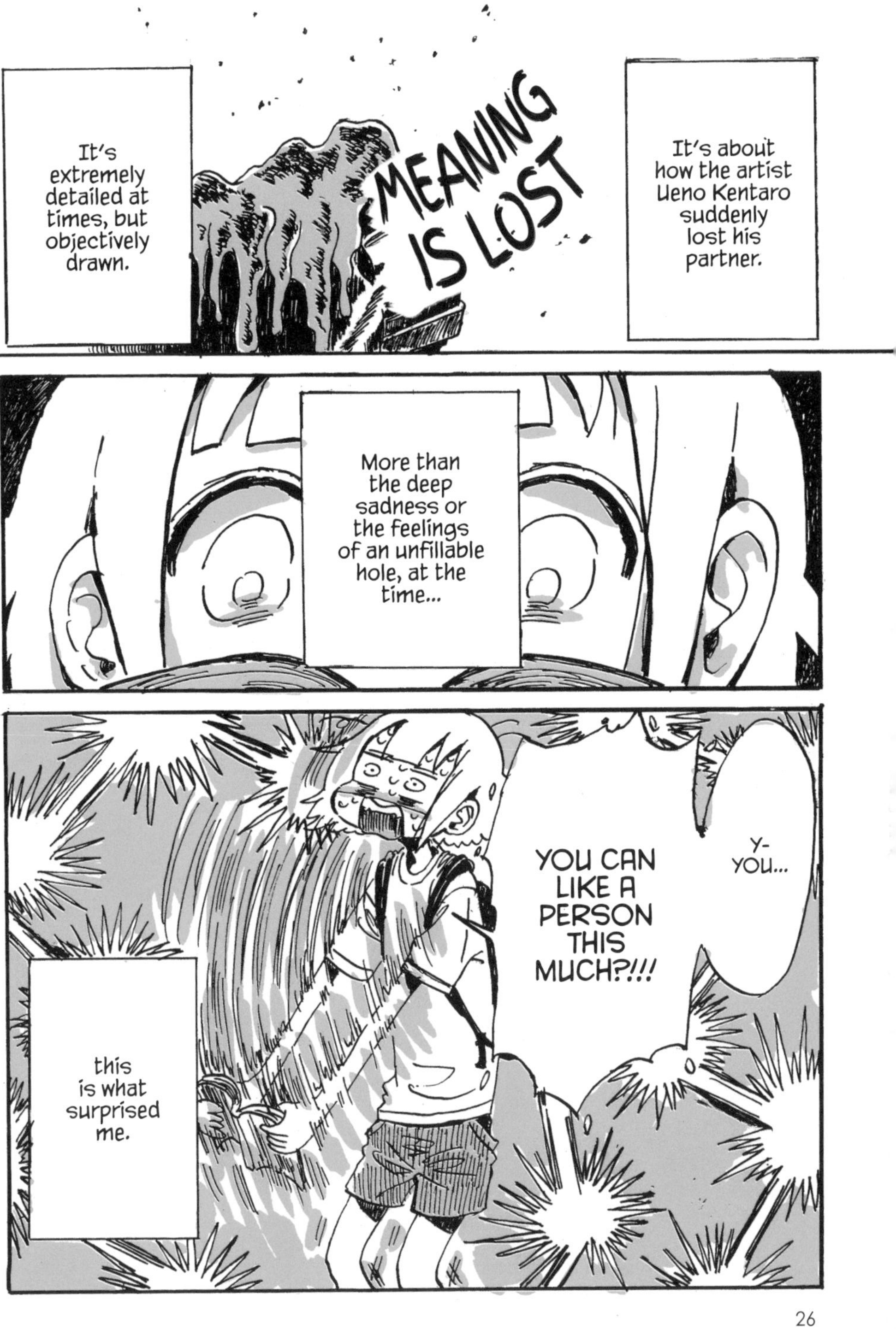
It's about how the artist Ueno Kentaro suddenly lost his partner.
MEANING IS LOST
It's extremely detailed at times, but objectively drawn.
More than the deep sadness or the feelings of an unfillable hole, at the time...
Y- YOU...
YOU CAN LIKE A PERSON THIS MUCH?!!!
this is what surprised me.

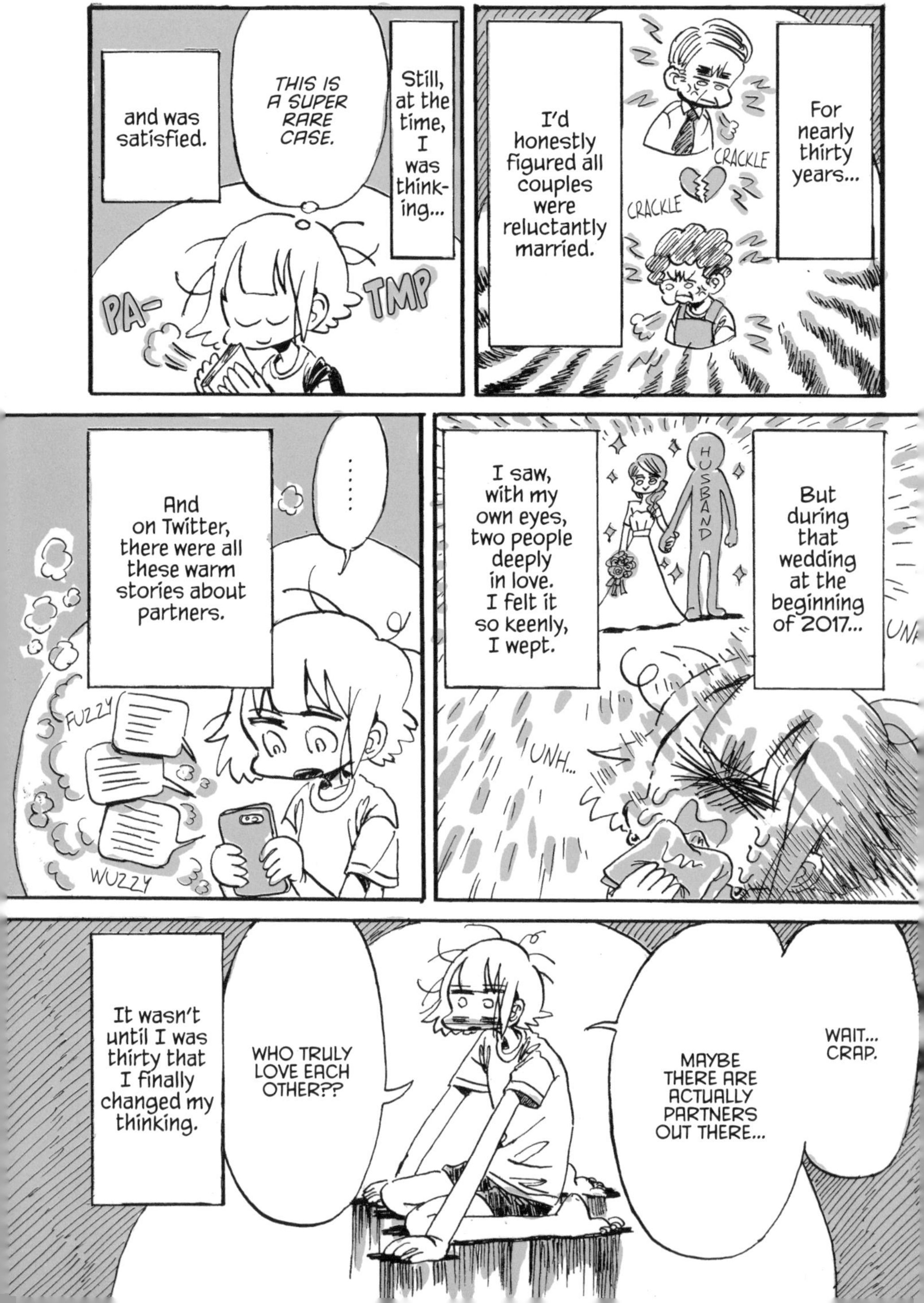

For nearly thirty years...
CRACKLE
CRACKLE
I'd honestly figured all couples were reluctantly married.
Still, at the time, I was thinking...
THIS IS A SUPER RARE CASE.
and was satisfied.
PA-TMP
But during that wedding at the beginning of 2017...
HUSBAND
I saw, with my own eyes, two people deeply in love. I felt it so keenly, I wept.
UNH...
......
And on Twitter, there were all these warm stories about partners.
FUZZY
WUZZY
WAIT... CRAP.
MAYBE THERE ARE ACTUALLY PARTNERS OUT THERE...
WHO TRULY LOVE EACH OTHER??
It wasn't until I was thirty that I finally changed my thinking.

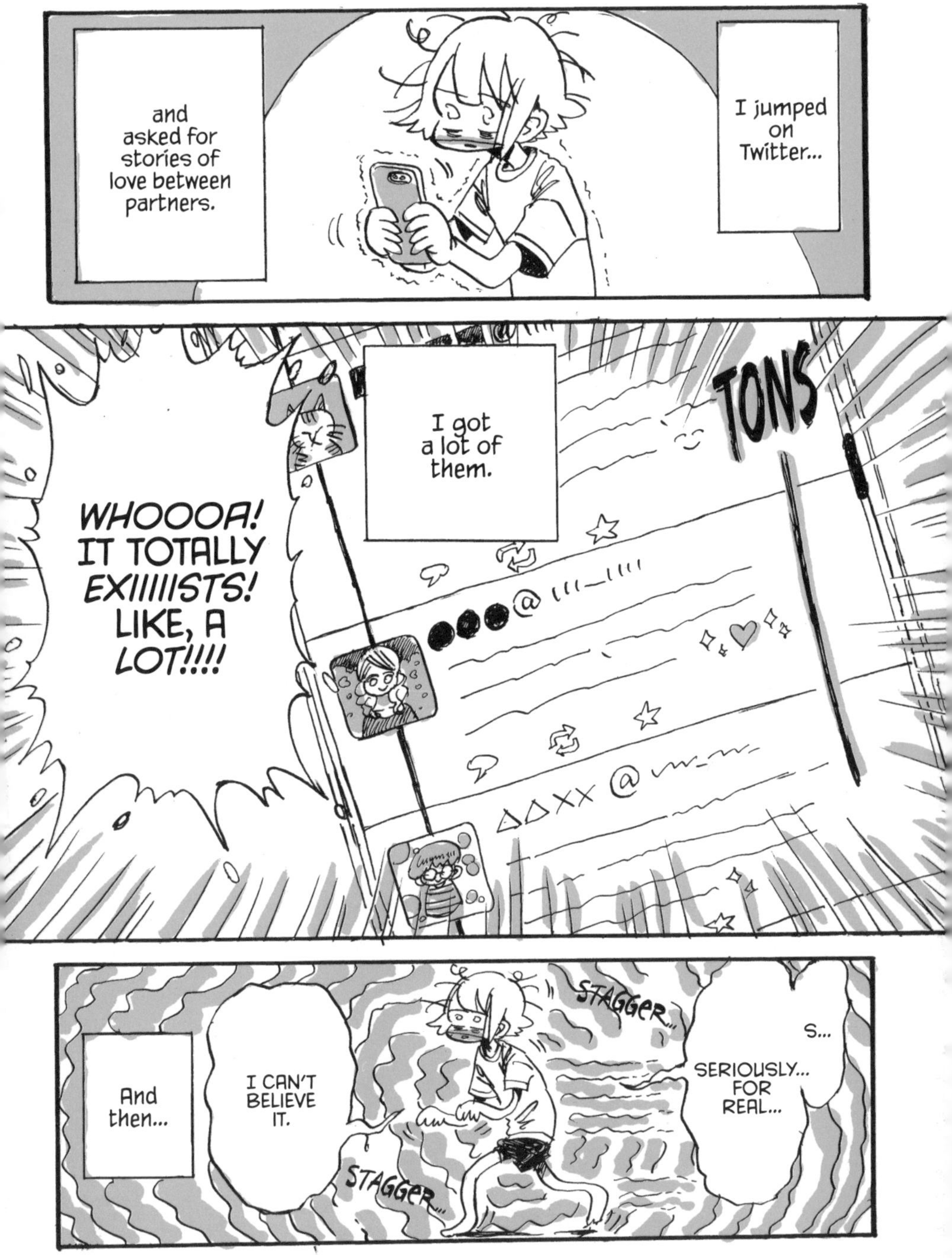
I jumped on Twitter...
and asked for stories of love between partners.
TONS
I got a lot of them.
WHOOOA! IT TOTALLY EXIIIIISTS! LIKE, A LOT!!!!
S...
SERIOUSLY... FOR REAL...
STAGGER...
I CAN'T BELIEVE IT.
STAGGER...
And then...

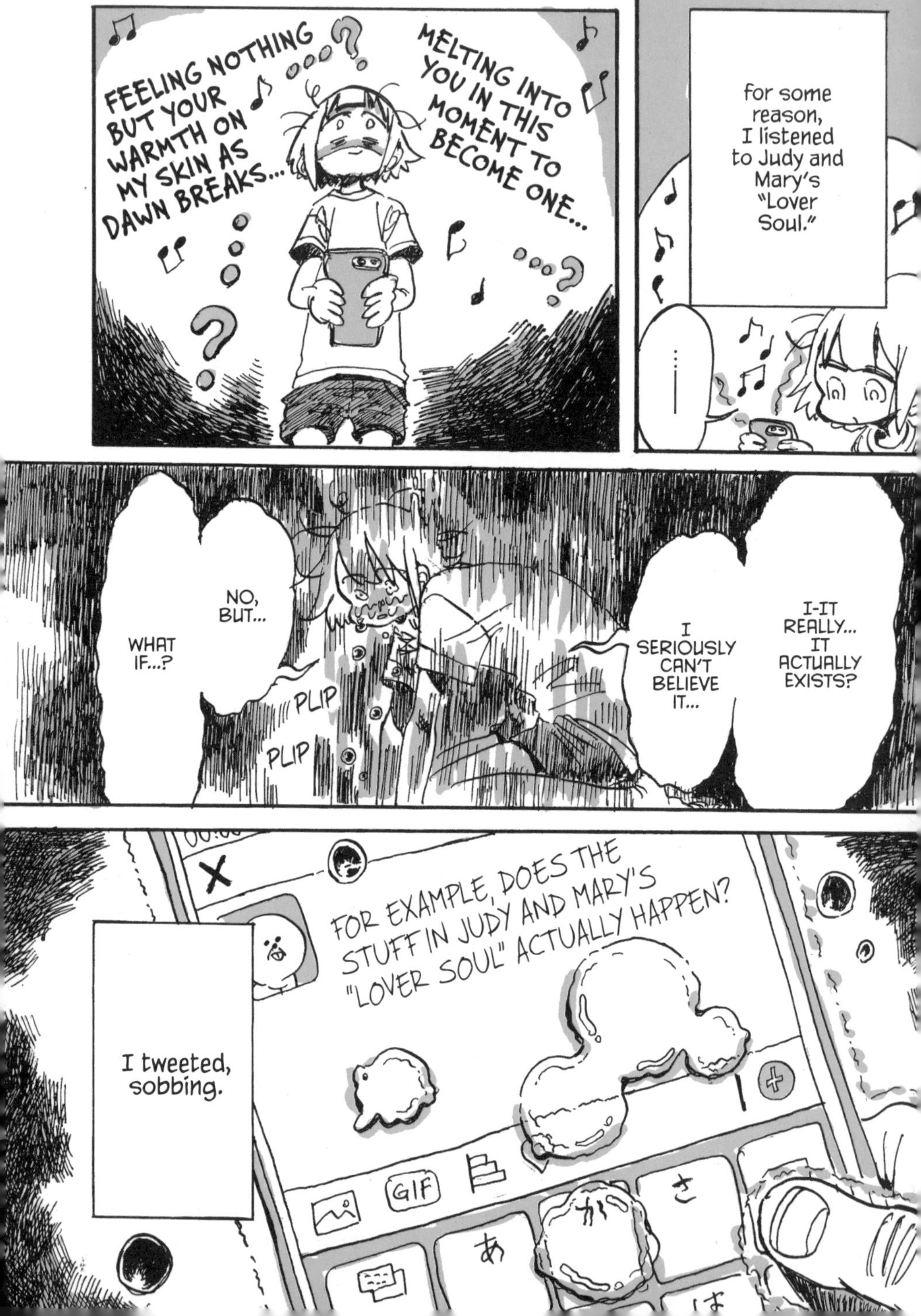

for some reason, I listened to Judy and Mary's "Lover Soul."
...
MELTING INTO YOU IN THIS MOMENT TO BECOME ONE...
FEELING NOTHING BUT YOUR WARMTH ON MY SKIN AS DAWN BREAKS...
I-IT REALLY... IT ACTUALLY EXISTS?
I SERIOUSLY CAN'T BELIEVE IT...
PLIP
PLIP
NO, BUT...
WHAT IF...?
FOR EXAMPLE, DOES THE STUFF IN JUDY AND MARY'S "LOVER SOUL" ACTUALLY HAPPEN?
I tweeted, sobbing.

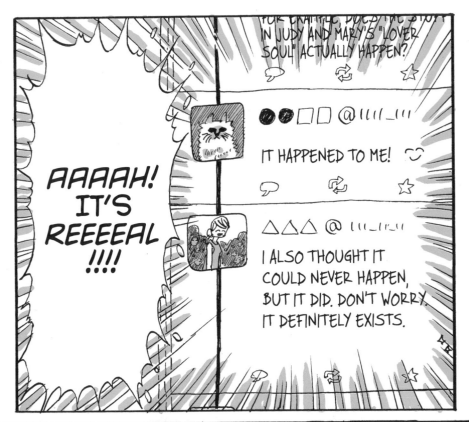

FOR EXAMPLE, DOES THE STORY IN JUDY AND MARY'S "LOVER SOUL" ACTUALLY HAPPEN?

●●□□ @||||_|||

IT HAPPENED TO ME!

△△△ @ |||_||_|

I ALSO THOUGHT IT COULD NEVER HAPPEN, BUT IT DID. DON'T WORRY, IT DEFINITELY EXISTS.

AAAAH! IT'S REEEEAL !!!!

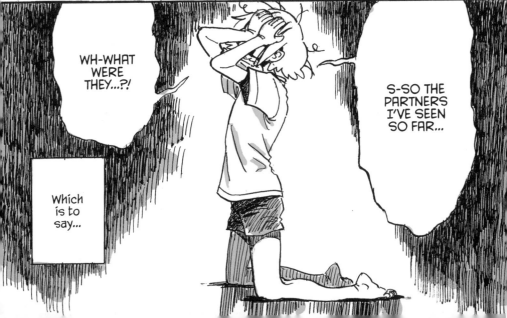

WH-WHAT WERE THEY...?!

S-SO THE PARTNERS I'VE SEEN SO FAR...

Which is to say...

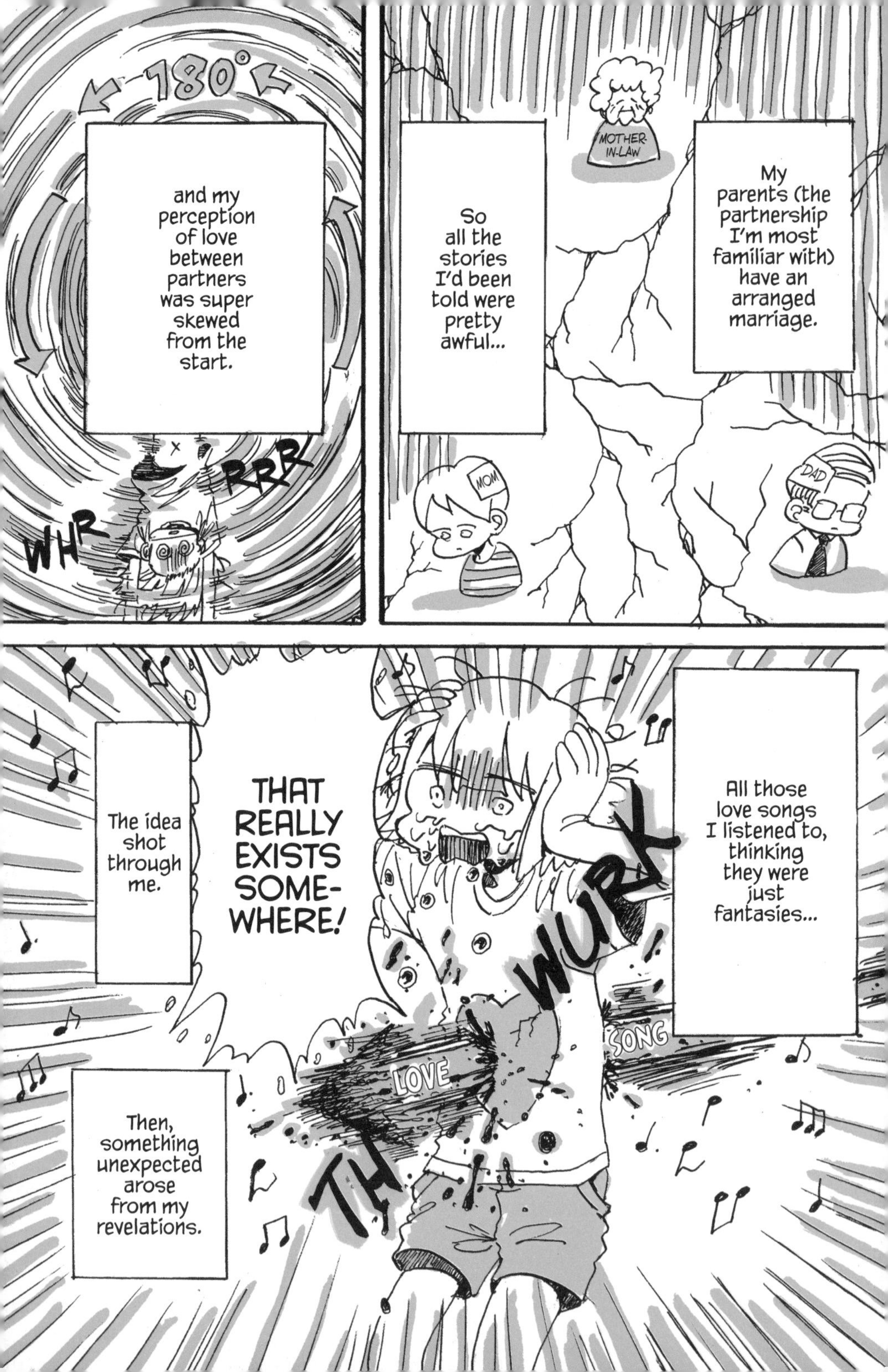
My parents (the partnership I'm most familiar with) have an arranged marriage.
MOTHER-IN-LAW
So all the stories I'd been told were pretty awful...
DAD
MOM
180°
and my perception of love between partners was super skewed from the start.
RRR
WHR
All those love songs I listened to, thinking they were just fantasies...
WURK
SONG
THAT REALLY EXISTS SOME-WHERE!
The idea shot through me.
LOVE
TH
Then, something unexpected arose from my revelations.

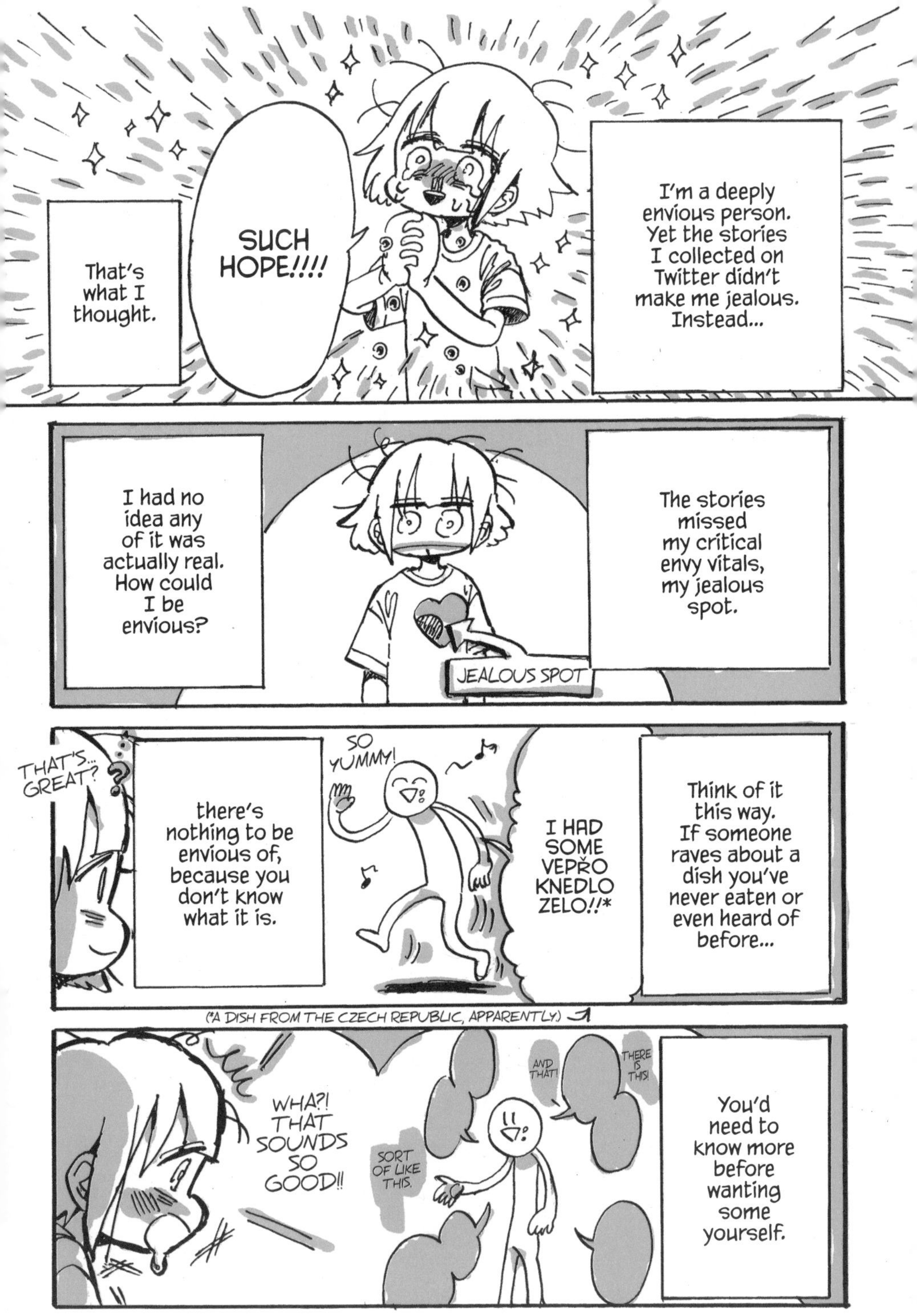
I'm a deeply envious person. Yet the stories I collected on Twitter didn't make me jealous. Instead...
SUCH HOPE!!!!
That's what I thought.
The stories missed my critical envy vitals, my jealous spot.
JEALOUS SPOT
I had no idea any of it was actually real. How could I be envious?
Think of it this way. If someone raves about a dish you've never eaten or even heard of before...
I HAD SOME VEPŘO KNEDLO ZELO!!*
SO YUMMY!
there's nothing to be envious of, because you don't know what it is.
THAT'S... GREAT?
(*A DISH FROM THE CZECH REPUBLIC, APPARENTLY.)
You'd need to know more before wanting some yourself.
THERE IS THIS!
AND THAT!
SORT OF LIKE THIS.
WHA?! THAT SOUNDS SO GOOD!!

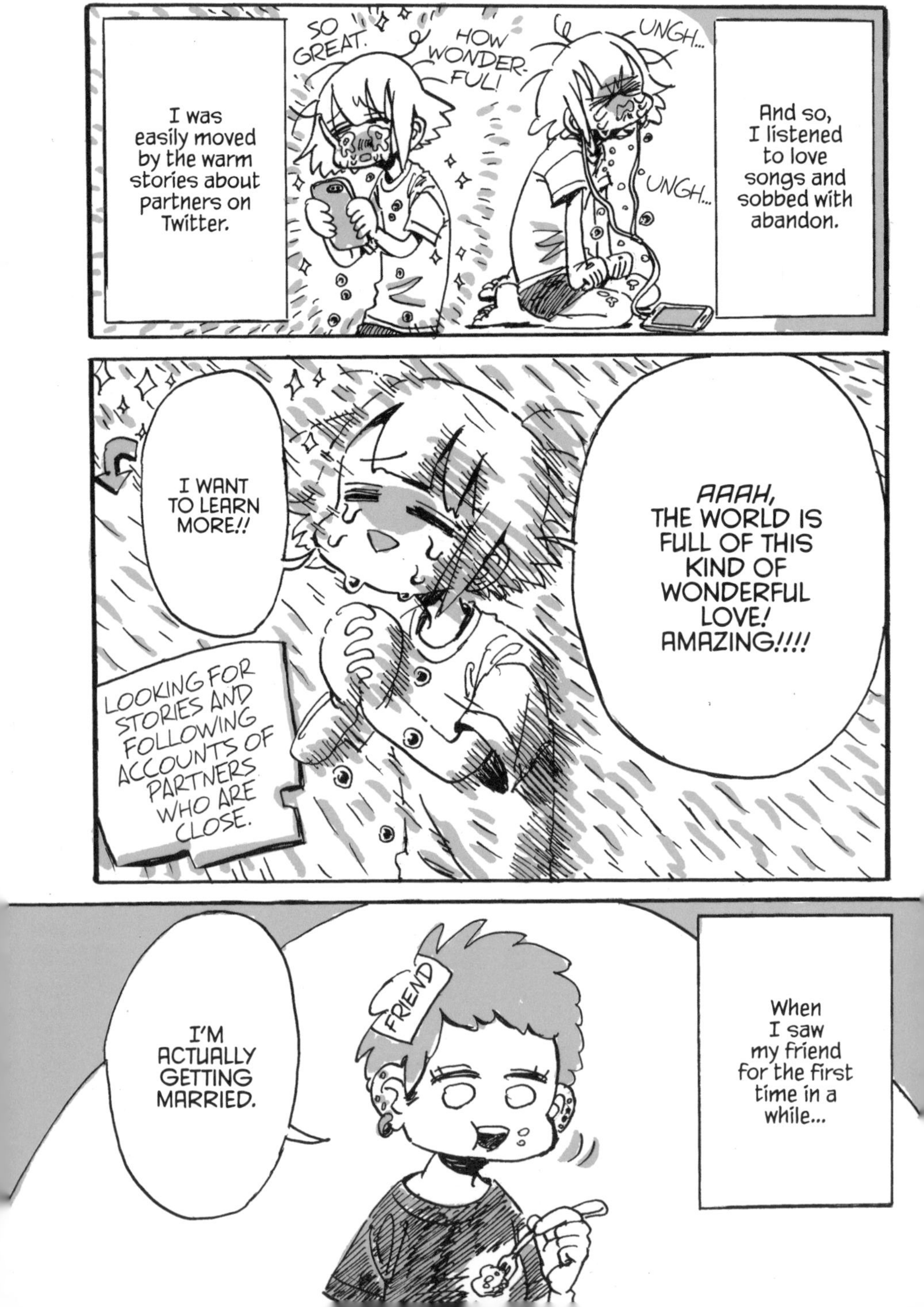
And so, I listened to love songs and sobbed with abandon.
UNGH...
UNGH...
HOW WONDER-FUL!
SO GREAT.
I was easily moved by the warm stories about partners on Twitter.
AAAH, THE WORLD IS FULL OF THIS KIND OF WONDERFUL LOVE! AMAZING!!!!
I WANT TO LEARN MORE!!
LOOKING FOR STORIES AND FOLLOWING ACCOUNTS OF PARTNERS WHO ARE CLOSE.
When I saw my friend for the first time in a while...
FRIEND
I'M ACTUALLY GETTING MARRIED.

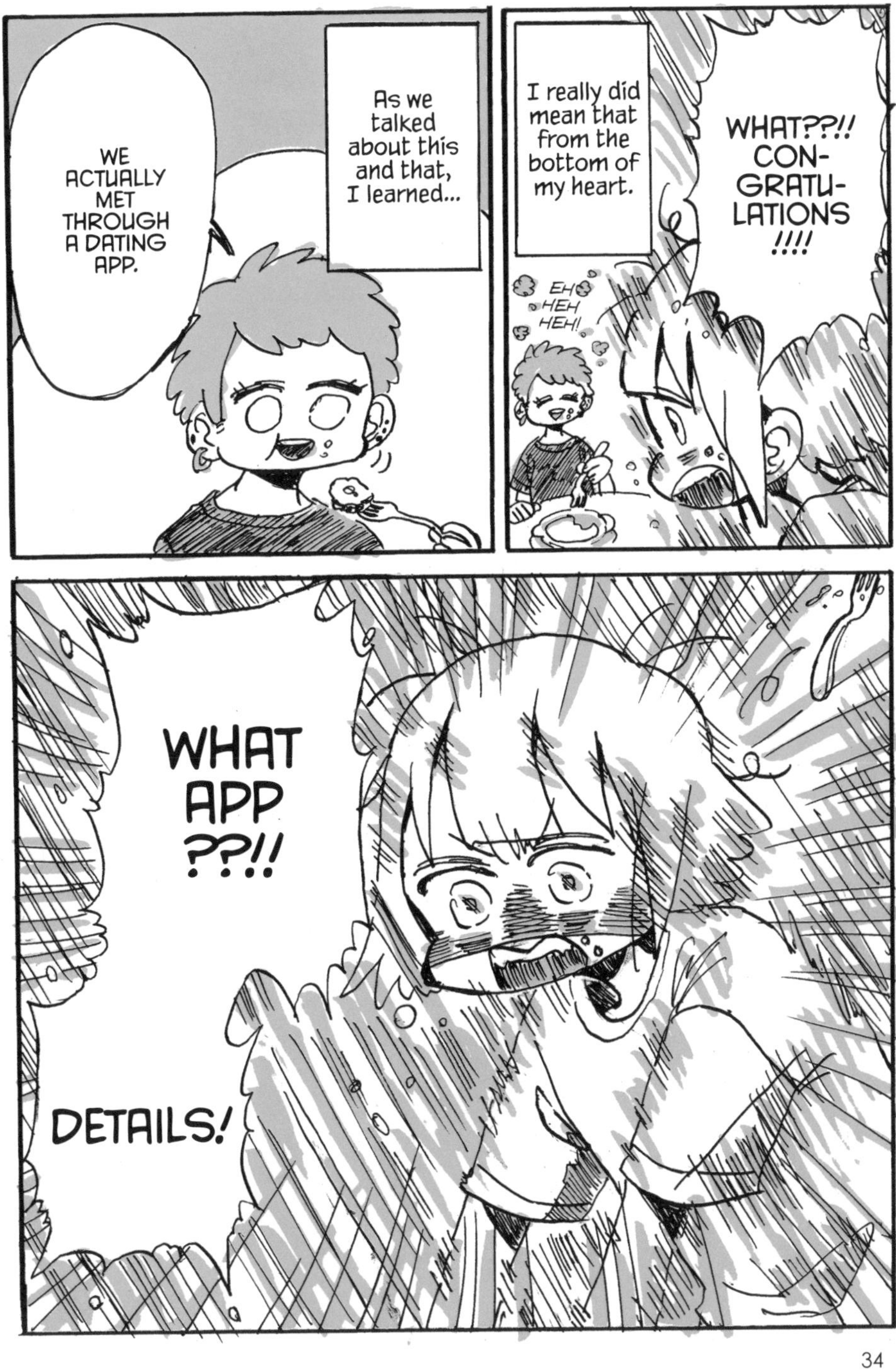

WHAT??!! CON-GRATU-LATIONS!!!!
I really did mean that from the bottom of my heart.
EH HEH HEH!
As we talked about this and that, I learned...
WE ACTUALLY MET THROUGH A DATING APP.
WHAT APP??!!
DETAILS!

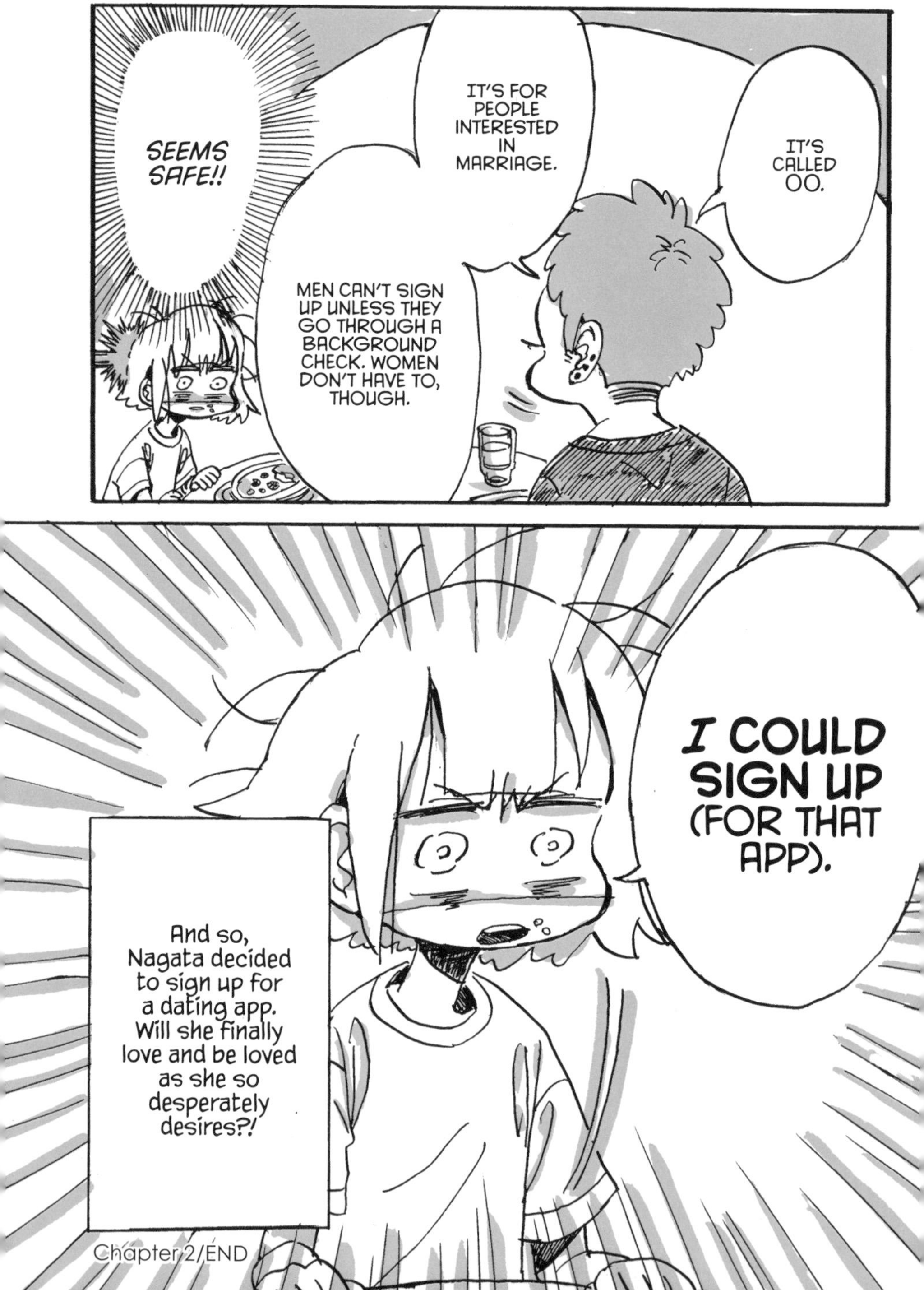
IT'S CALLED OO.
IT'S FOR PEOPLE INTERESTED IN MARRIAGE.
MEN CAN'T SIGN UP UNLESS THEY GO THROUGH A BACKGROUND CHECK. WOMEN DON'T HAVE TO, THOUGH.
SEEMS SAFE!!
I COULD SIGN UP (FOR THAT APP).
And so, Nagata decided to sign up for a dating app. Will she finally love and be loved as she so desperately desires?!
Chapter 2/END

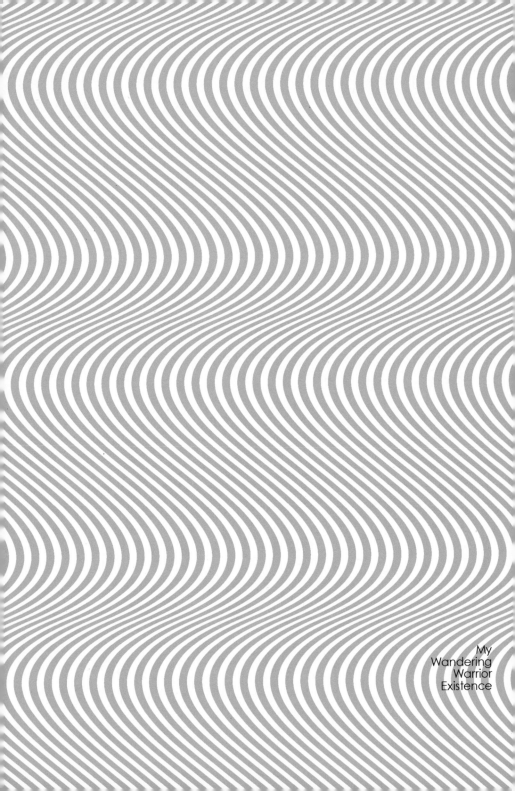

My
Wandering
Warrior
Existence

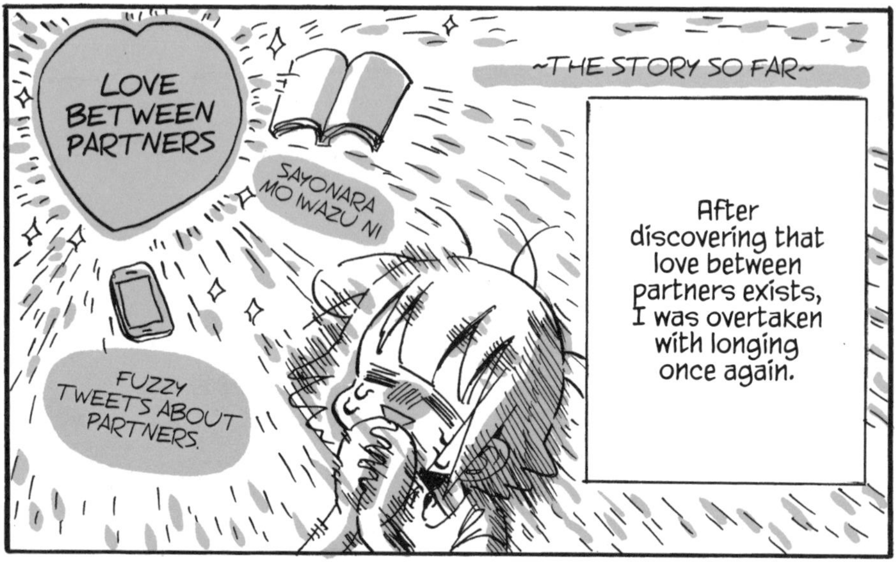
~THE STORY SO FAR~
After discovering that love between partners exists, I was overtaken with longing once again.
LOVE BETWEEN PARTNERS
SAYONARA MO IWAZU NI
FUZZY TWEETS ABOUT PARTNERS.

Chapter 3: I Tried a Dating App

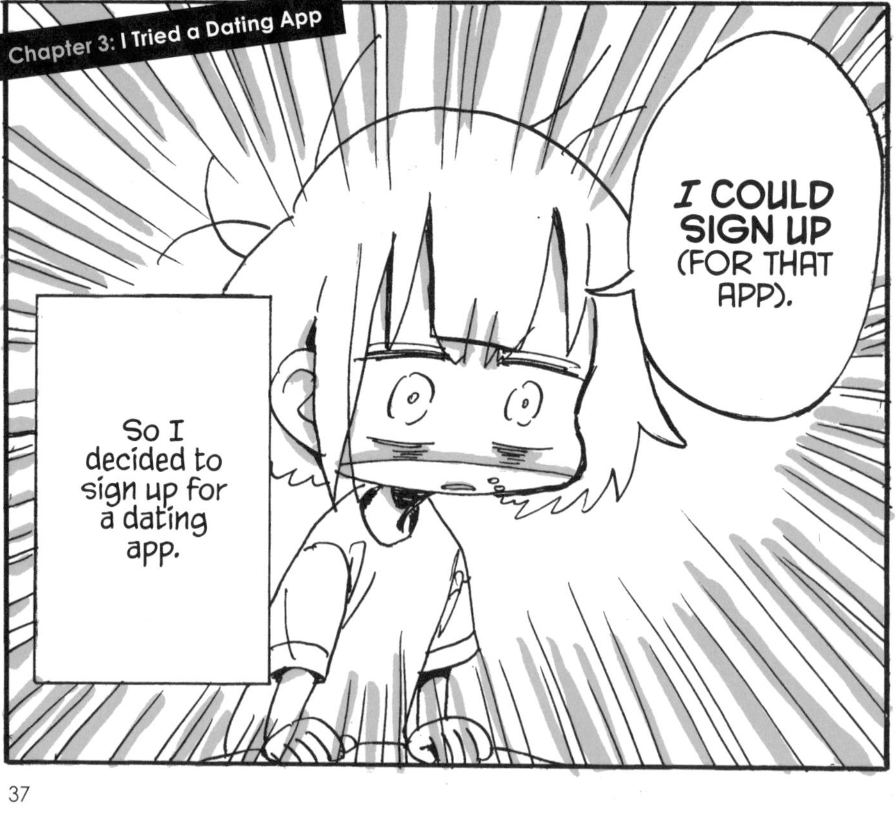
I COULD SIGN UP (FOR THAT APP).
So I decided to sign up for a dating app.

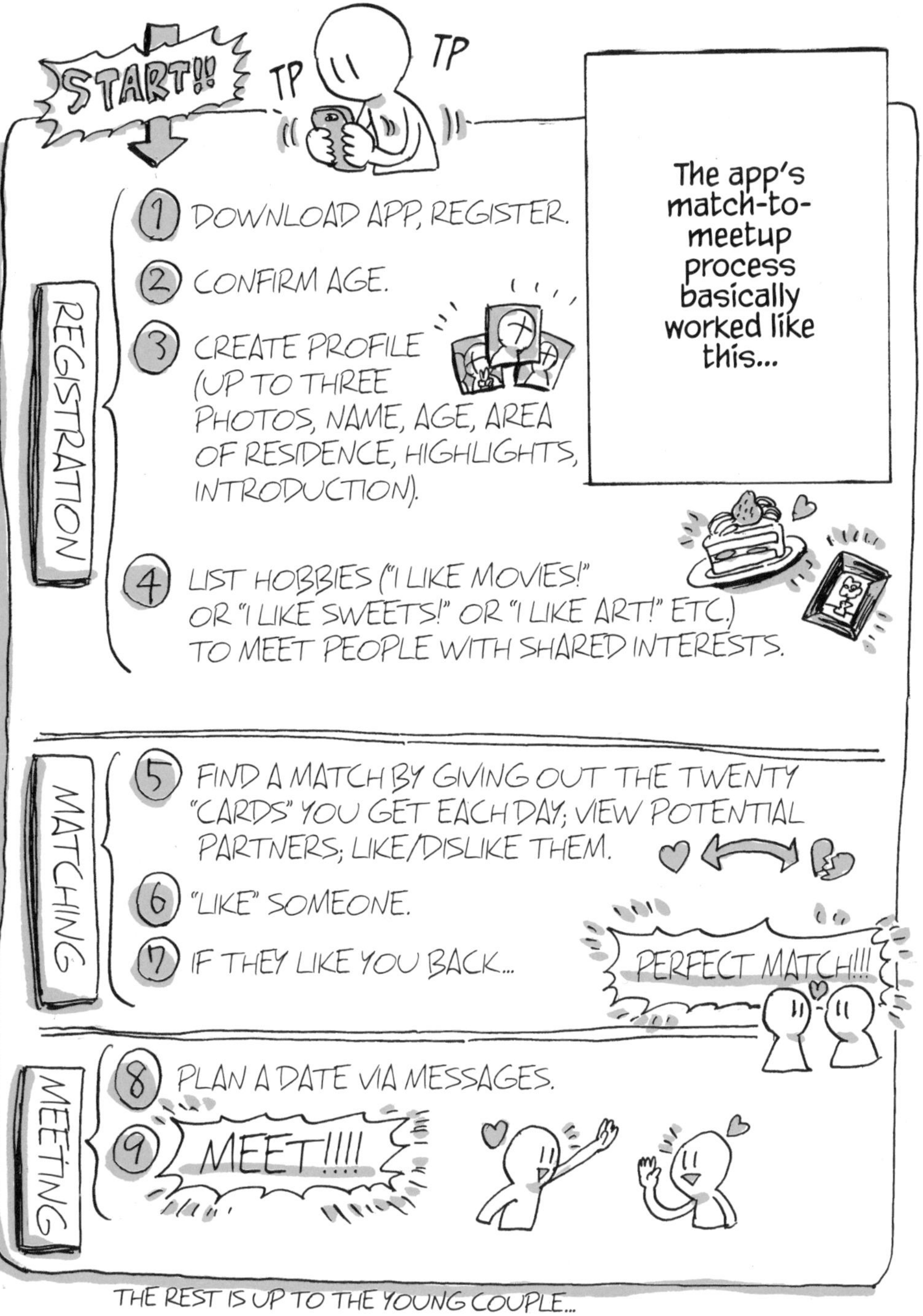
The app's match-to-meetup process basically worked like this...
START!!
TP
TP
REGISTRATION
1 DOWNLOAD APP, REGISTER.
2 CONFIRM AGE.
3 CREATE PROFILE (UP TO THREE PHOTOS, NAME, AGE, AREA OF RESIDENCE, HIGHLIGHTS, INTRODUCTION).
4 LIST HOBBIES ("I LIKE MOVIES!" OR "I LIKE SWEETS!" OR "I LIKE ART!" ETC.) TO MEET PEOPLE WITH SHARED INTERESTS.
MATCHING
5 FIND A MATCH BY GIVING OUT THE TWENTY "CARDS" YOU GET EACH DAY; VIEW POTENTIAL PARTNERS; LIKE/DISLIKE THEM.
6 "LIKE" SOMEONE.
7 IF THEY LIKE YOU BACK...
PERFECT MATCH!!!
MEETING
8 PLAN A DATE VIA MESSAGES.
9 MEET!!!!
THE REST IS UP TO THE YOUNG COUPLE...

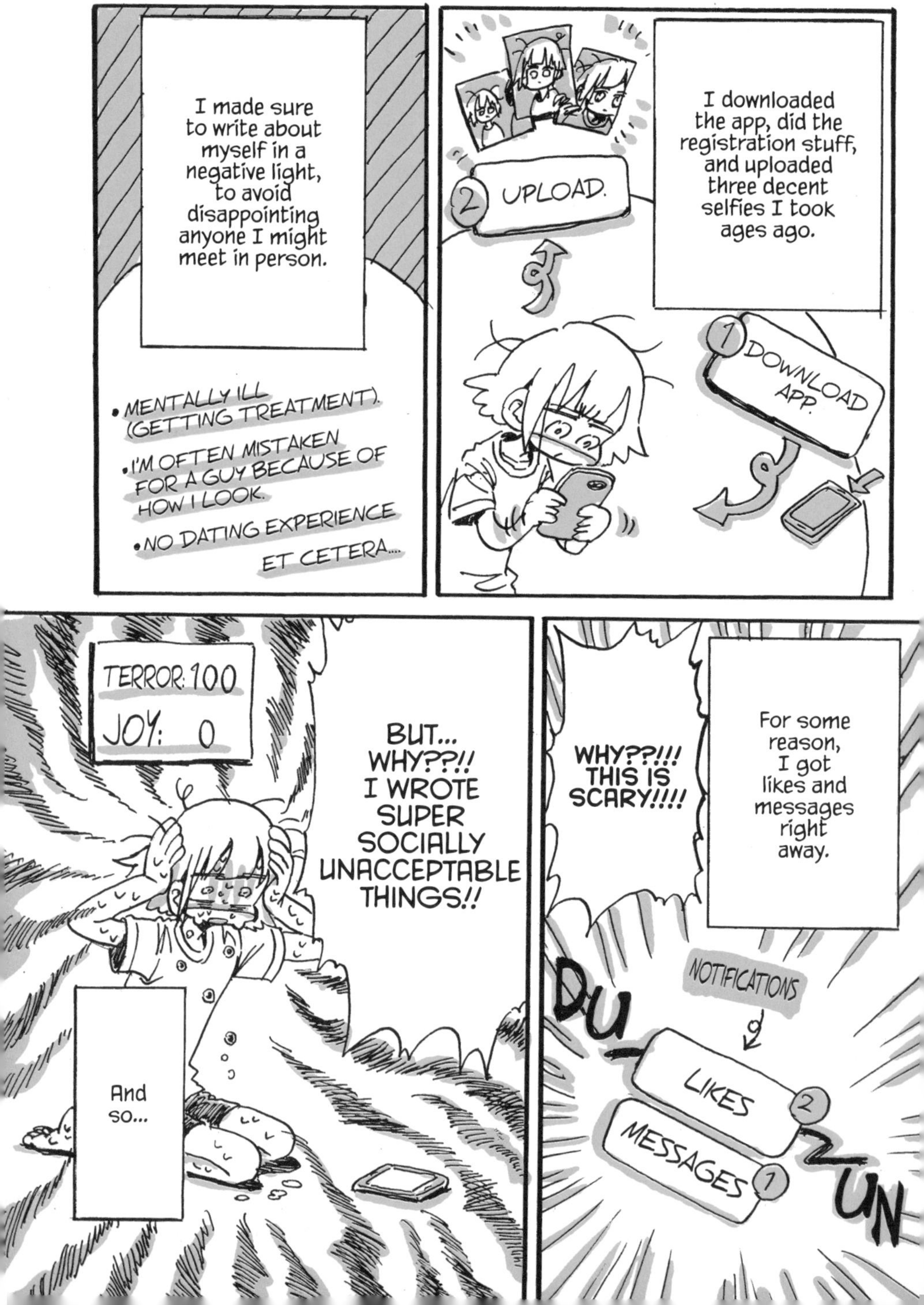
I downloaded the app, did the registration stuff, and uploaded three decent selfies I took ages ago.
1 DOWNLOAD APP.
2 UPLOAD.
I made sure to write about myself in a negative light, to avoid disappointing anyone I might meet in person.
• MENTALLY ILL (GETTING TREATMENT).
• I'M OFTEN MISTAKEN FOR A GUY BECAUSE OF HOW I LOOK.
• NO DATING EXPERIENCE
ET CETERA...
For some reason, I got likes and messages right away.
WHY??!!! THIS IS SCARY!!!!
NOTIFICATIONS
LIKES 2
MESSAGES 1
DU-UN
BUT... WHY??!! I WROTE SUPER SOCIALLY UNACCEPTABLE THINGS!!
TERROR: 100
JOY: 0
And so...

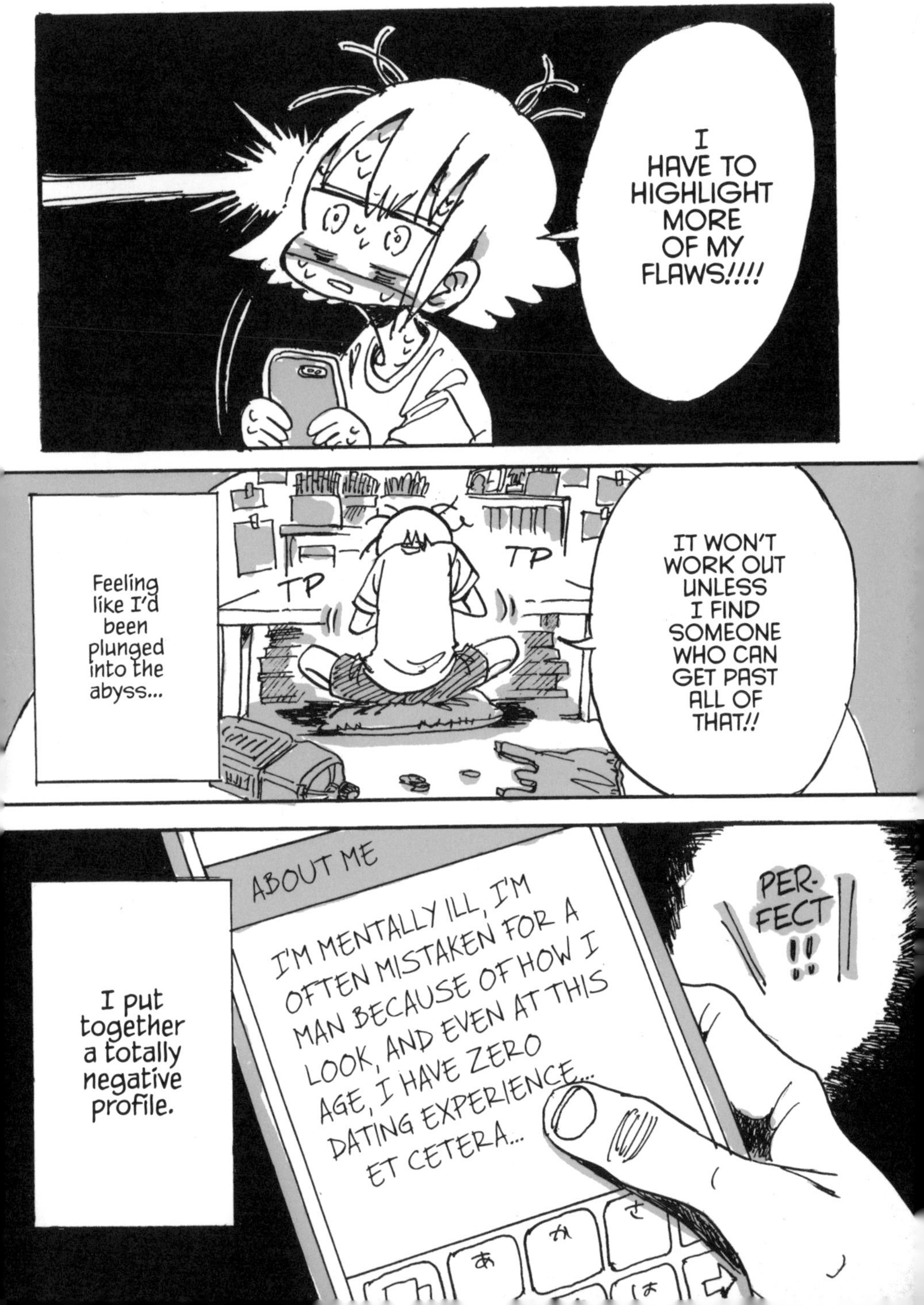
I HAVE TO HIGHLIGHT MORE OF MY FLAWS!!!!
IT WON'T WORK OUT UNLESS I FIND SOMEONE WHO CAN GET PAST ALL OF THAT!!
TP
TP
Feeling like I'd been plunged into the abyss...
PER-FECT!!
ABOUT ME
I'M MENTALLY ILL, I'M OFTEN MISTAKEN FOR A MAN BECAUSE OF HOW I LOOK, AND EVEN AT THIS AGE, I HAVE ZERO DATING EXPERIENCE... ET CETERA...
あ か さ
は
I put together a totally negative profile.

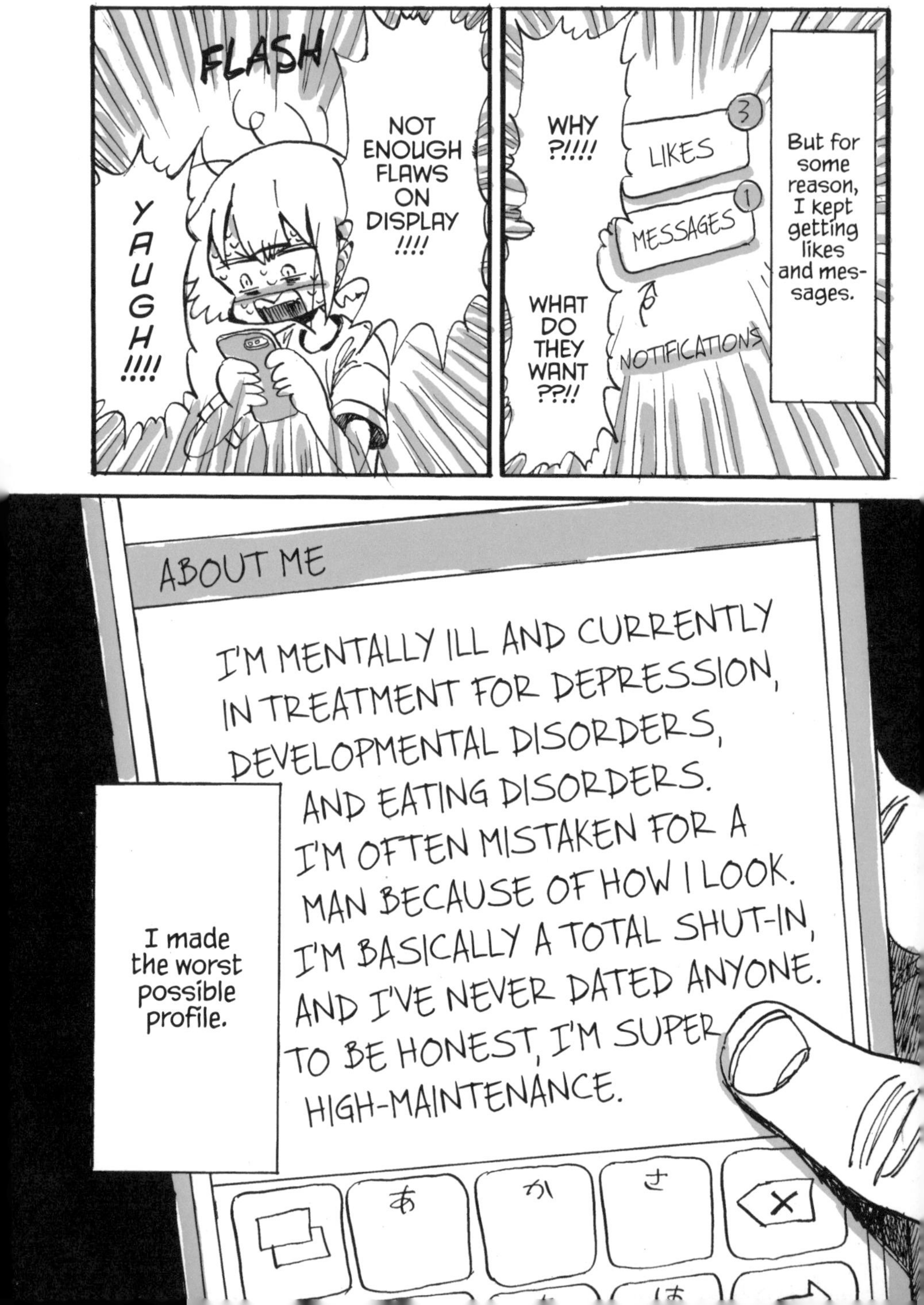
But for some reason, I kept getting likes and messages.
LIKES 3
MESSAGES 1
NOTIFICATIONS
WHY?!!!!
WHAT DO THEY WANT??!!
FLASH
NOT ENOUGH FLAWS ON DISPLAY!!!!
YAUGH!!!!
ABOUT ME
I'M MENTALLY ILL AND CURRENTLY IN TREATMENT FOR DEPRESSION, DEVELOPMENTAL DISORDERS, AND EATING DISORDERS. I'M OFTEN MISTAKEN FOR A MAN BECAUSE OF HOW I LOOK. I'M BASICALLY A TOTAL SHUT-IN, AND I'VE NEVER DATED ANYONE. TO BE HONEST, I'M SUPER HIGH-MAINTENANCE.
I made the worst possible profile.
あ
か
さ

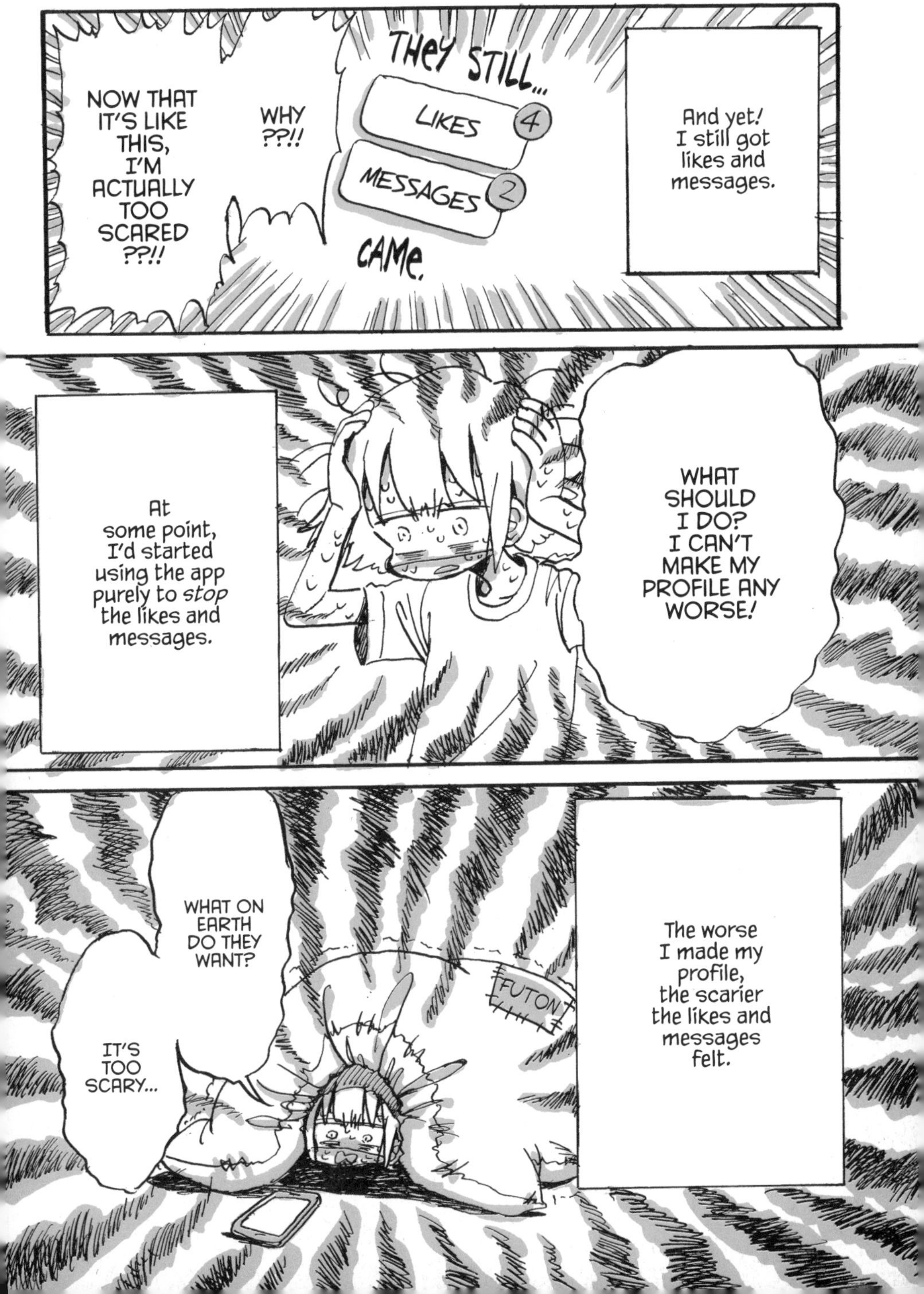
And yet! I still got likes and messages.
THEY STILL...
LIKES 4
MESSAGES 2
CAME.
WHY ??!!
NOW THAT IT'S LIKE THIS, I'M ACTUALLY TOO SCARED ??!!
WHAT SHOULD I DO? I CAN'T MAKE MY PROFILE ANY WORSE!
At some point, I'd started using the app purely to *stop* the likes and messages.
The worse I made my profile, the scarier the likes and messages felt.
WHAT ON EARTH DO THEY WANT?
FUTON
IT'S TOO SCARY...

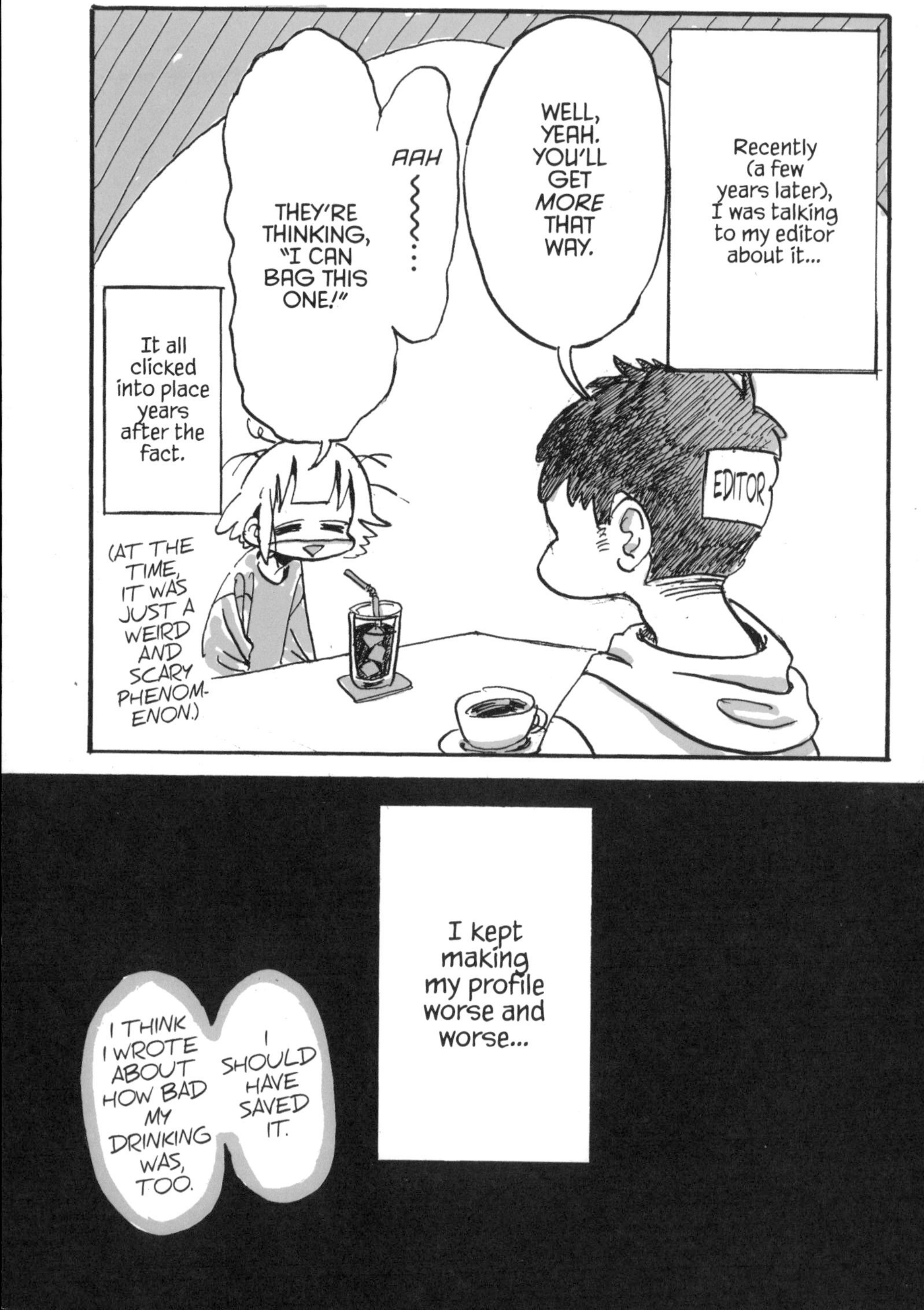

Recently (a few years later), I was talking to my editor about it...
WELL, YEAH. YOU'LL GET MORE THAT WAY.
AAH ~~~.....
THEY'RE THINKING, "I CAN BAG THIS ONE!"
EDITOR
It all clicked into place years after the fact.
(AT THE TIME, IT WAS JUST A WEIRD AND SCARY PHENOM-ENON.)
I kept making my profile worse and worse...
I SHOULD HAVE SAVED IT.
I THINK I WROTE ABOUT HOW BAD MY DRINKING WAS, TOO.

I can't remember my profile's final form, but it was the absolute worst one I could think up.

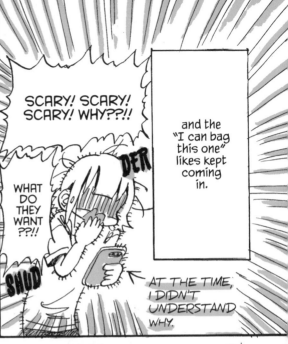

SCARY! SCARY! SCARY! WHY??!!

DER

WHAT DO THEY WANT ??!!

SHUD

and the "I can bag this one" likes kept coming in.

AT THE TIME, I DIDN'T UNDERSTAND WHY.

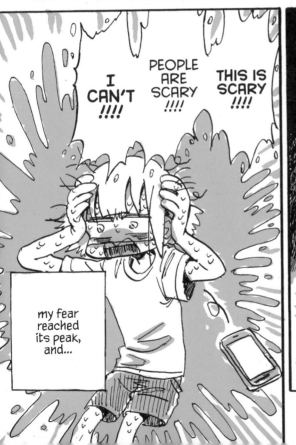

I CAN'T !!!!

PEOPLE ARE SCARY !!!!

THIS IS SCARY !!!!

my fear reached its peak, and...

Due to the increasing "I can bag this one" likes...

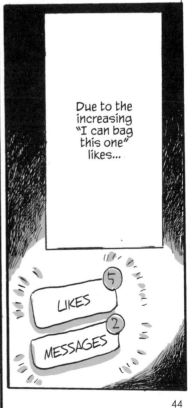

LIKES 5

MESSAGES 2

44

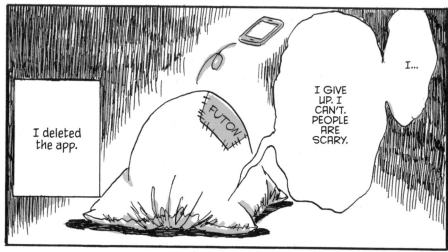

I deleted the app.

I GIVE UP. I CAN'T. PEOPLE ARE SCARY.

I...

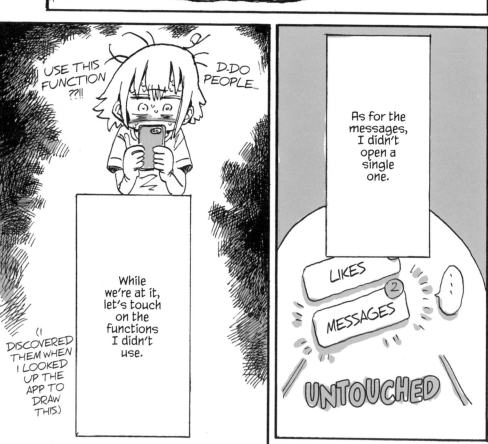

USE THIS FUNCTION ??!!

D-DO PEOPLE...

While we're at it, let's touch on the functions I didn't use.

(I DISCOVERED THEM WHEN I LOOKED UP THE APP TO DRAW THIS.)

As for the messages, I didn't open a single one.

LIKES

MESSAGES 2

UNTOUCHED

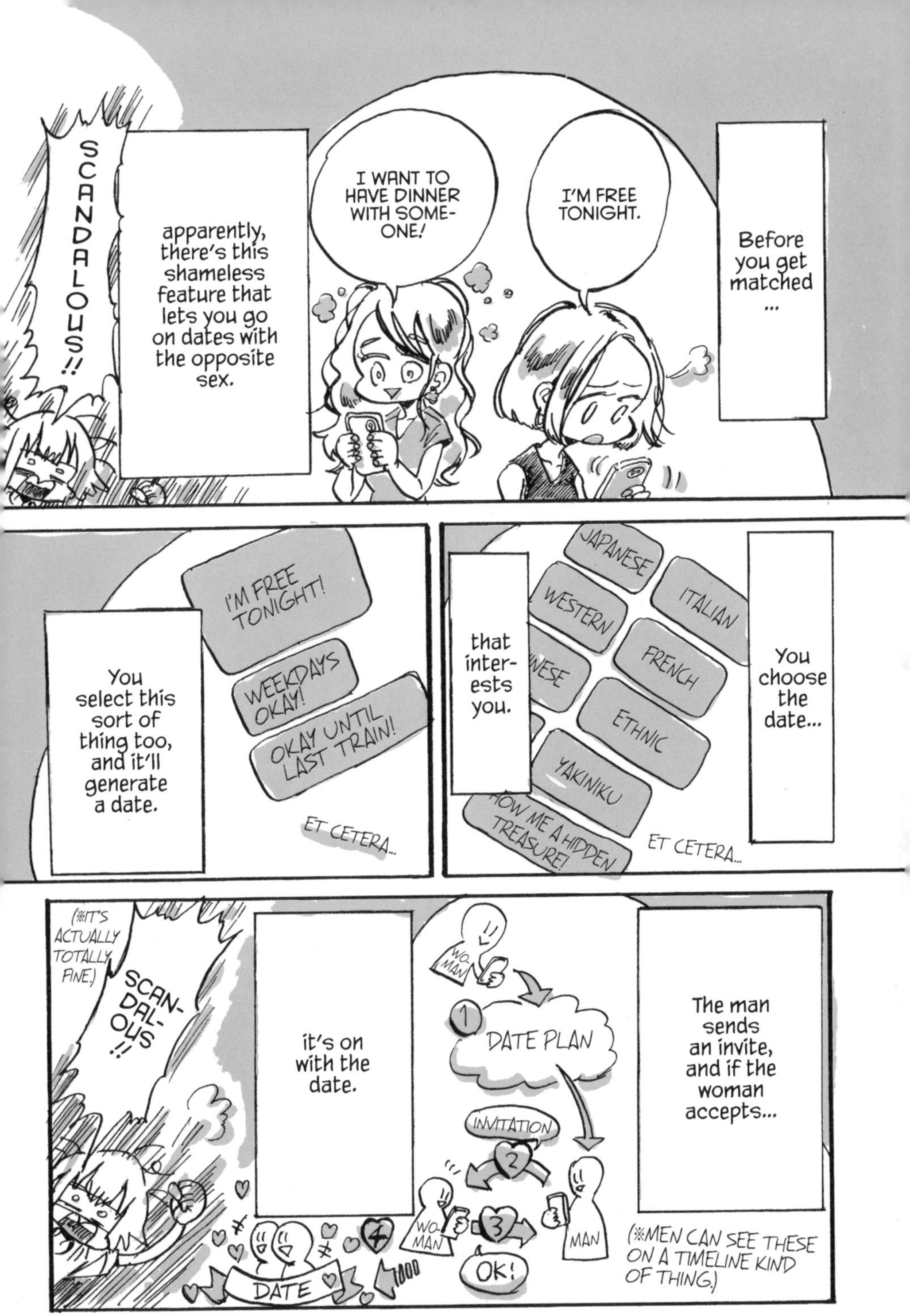
Before you get matched ...
I'M FREE TONIGHT.
I WANT TO HAVE DINNER WITH SOME-ONE!
apparently, there's this shameless feature that lets you go on dates with the opposite sex.
SCANDALOUS!!
You choose the date...
JAPANESE
ITALIAN
WESTERN
FRENCH
ETHNIC
YAKINIKU
HOW ME A HIDDEN TREASURE!
that inter-ests you.
ET CETERA...
I'M FREE TONIGHT!
WEEKDAYS OKAY!
OKAY UNTIL LAST TRAIN!
You select this sort of thing too, and it'll generate a date.
ET CETERA...
The man sends an invite, and if the woman accepts...
WO-MAN
1
DATE PLAN
INVITATION
2
MAN
WO-MAN
3
OK!
4
DATE
(※MEN CAN SEE THESE ON A TIMELINE KIND OF THING.)
it's on with the date.
SCAN-DAL-OUS!!
(※IT'S ACTUALLY TOTALLY FINE.)

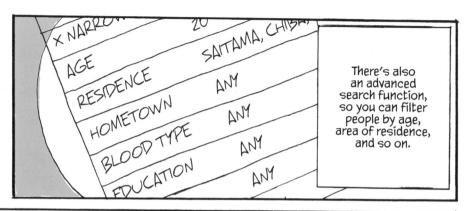

There's also an advanced search function, so you can filter people by age, area of residence, and so on.
20
SAITAMA,
AGE
RESIDENCE
ANY
HOMETOWN
ANY
BLOOD TYPE
ANY
EDUCATION
ANY
The basic function (which I never used) that leads to a match works like this.
MATCHING
1 WHEN YOU TAP "LIKE," A NOTIFICATION IS SENT TO THE PERSON YOU LIKED.
GOT LOTS OF THOSE.
2 IF YOU SEND A LIKE BACK
THAT'S A MATCH!!
APPARENTLY!!
KIND OF FAST?!
3 YOU'RE NOW ABLE TO EXCHANGE MESSAGES.
(AND MEET IN PERSON AND STUFF--APPARENTLY.)
If I divided **what I could do** and **what fear kept me from doing** into zones...
MENDELSSOHN
(1809-1847)

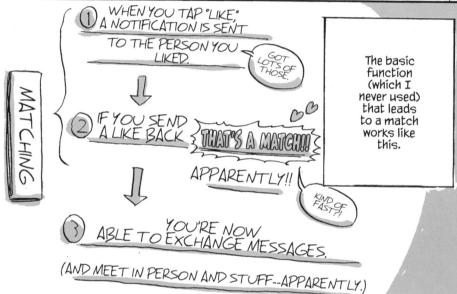

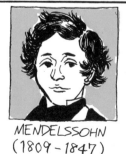

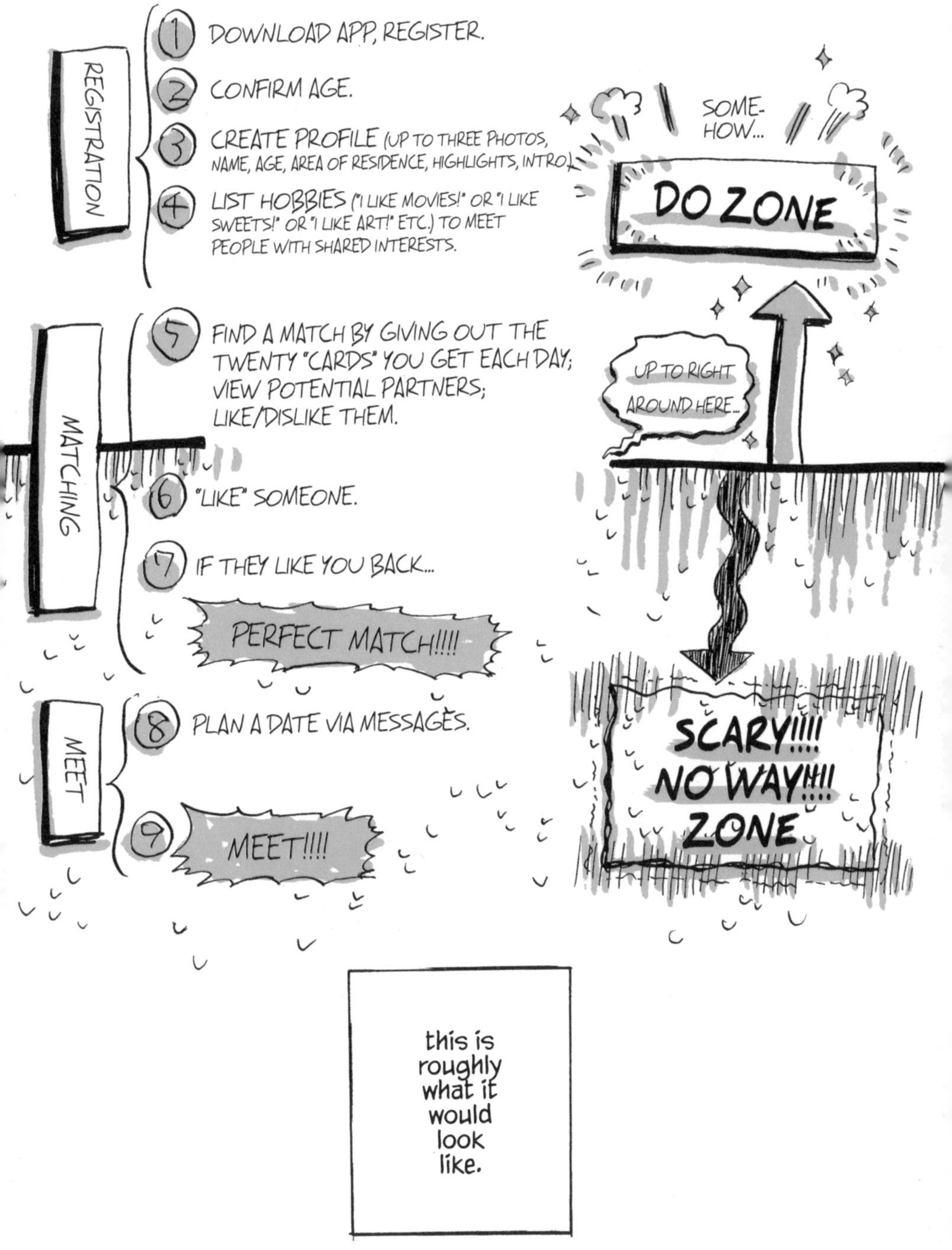
SOME-HOW...
DO ZONE
UP TO RIGHT AROUND HERE...
SCARY!!!! NO WAY!!!! ZONE
REGISTRATION
1 DOWNLOAD APP, REGISTER.
2 CONFIRM AGE.
3 CREATE PROFILE (UP TO THREE PHOTOS, NAME, AGE, AREA OF RESIDENCE, HIGHLIGHTS, INTRO)
4 LIST HOBBIES ("I LIKE MOVIES!" OR "I LIKE SWEETS!" OR "I LIKE ART!" ETC.) TO MEET PEOPLE WITH SHARED INTERESTS.
MATCHING
5 FIND A MATCH BY GIVING OUT THE TWENTY "CARDS" YOU GET EACH DAY; VIEW POTENTIAL PARTNERS; LIKE/DISLIKE THEM.
6 "LIKE" SOMEONE.
7 IF THEY LIKE YOU BACK...
PERFECT MATCH!!!!
MEET
8 PLAN A DATE VIA MESSAGES.
9 MEET!!!!
this is roughly what it would look like.

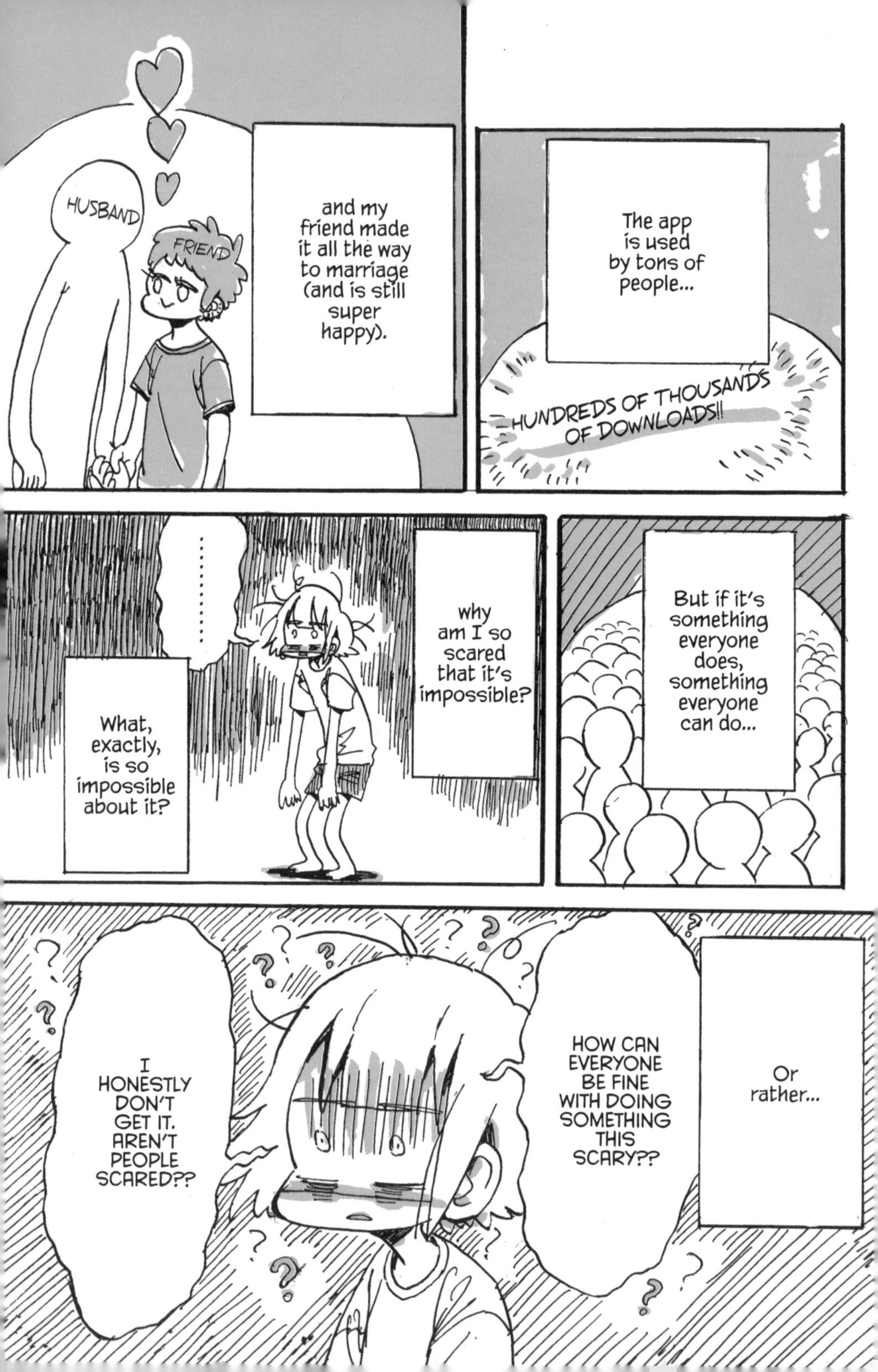
The app is used by tons of people...
HUNDREDS OF THOUSANDS OF DOWNLOADS!!
and my friend made it all the way to marriage (and is still super happy).
HUSBAND
FRIEND
But if it's something everyone does, something everyone can do...
why am I so scared that it's impossible?
......
What, exactly, is so impossible about it?
Or rather...
HOW CAN EVERYONE BE FINE WITH DOING SOMETHING THIS SCARY??
I HONESTLY DON'T GET IT. AREN'T PEOPLE SCARED??

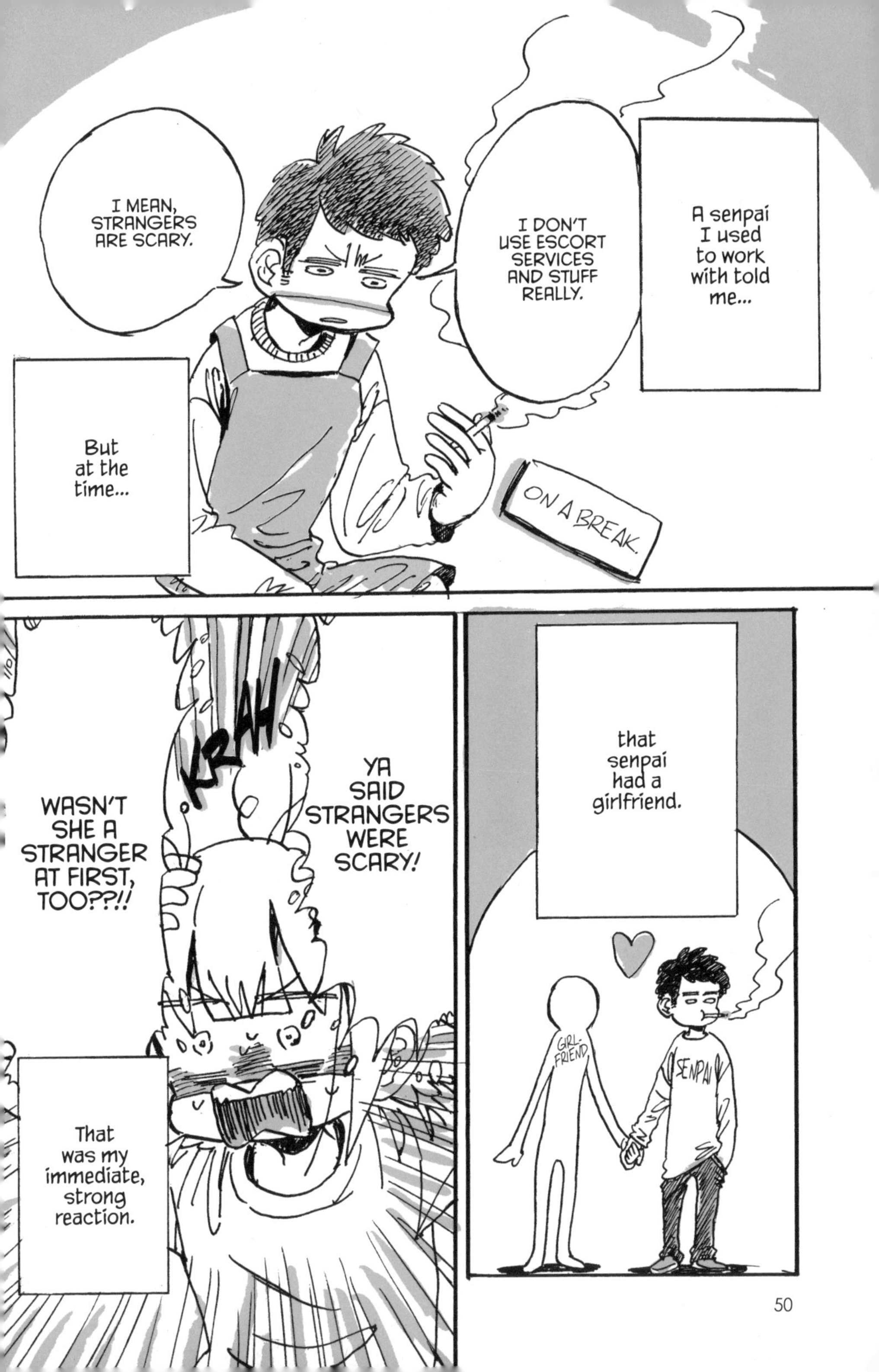

A senpai I used to work with told me...
I DON'T USE ESCORT SERVICES AND STUFF REALLY.
I MEAN, STRANGERS ARE SCARY.
ON A BREAK.
But at the time...
that senpai had a girlfriend.
GIRL-FRIEND
SENPAI
YA SAID STRANGERS WERE SCARY!
KRAH
WASN'T SHE A STRANGER AT FIRST, TOO??!!
That was my immediate, strong reaction.

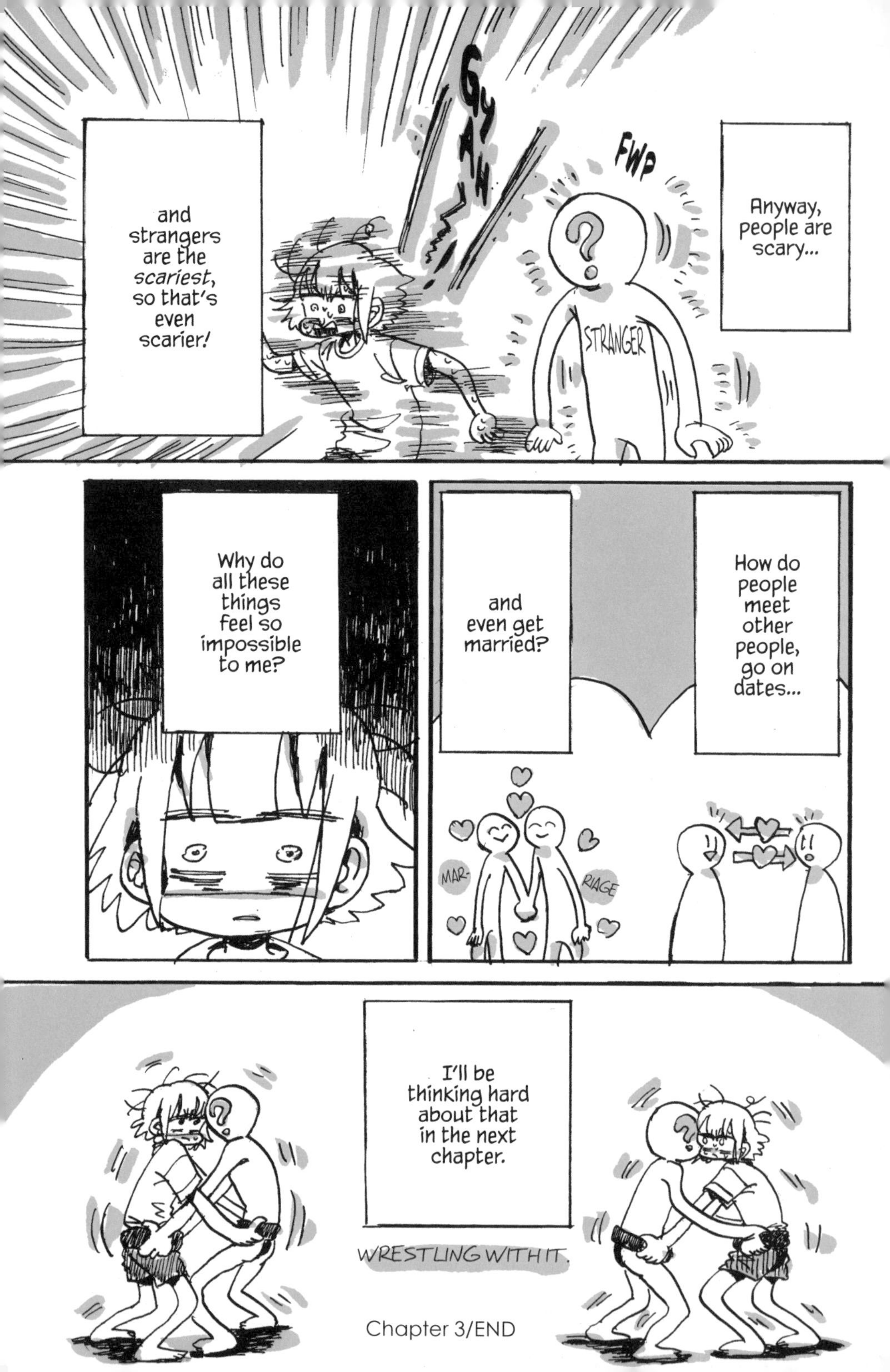
Anyway, people are scary...
FWP
STRANGER
GYAH
and strangers are the *scariest*, so that's even scarier!
How do people meet other people, go on dates...
and even get married?
MAR-
RIAGE
Why do all these things feel so impossible to me?
I'll be thinking hard about that in the next chapter.
WRESTLING WITH IT.
Chapter 3/END

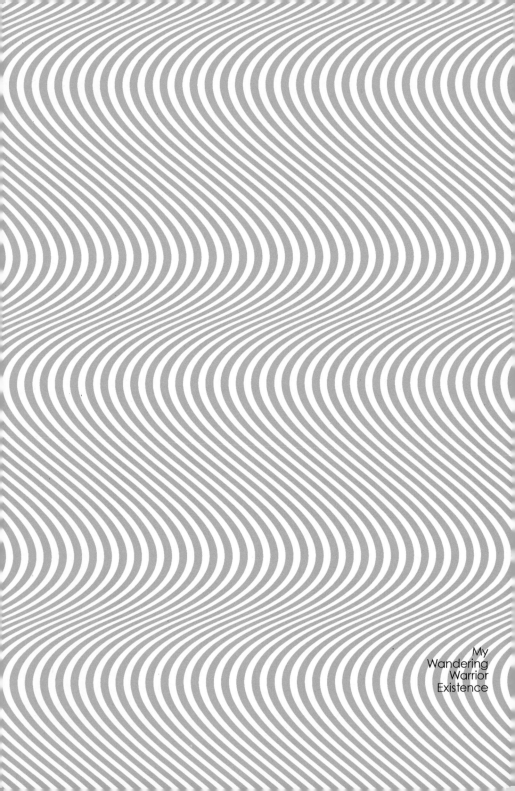

My
Wandering
Warrior
Existence

Chapter 4: Thinking About Why I...

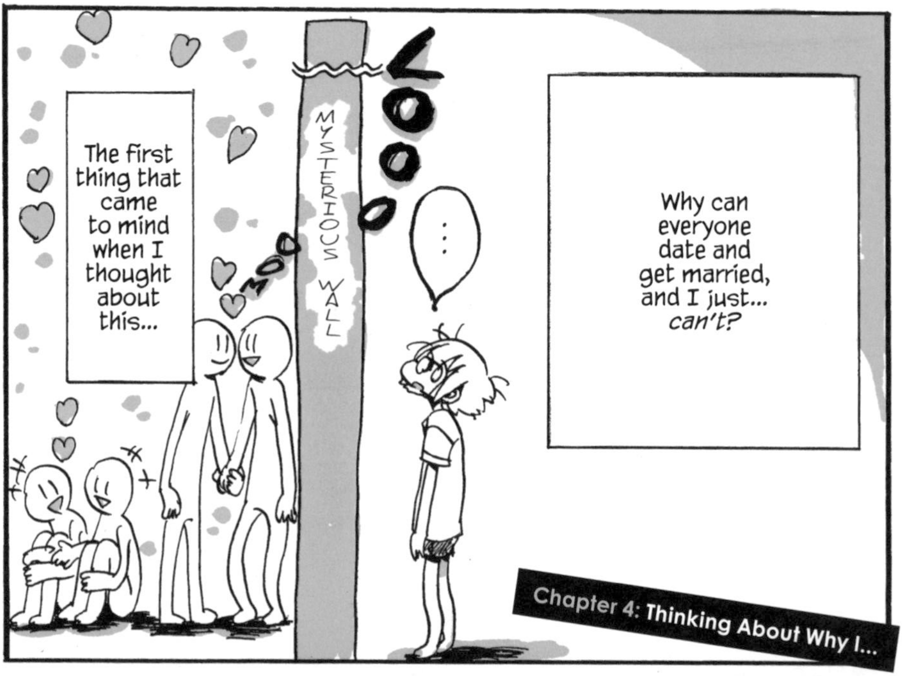
Why can everyone date and get married, and I just... *can't?*
...
LOOOO
MYSTERIOUS WALL
MOOO
The first thing that came to mind when I thought about this...

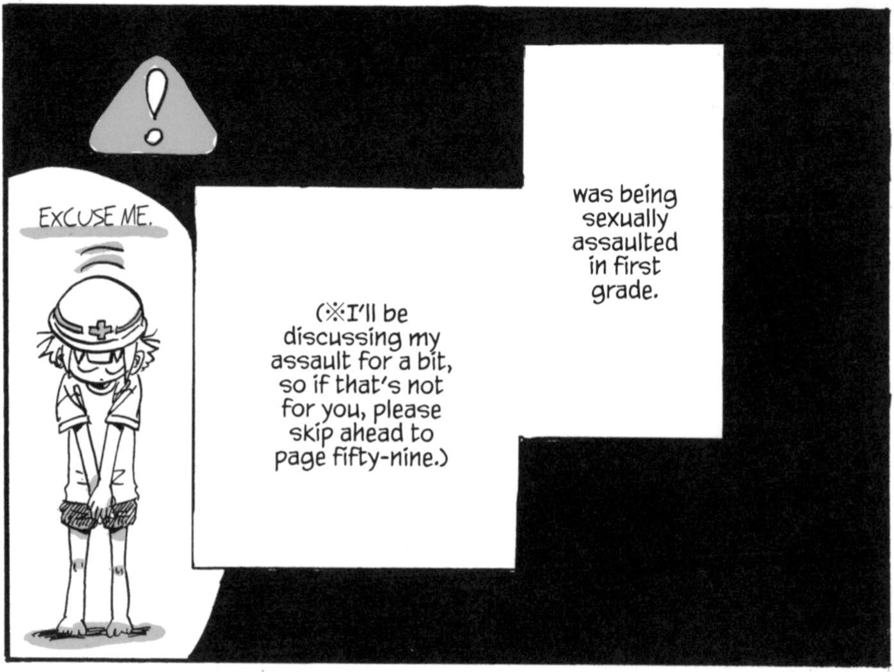
was being sexually assaulted in first grade.
(※I'll be discussing my assault for a bit, so if that's not for you, please skip ahead to page fifty-nine.)
EXCUSE ME.

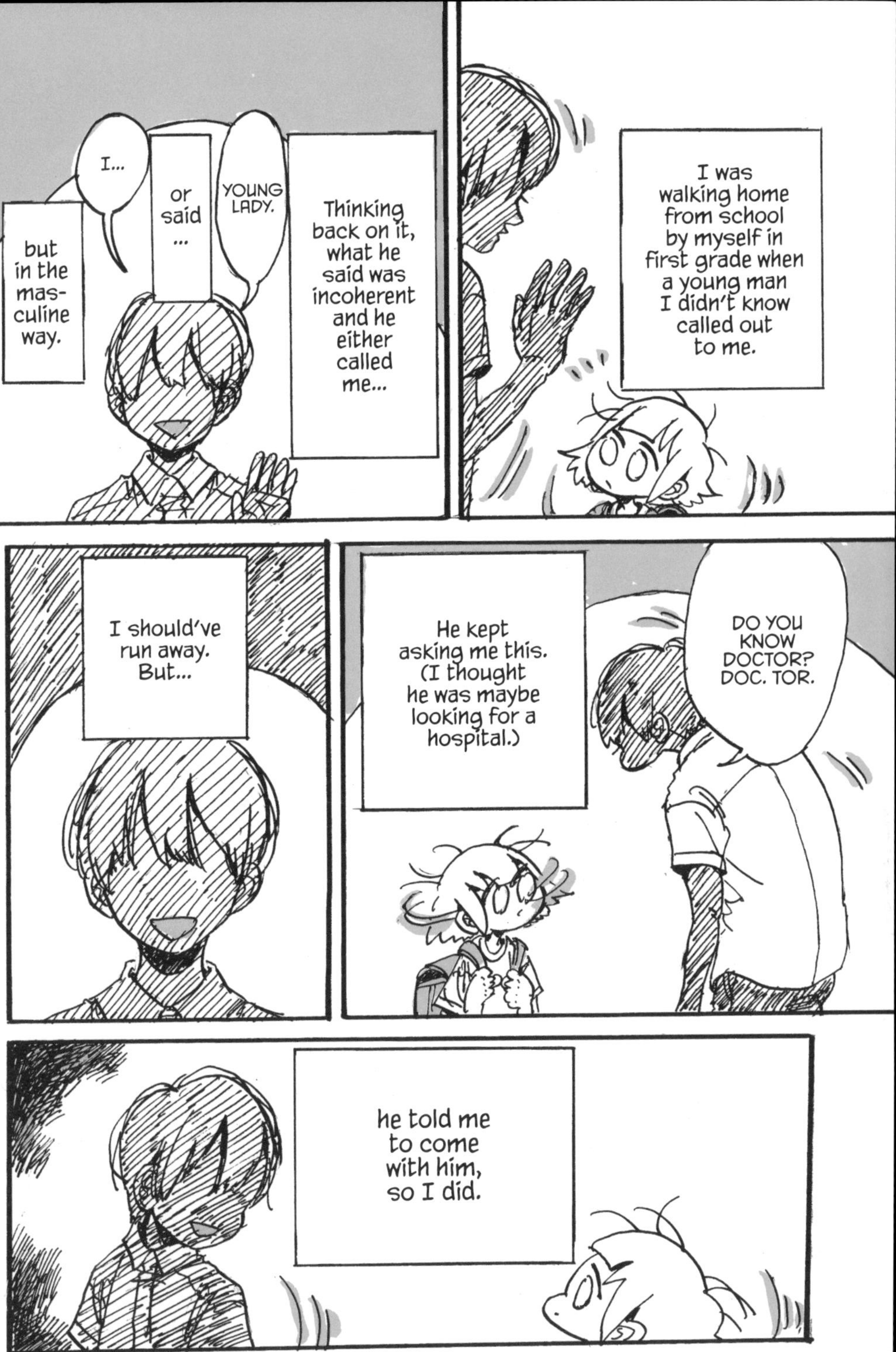
I was walking home from school by myself in first grade when a young man I didn't know called out to me.
Thinking back on it, what he said was incoherent and he either called me...
YOUNG LADY.
or said ...
I...
but in the masculine way.
DO YOU KNOW DOCTOR? DOC. TOR.
He kept asking me this. (I thought he was maybe looking for a hospital.)
I should've run away. But...
he told me to come with him, so I did.

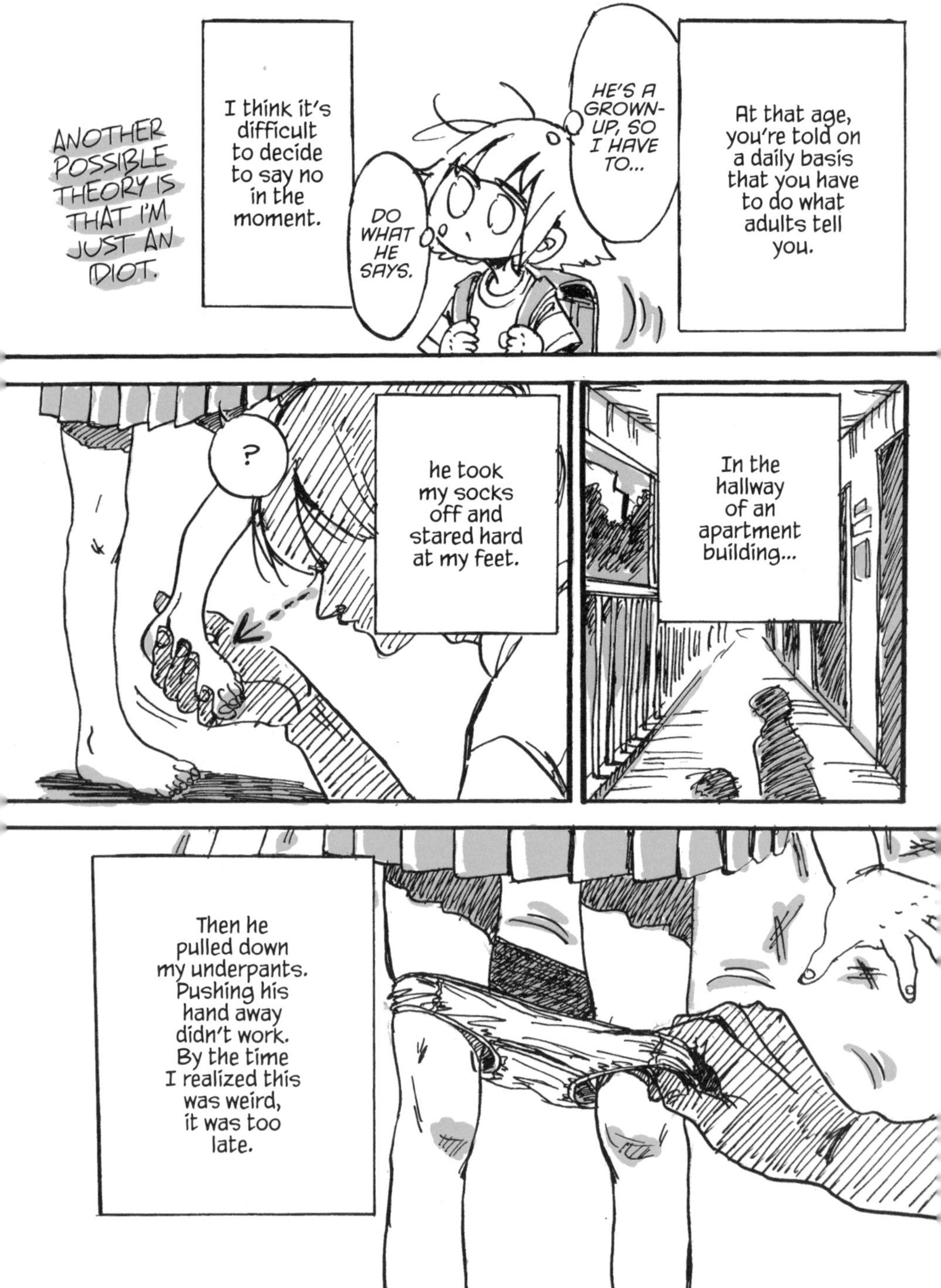
At that age, you're told on a daily basis that you have to do what adults tell you.
HE'S A GROWN-UP, SO I HAVE TO...
DO WHAT HE SAYS.
I think it's difficult to decide to say no in the moment.
ANOTHER POSSIBLE THEORY IS THAT I'M JUST AN IDIOT.
In the hallway of an apartment building...
he took my socks off and stared hard at my feet.
?
Then he pulled down my underpants. Pushing his hand away didn't work. By the time I realized this was weird, it was too late.

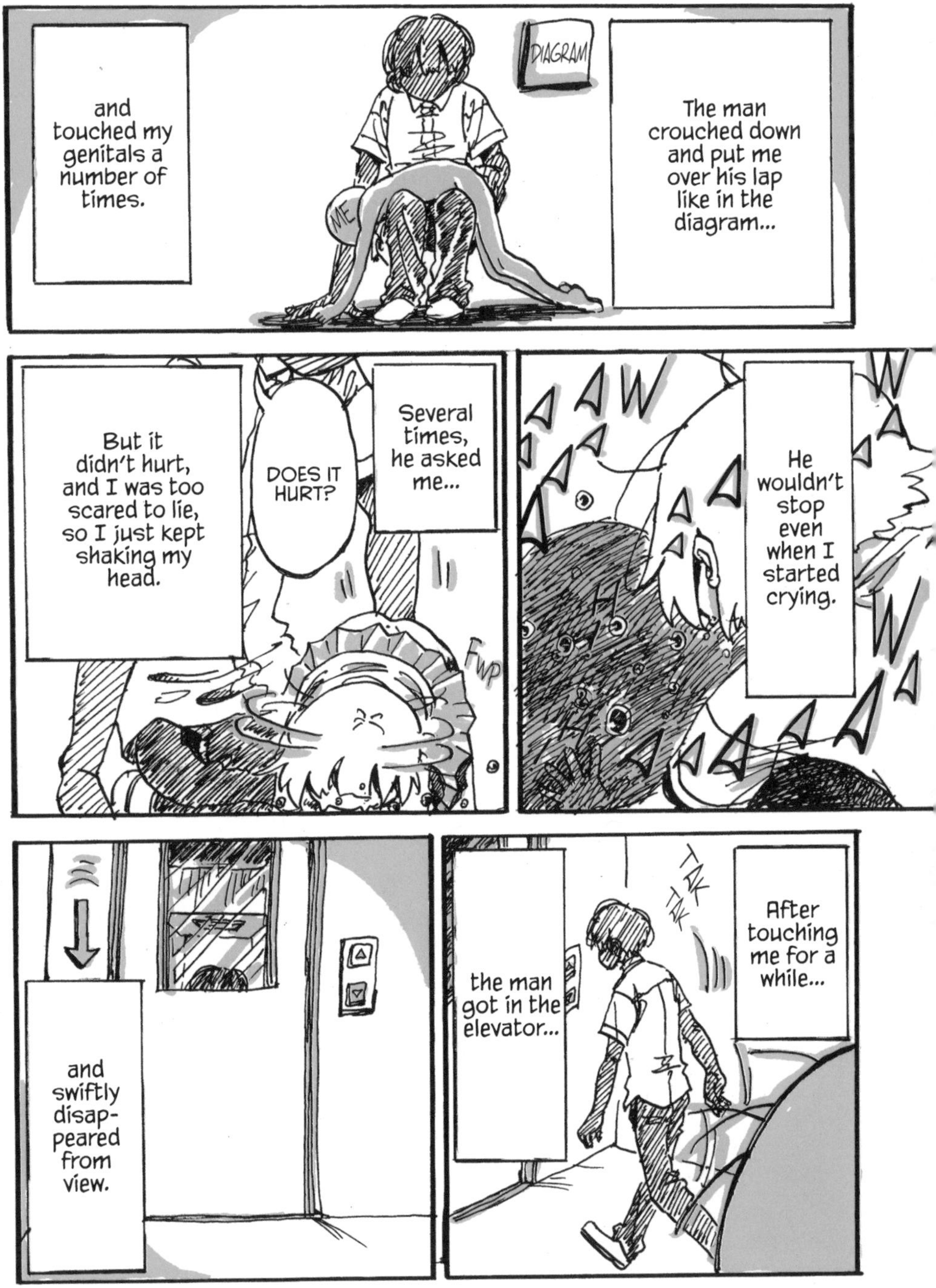
The man crouched down and put me over his lap like in the diagram...
DIAGRAM
ME
and touched my genitals a number of times.
He wouldn't stop even when I started crying.
Several times, he asked me...
DOES IT HURT?
But it didn't hurt, and I was too scared to lie, so I just kept shaking my head.
FWP
After touching me for a while...
the man got in the elevator...
and swiftly disap-peared from view.

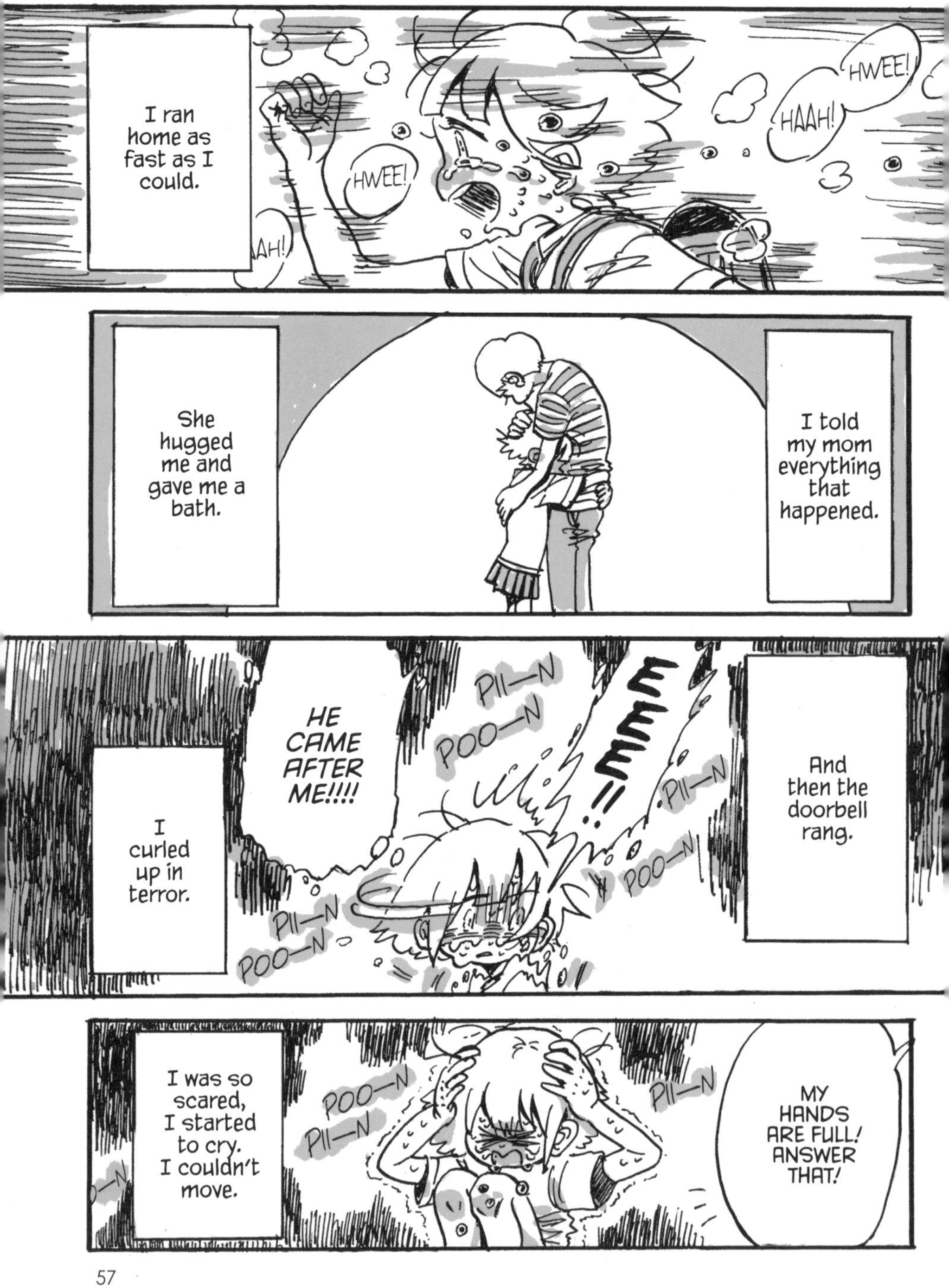
HWEE!
HAAH!
HWEE!
I ran home as fast as I could.
AH!
I told my mom everything that happened.
She hugged me and gave me a bath.
And then the doorbell rang.
PII—N
POO—N
PII—N
POO—N
EEEE!!
HE CAME AFTER ME!!!!
I curled up in terror.
PII—N
POO—N
MY HANDS ARE FULL! ANSWER THAT!
PII—N
POO—N
PII—N
I was so scared, I started to cry. I couldn't move.

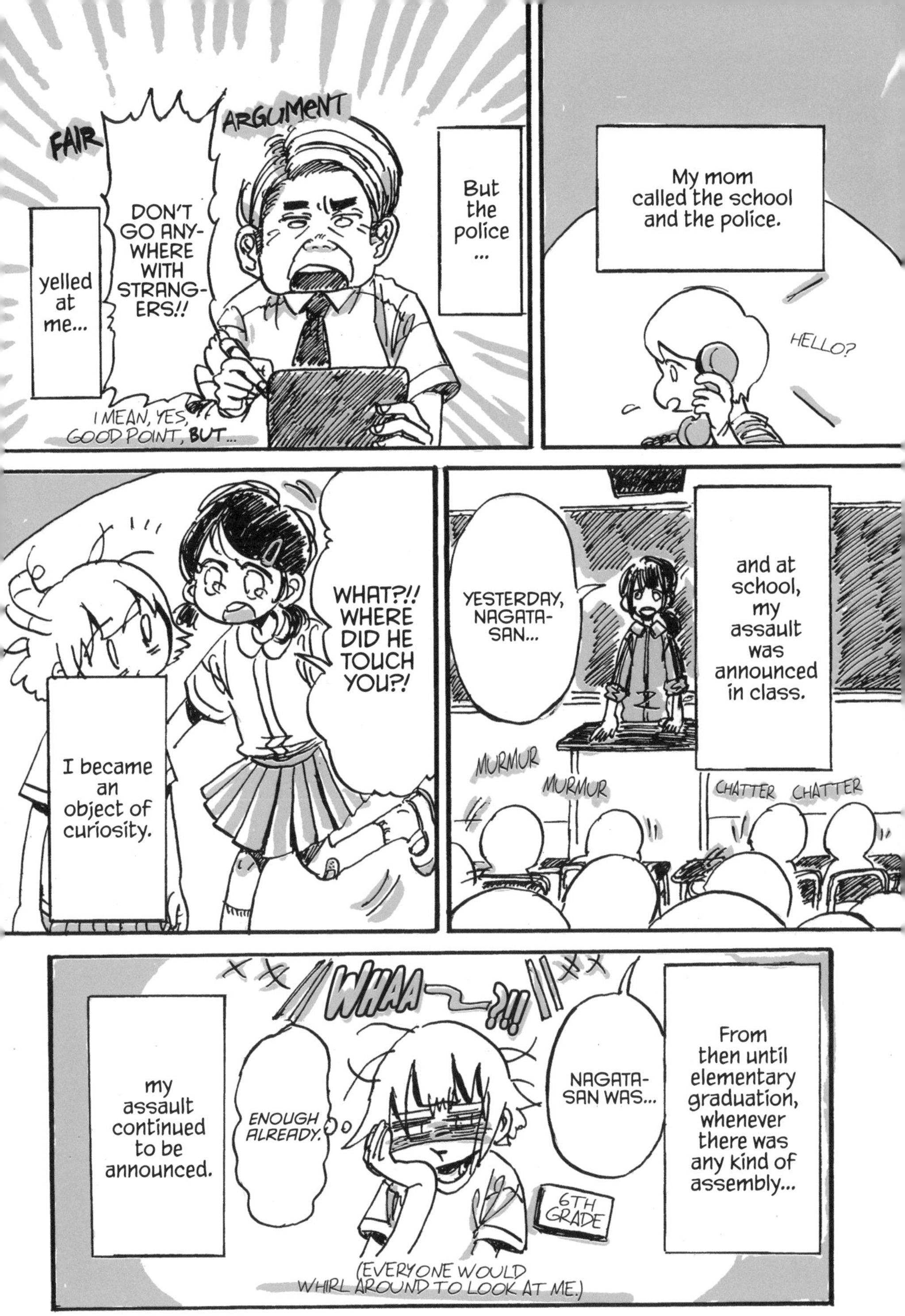
My mom called the school and the police.
HELLO?
But the police ...
FAIR ARGUMENT
DON'T GO ANYWHERE WITH STRANGERS!!
yelled at me...
I MEAN, YES, GOOD POINT, BUT...
and at school, my assault was announced in class.
YESTERDAY, NAGATA-SAN...
MURMUR
MURMUR
CHATTER CHATTER
WHAT?!! WHERE DID HE TOUCH YOU?!
I became an object of curiosity.
From then until elementary graduation, whenever there was any kind of assembly...
NAGATA-SAN WAS...
WHAA~?!!
6TH GRADE
ENOUGH ALREADY.
my assault continued to be announced.
(EVERYONE WOULD WHIRL AROUND TO LOOK AT ME.)

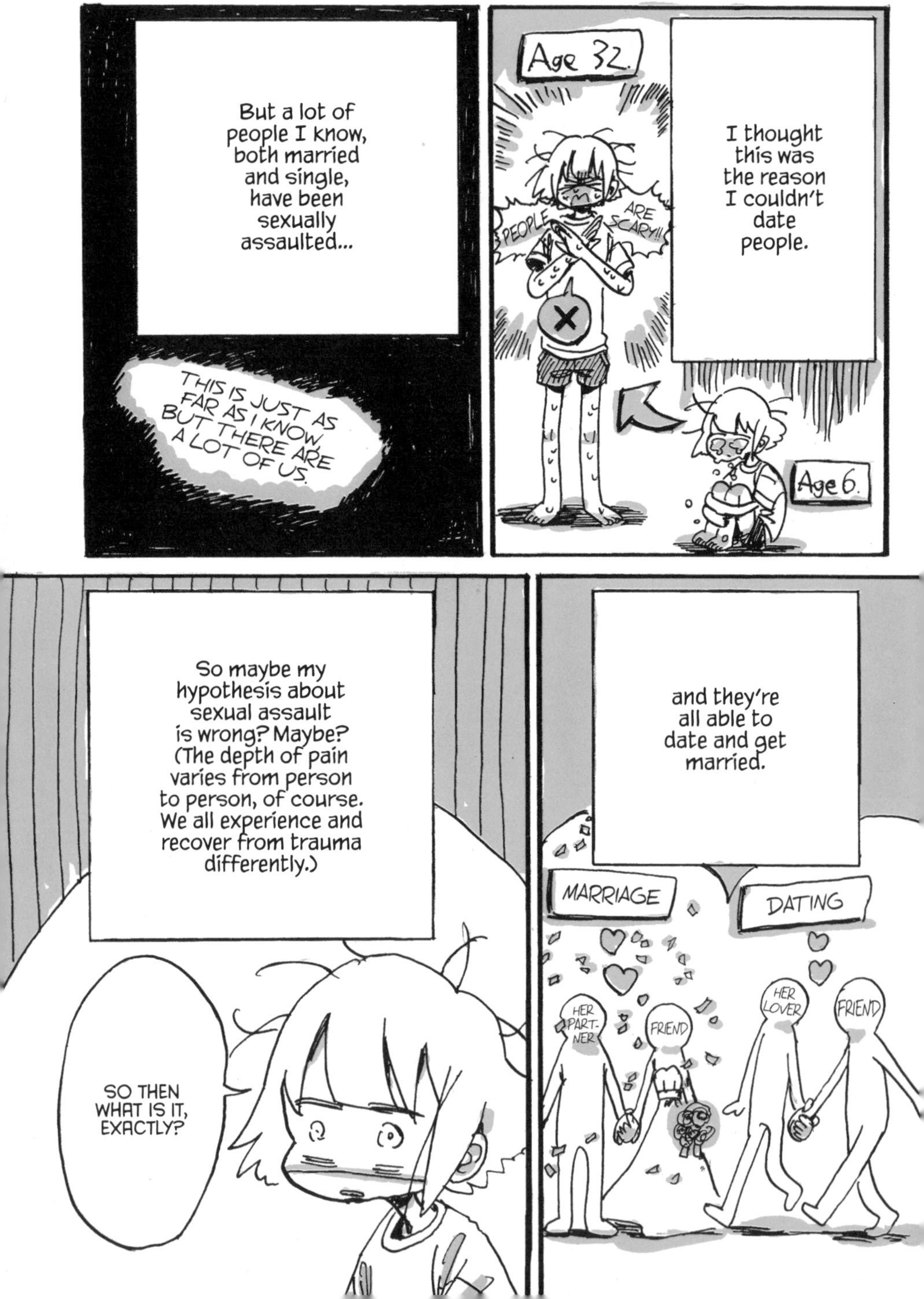
I thought this was the reason I couldn't date people.
Age 32.
PEOPLE ARE SCARY!!
Age 6.
But a lot of people I know, both married and single, have been sexually assaulted...
THIS IS JUST AS FAR AS I KNOW, BUT THERE ARE A LOT OF US.
and they're all able to date and get married.
DATING
MARRIAGE
HER LOVER
FRIEND
FRIEND
HER PART-NER
So maybe my hypothesis about sexual assault is wrong? Maybe? (The depth of pain varies from person to person, of course. We all experience and recover from trauma differently.)
SO THEN WHAT IS IT, EXACTLY?

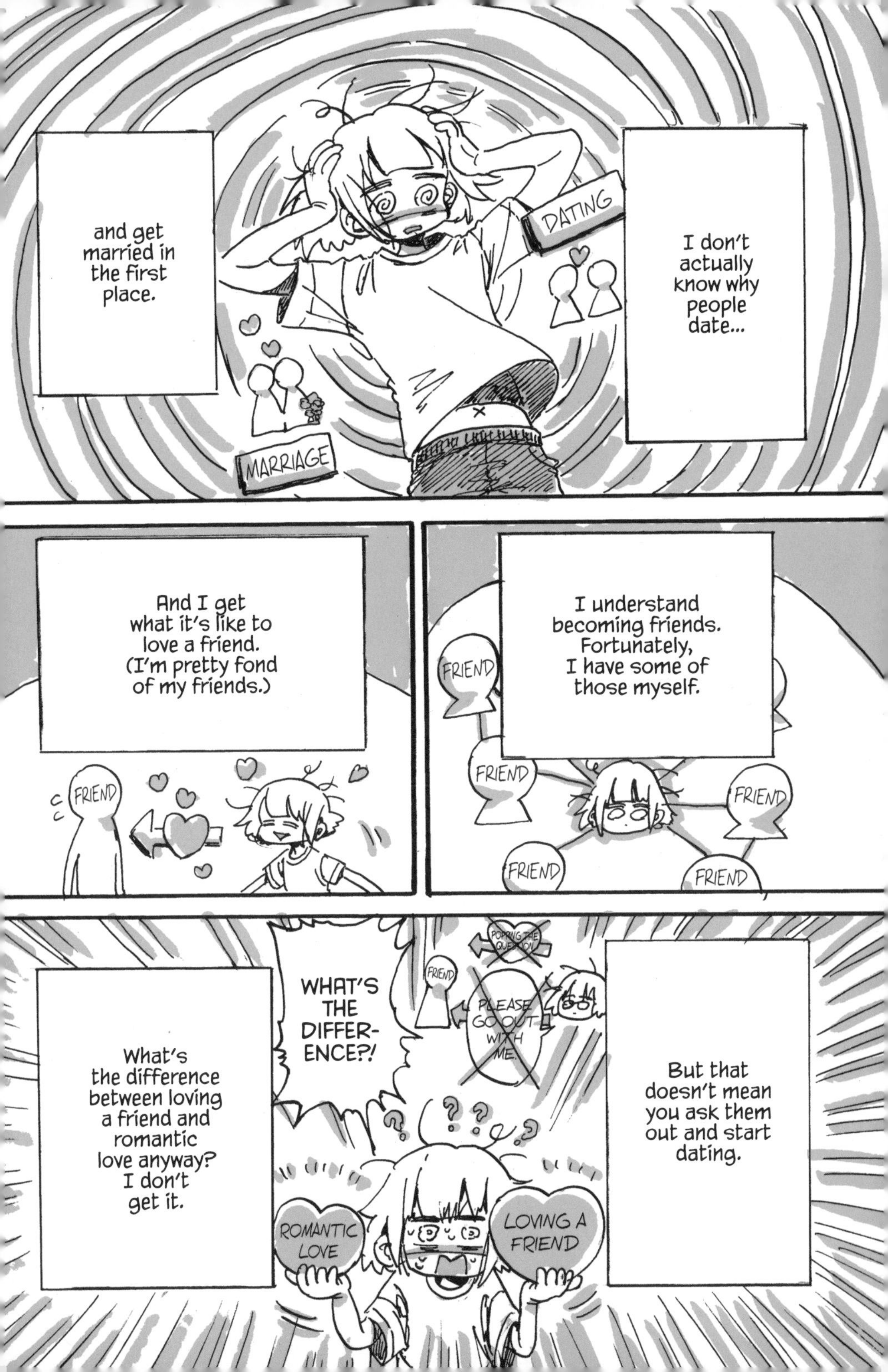
I don't actually know why people date...
DATING
and get married in the first place.
MARRIAGE
I understand becoming friends. Fortunately, I have some of those myself.
FRIEND
FRIEND
FRIEND
FRIEND
FRIEND
And I get what it's like to love a friend. (I'm pretty fond of my friends.)
FRIEND
But that doesn't mean you ask them out and start dating.
POPPING THE QUESTION
FRIEND
PLEASE GO OUT WITH ME.
WHAT'S THE DIFFER-ENCE?!
What's the difference between loving a friend and romantic love anyway? I don't get it.
LOVING A FRIEND
ROMANTIC LOVE

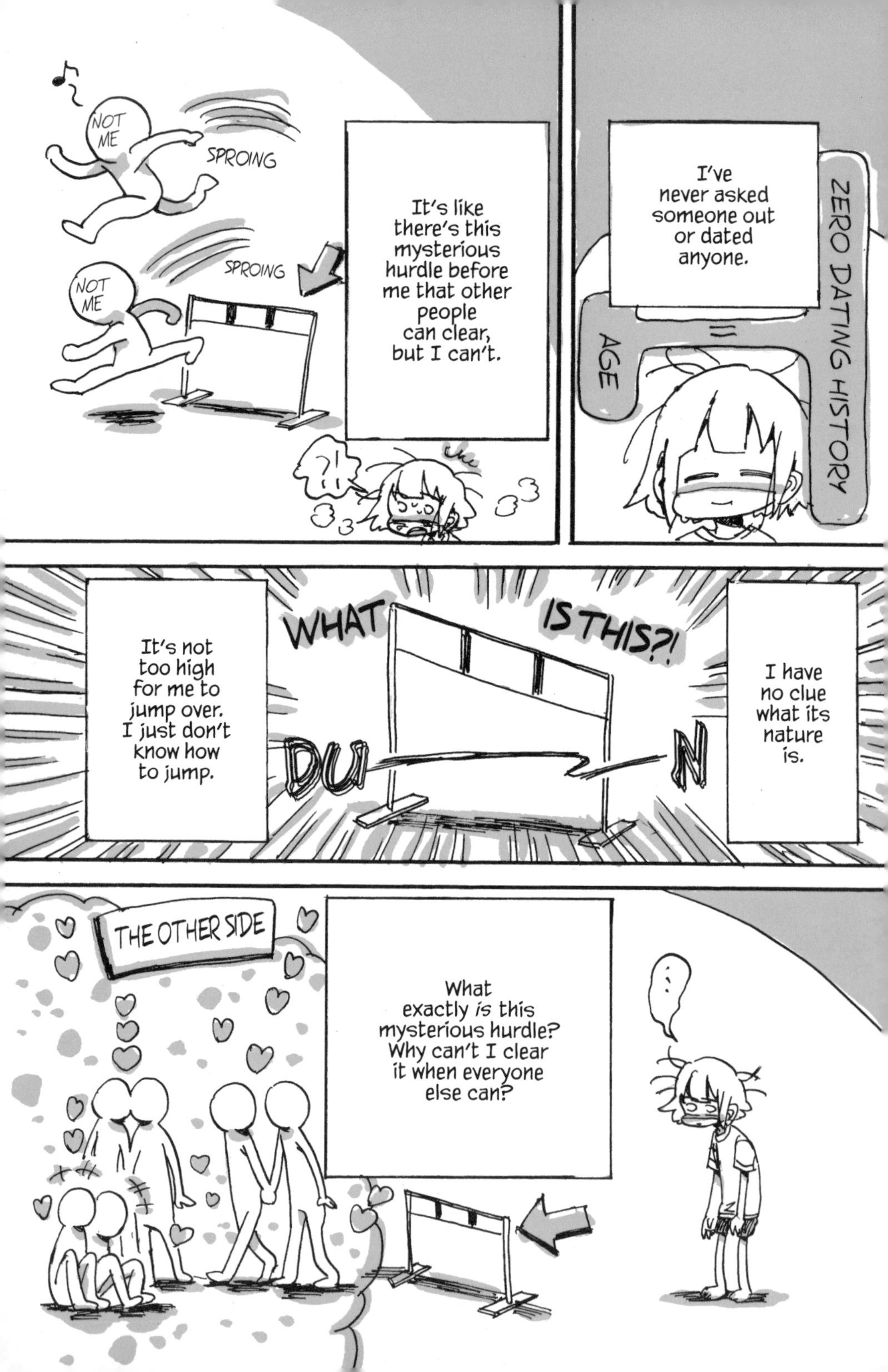

I've never asked someone out or dated anyone.
ZERO DATING HISTORY
=
AGE
It's like there's this mysterious hurdle before me that other people can clear, but I can't.
NOT ME
SPROING
NOT ME
SPROING
?!
I have no clue what its nature is.
WHAT IS THIS?!
DU——N
It's not too high for me to jump over. I just don't know how to jump.
...
What exactly *is* this mysterious hurdle? Why can't I clear it when everyone else can?
THE OTHER SIDE

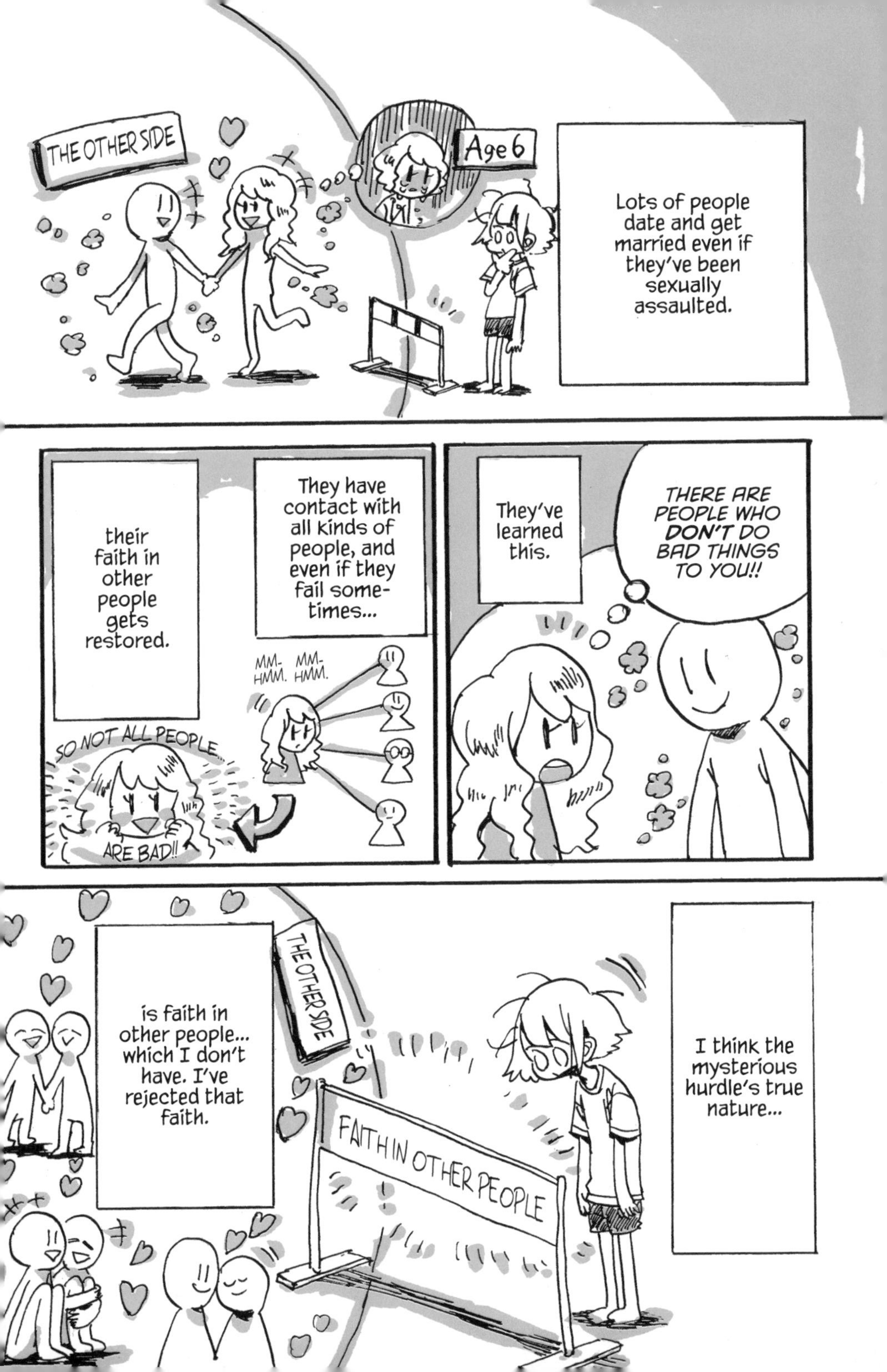
Lots of people date and get married even if they've been sexually assaulted.
Age 6
THE OTHER SIDE
THERE ARE PEOPLE WHO **DON'T** DO BAD THINGS TO YOU!!
They've learned this.
They have contact with all kinds of people, and even if they fail sometimes...
MM-HMM. MM-HMM.
their faith in other people gets restored.
SO NOT ALL PEOPLE... ARE BAD!!
I think the mysterious hurdle's true nature...
FAITH IN OTHER PEOPLE
THE OTHER SIDE
is faith in other people... which I don't have. I've rejected that faith.

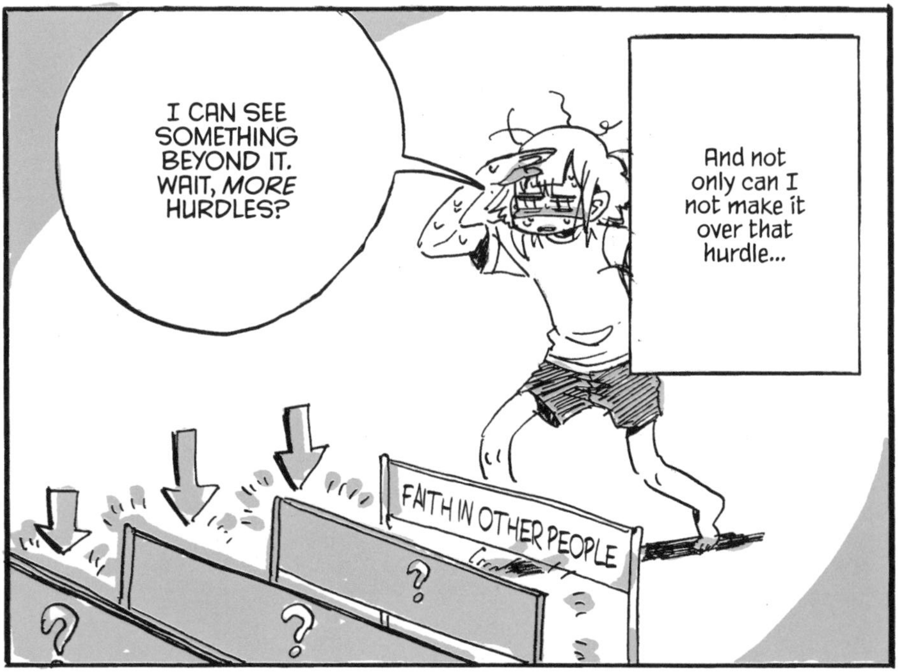
And not only can I not make it over that hurdle...
I CAN SEE SOMETHING BEYOND IT. WAIT, *MORE* HURDLES?
FAITH IN OTHER PEOPLE

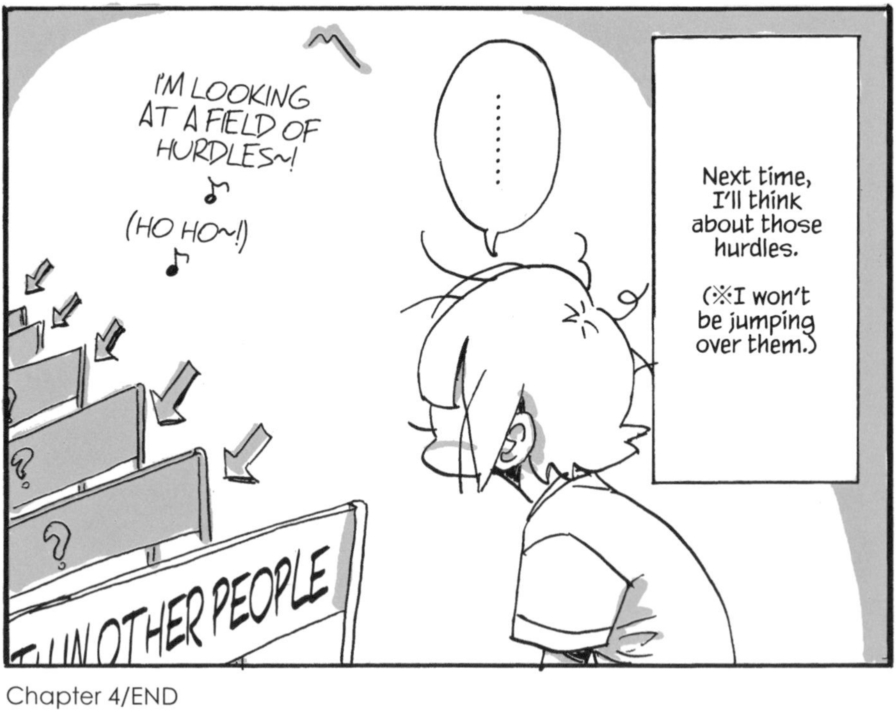
Next time, I'll think about those hurdles.
(※I won't be jumping over them.)
......
I'M LOOKING AT A FIELD OF HURDLES~!
(HO HO~!)
IN OTHER PEOPLE

Chapter 4/END

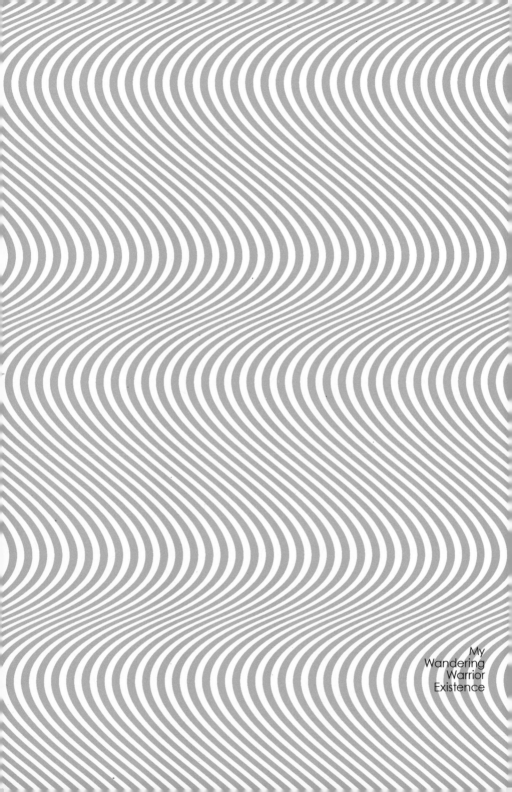

My
Wandering
Warrior
Existence

Chapter 5: I Take a Good Look at the Countless Hurdles

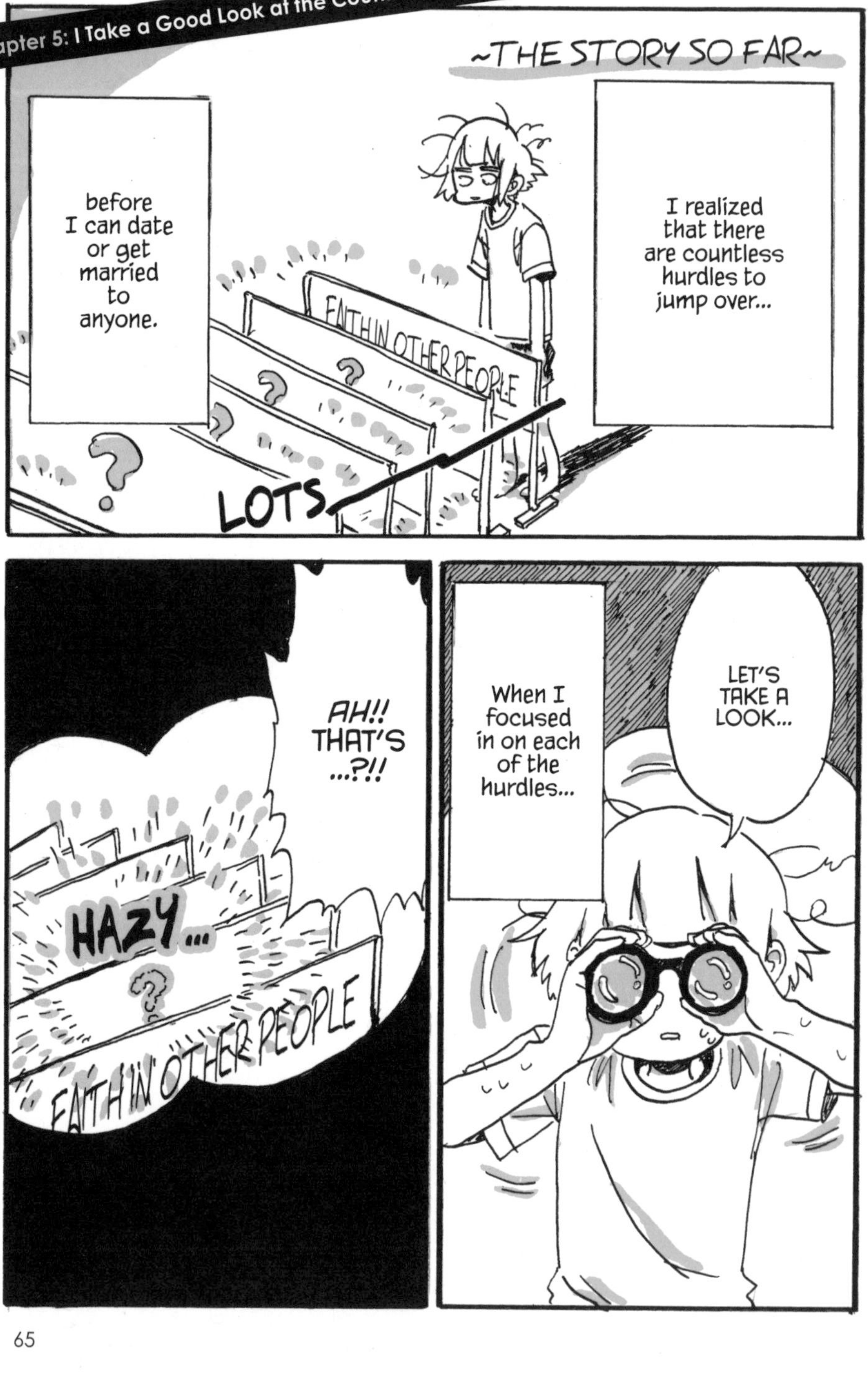
~THE STORY SO FAR~
I realized that there are countless hurdles to jump over...
before I can date or get married to anyone.
FAITH IN OTHER PEOPLE
LOTS
LET'S TAKE A LOOK...
When I focused in on each of the hurdles...
AH!! THAT'S ...?!!
HAZY...
FAITH IN OTHER PEOPLE

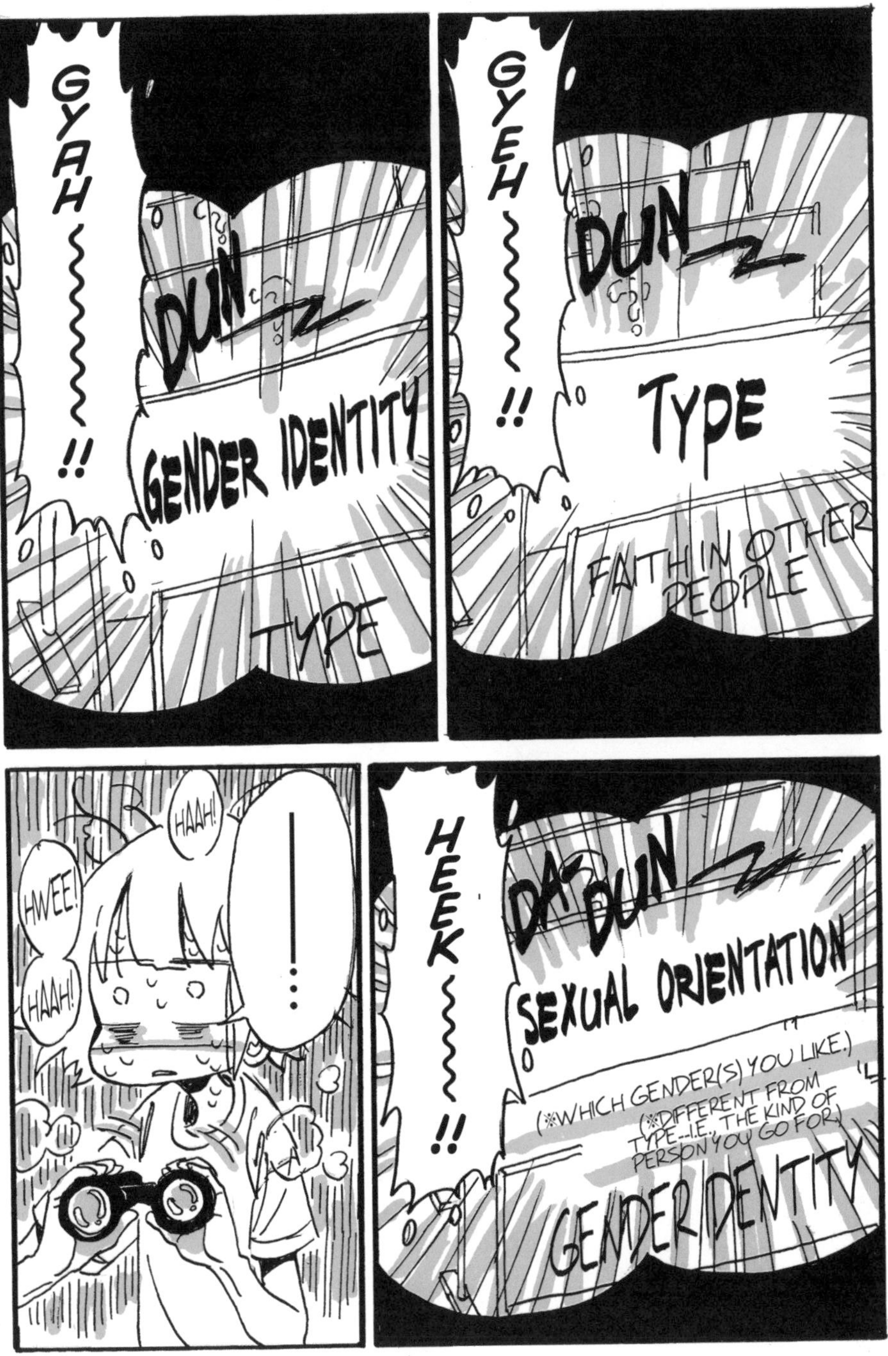
GYEH~!!
DUN
TYPE
FAITH IN OTHER PEOPLE
GYAH~!!
DUN
GENDER IDENTITY
TYPE
HEEK~!!
DA-DUN
SEXUAL ORIENTATION
(※WHICH GENDER(S) YOU LIKE.)
(※DIFFERENT FROM TYPE--I.E., THE KIND OF PERSON YOU GO FOR.)
GENDER IDENTITY
HAAH!
—...
HWEE!
HAAH!

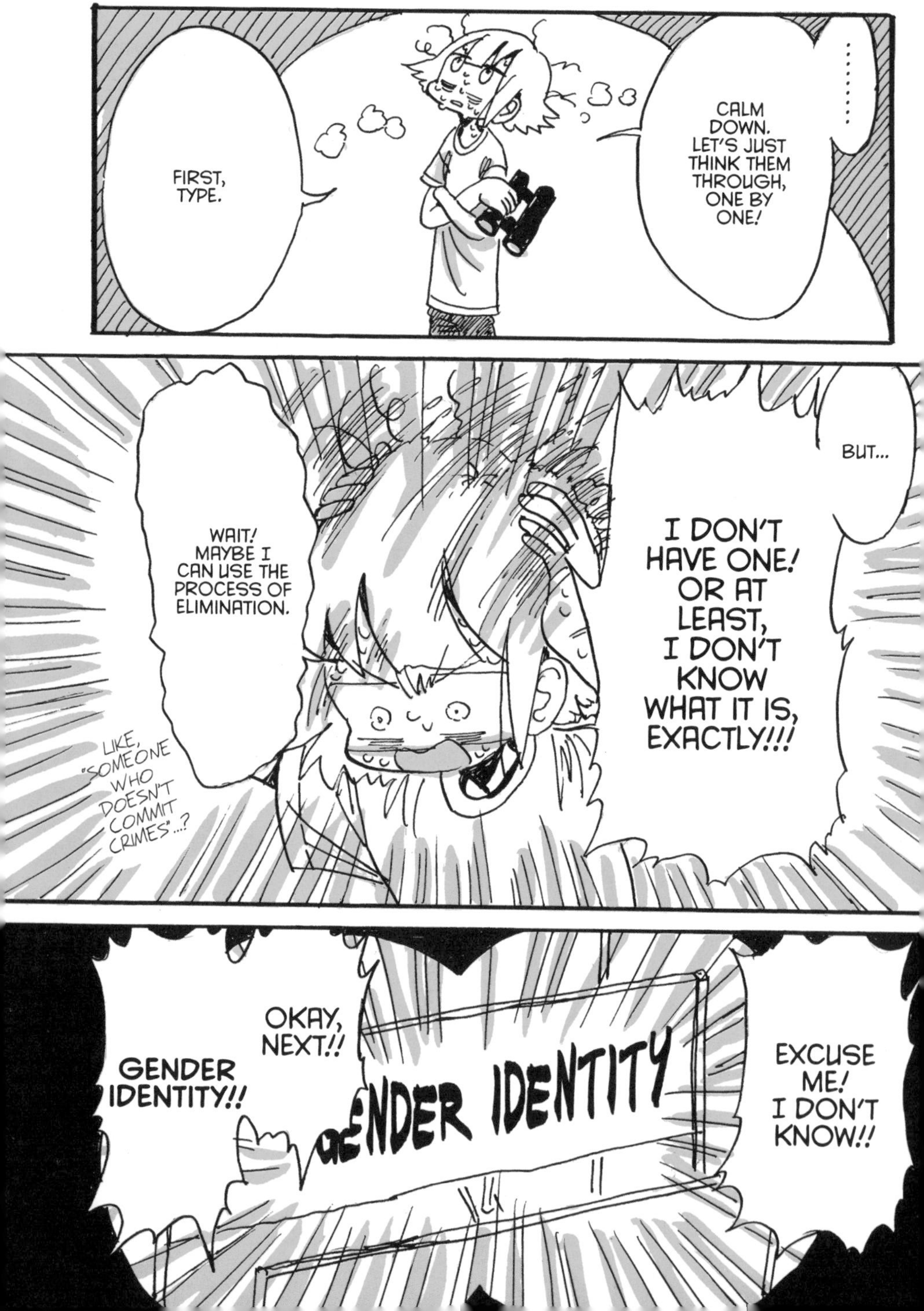
......
CALM DOWN. LET'S JUST THINK THEM THROUGH, ONE BY ONE!
FIRST, TYPE.
BUT...
I DON'T HAVE ONE! OR AT LEAST, I DON'T KNOW WHAT IT IS, EXACTLY!!!
WAIT! MAYBE I CAN USE THE PROCESS OF ELIMINATION.
LIKE, "SOMEONE WHO DOESN'T COMMIT CRIMES"...?
EXCUSE ME! I DON'T KNOW!!
GENDER IDENTITY
OKAY, NEXT!!
GENDER IDENTITY!!

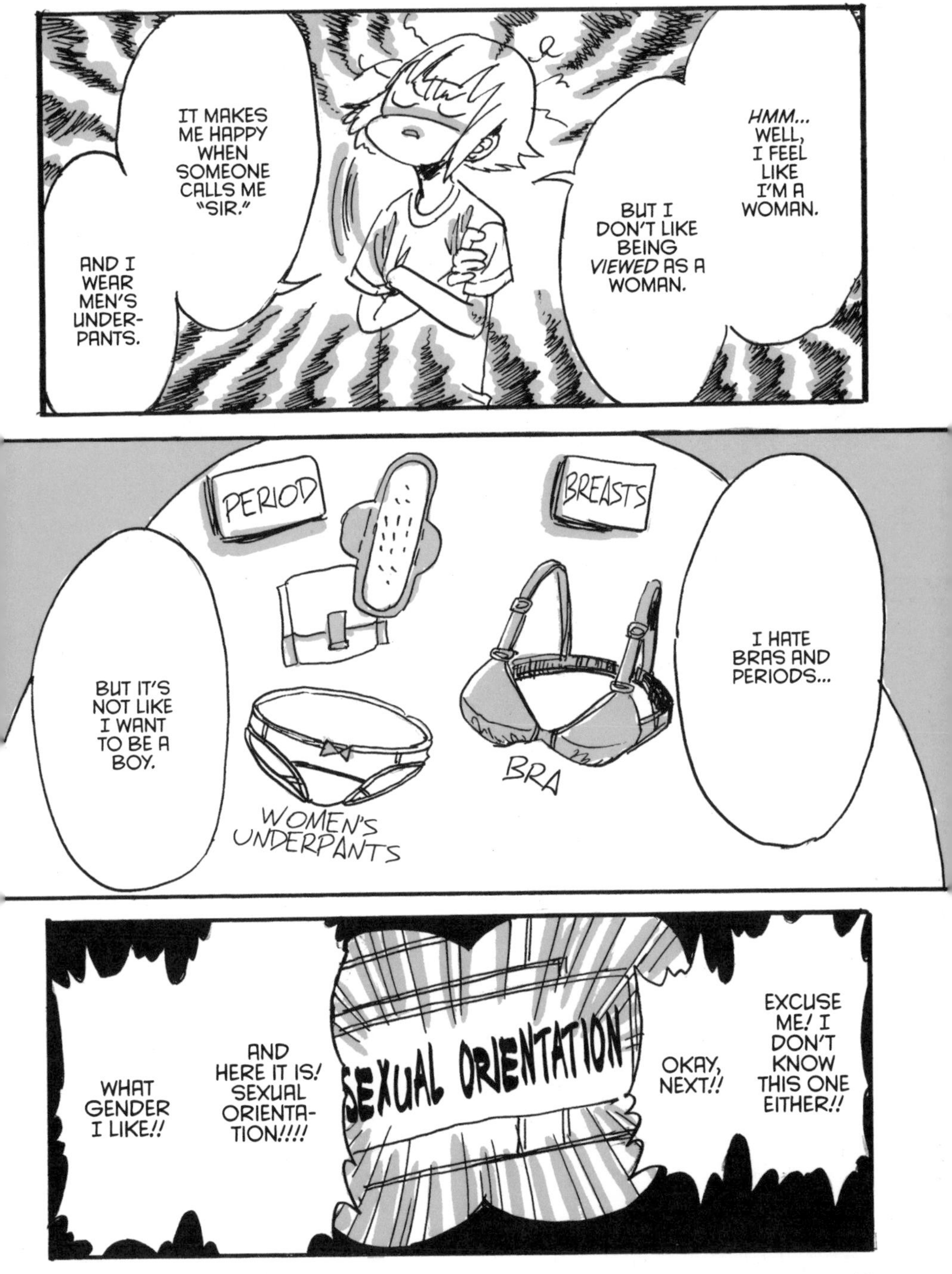
HMM... WELL, I FEEL LIKE I'M A WOMAN.
BUT I DON'T LIKE BEING *VIEWED* AS A WOMAN.
IT MAKES ME HAPPY WHEN SOMEONE CALLS ME "SIR."
AND I WEAR MEN'S UNDER-PANTS.
I HATE BRAS AND PERIODS...
BREASTS
BRA
PERIOD
WOMEN'S UNDERPANTS
BUT IT'S NOT LIKE I WANT TO BE A BOY.
EXCUSE ME! I DON'T KNOW THIS ONE EITHER!!
OKAY, NEXT!!
SEXUAL ORIENTATION
AND HERE IT IS! SEXUAL ORIENTA-TION!!!!
WHAT GENDER I LIKE!!

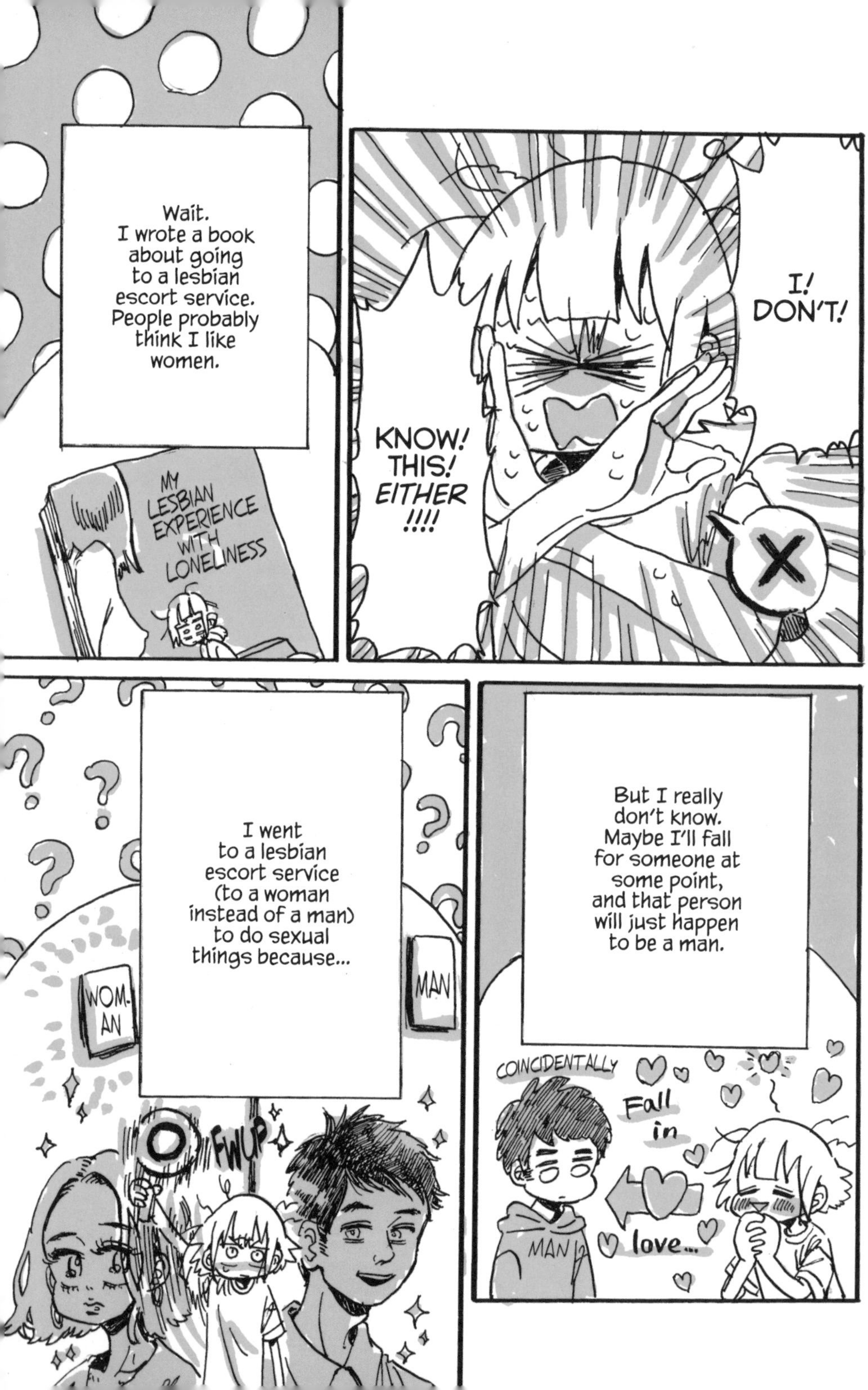
I! DON'T!
KNOW! THIS! EITHER!!!!
Wait. I wrote a book about going to a lesbian escort service. People probably think I like women.
MY LESBIAN EXPERIENCE WITH LONELINESS
But I really don't know. Maybe I'll fall for someone at some point, and that person will just happen to be a man.
COINCIDENTALLY
Fall in love...
MAN
I went to a lesbian escort service (to a woman instead of a man) to do sexual things because...
WOM-AN
MAN
FWUP

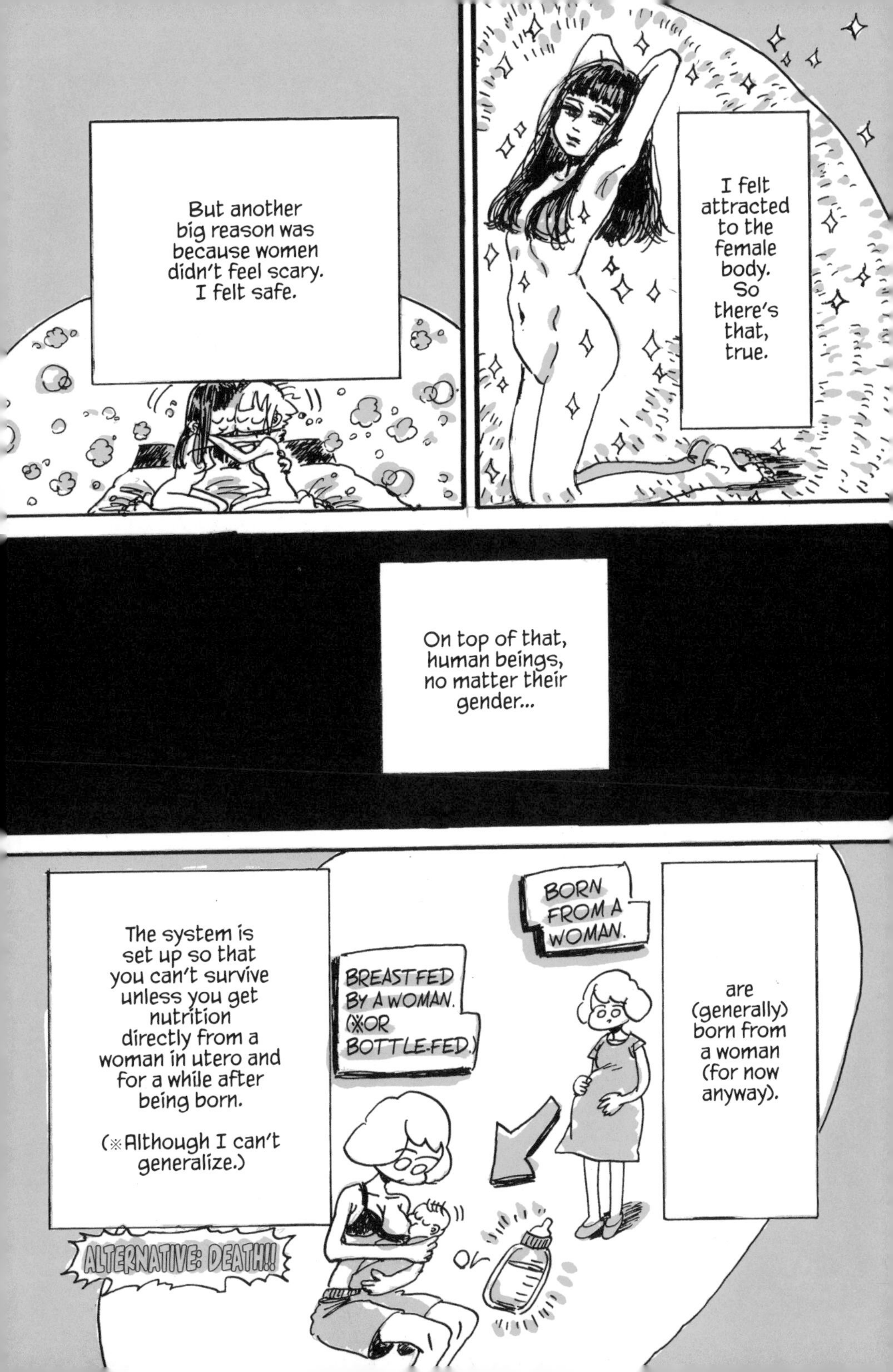

I felt attracted to the female body. So there's that, true.
But another big reason was because women didn't feel scary. I felt safe.
On top of that, human beings, no matter their gender...
are (generally) born from a woman (for now anyway).
BORN FROM A WOMAN.
BREASTFED BY A WOMAN. (※OR BOTTLE-FED.)
The system is set up so that you can't survive unless you get nutrition directly from a woman in utero and for a while after being born.
(※Although I can't generalize.)
ALTERNATIVE: DEATH!!
or

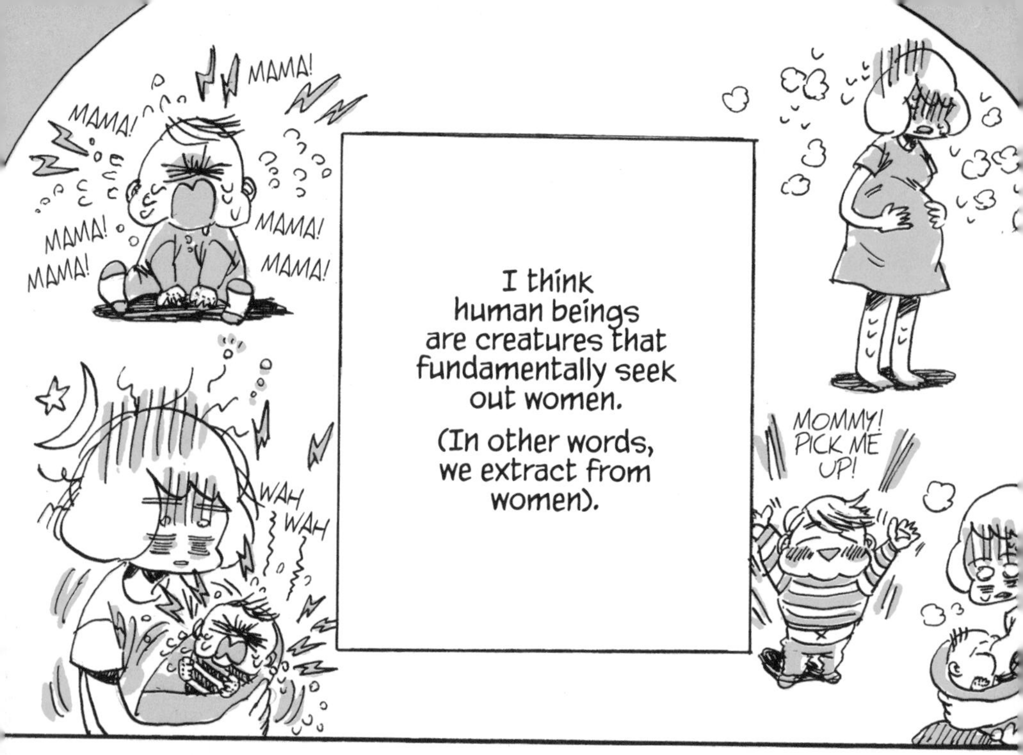
I think
human beings
are creatures that
fundamentally seek
out women.
(In other words,
we extract from
women).
MOMMY! PICK ME UP!
MAMA!
MAMA!
MAMA!
MAMA!
MAMA!
MAMA!
WAH WAH

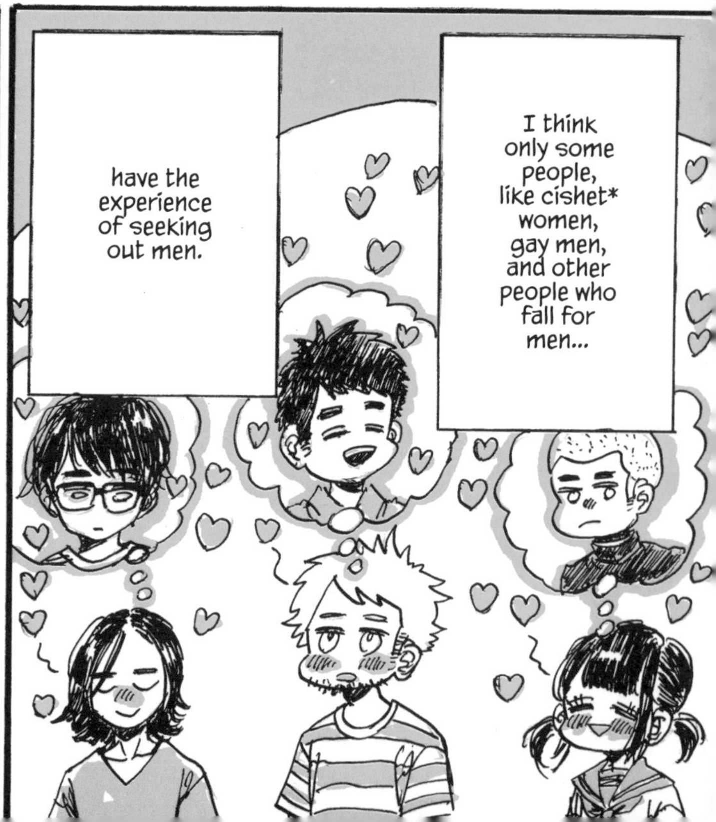
I think only some people, like cishet* women, gay men, and other people who fall for men...
have the experience of seeking out men.

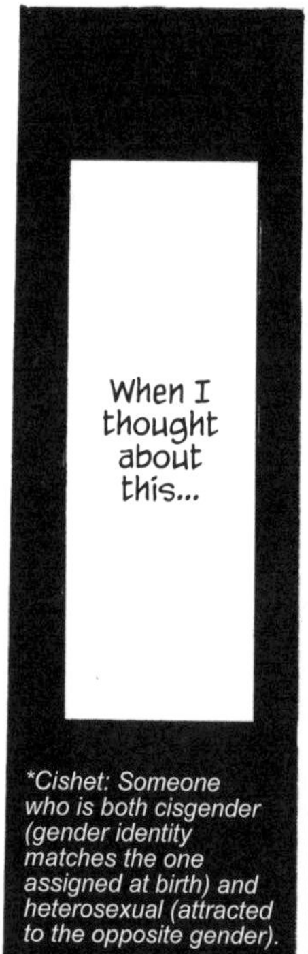
When I thought about this...

*Cishet: Someone who is both cisgender (gender identity matches the one assigned at birth) and heterosexual (attracted to the opposite gender).

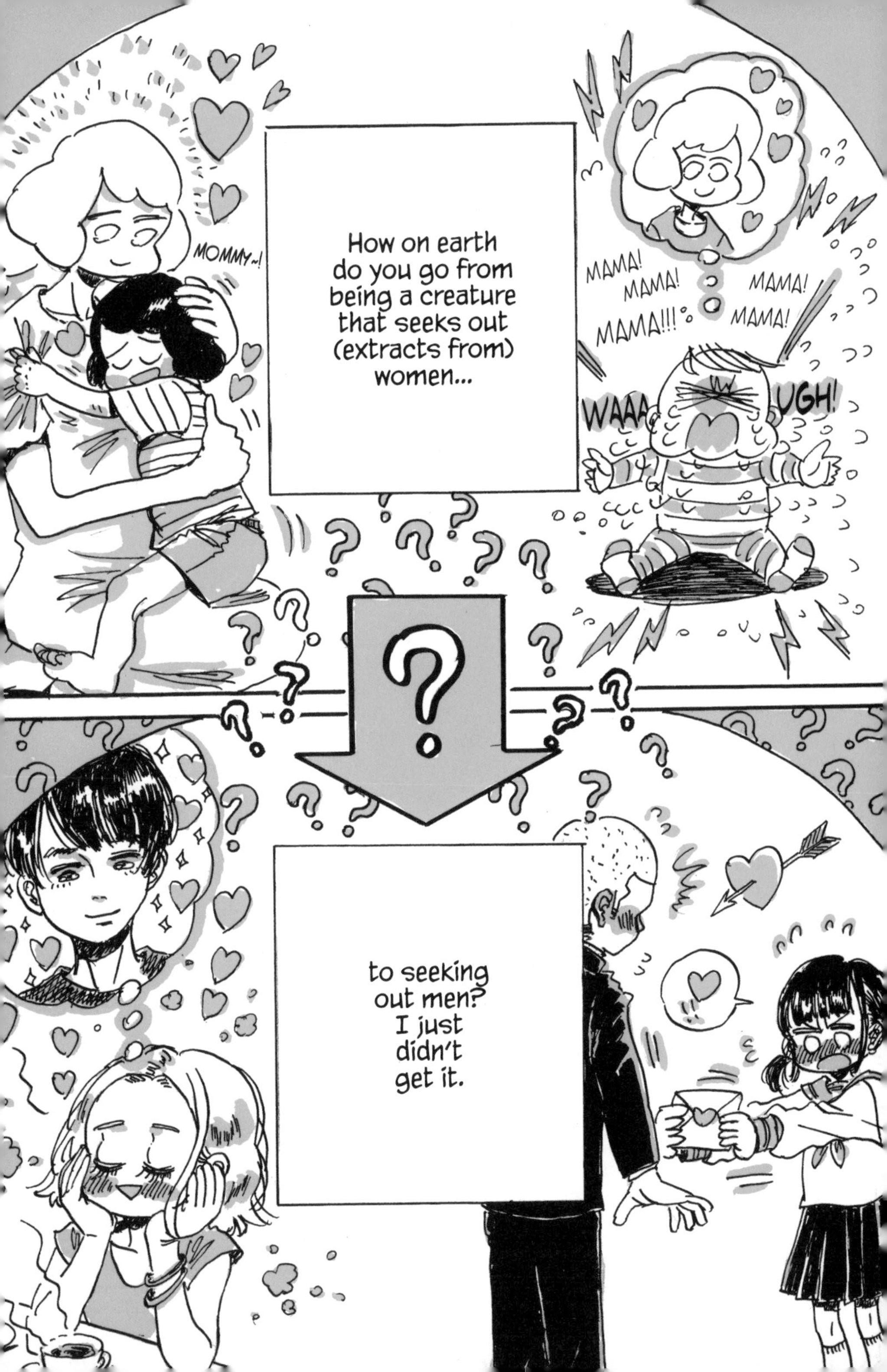
MAMA!
MAMA!
MAMA!
MAMA!
MAMA!!!
WAAAUGH!
How on earth do you go from being a creature that seeks out (extracts from) women...
MOMMY~!
to seeking out men? I just didn't get it.

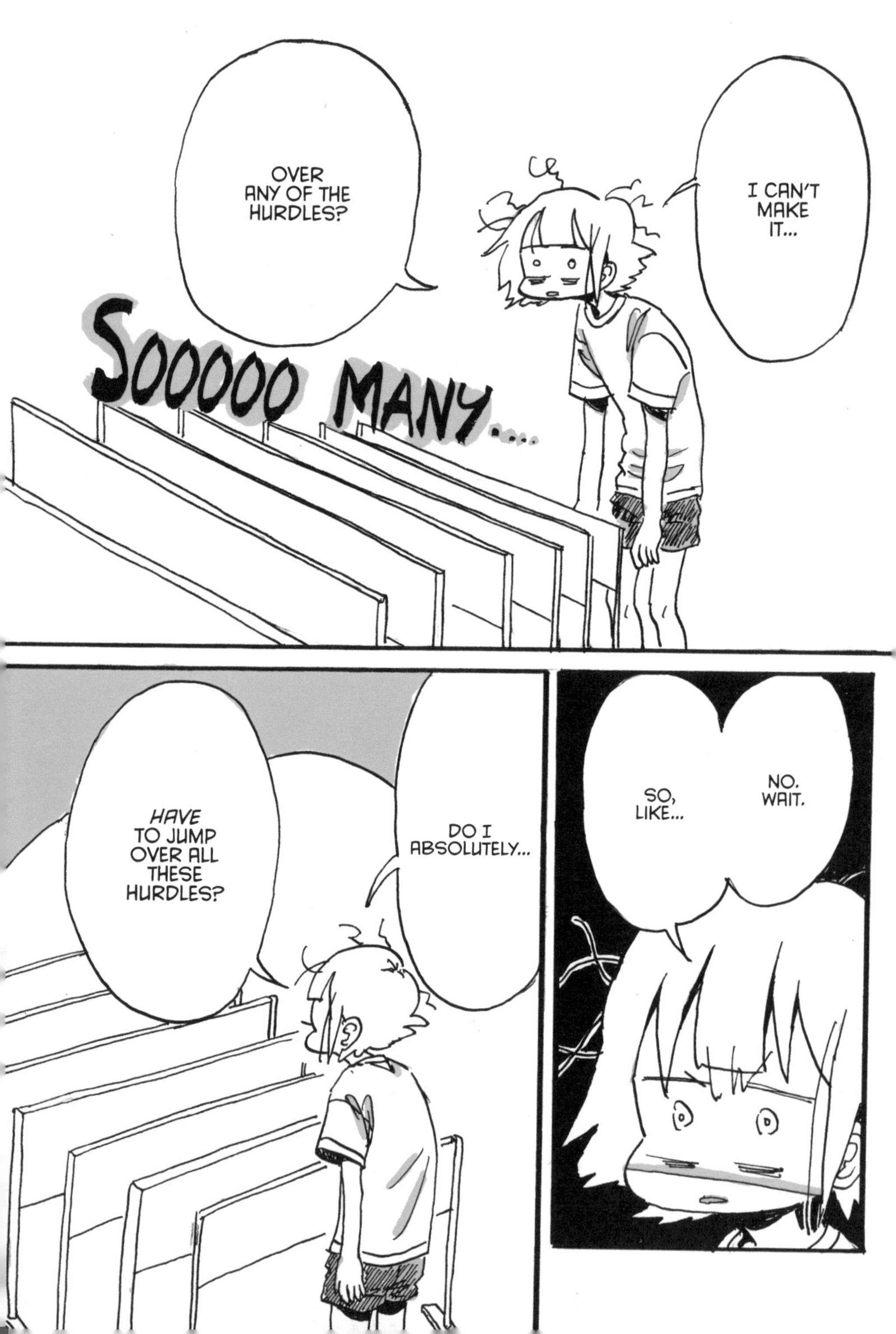
I CAN'T MAKE IT...
OVER ANY OF THE HURDLES?
SOOOOO MANY....
NO. WAIT.
SO, LIKE...
DO I ABSOLUTELY...
HAVE TO JUMP OVER ALL THESE HURDLES?

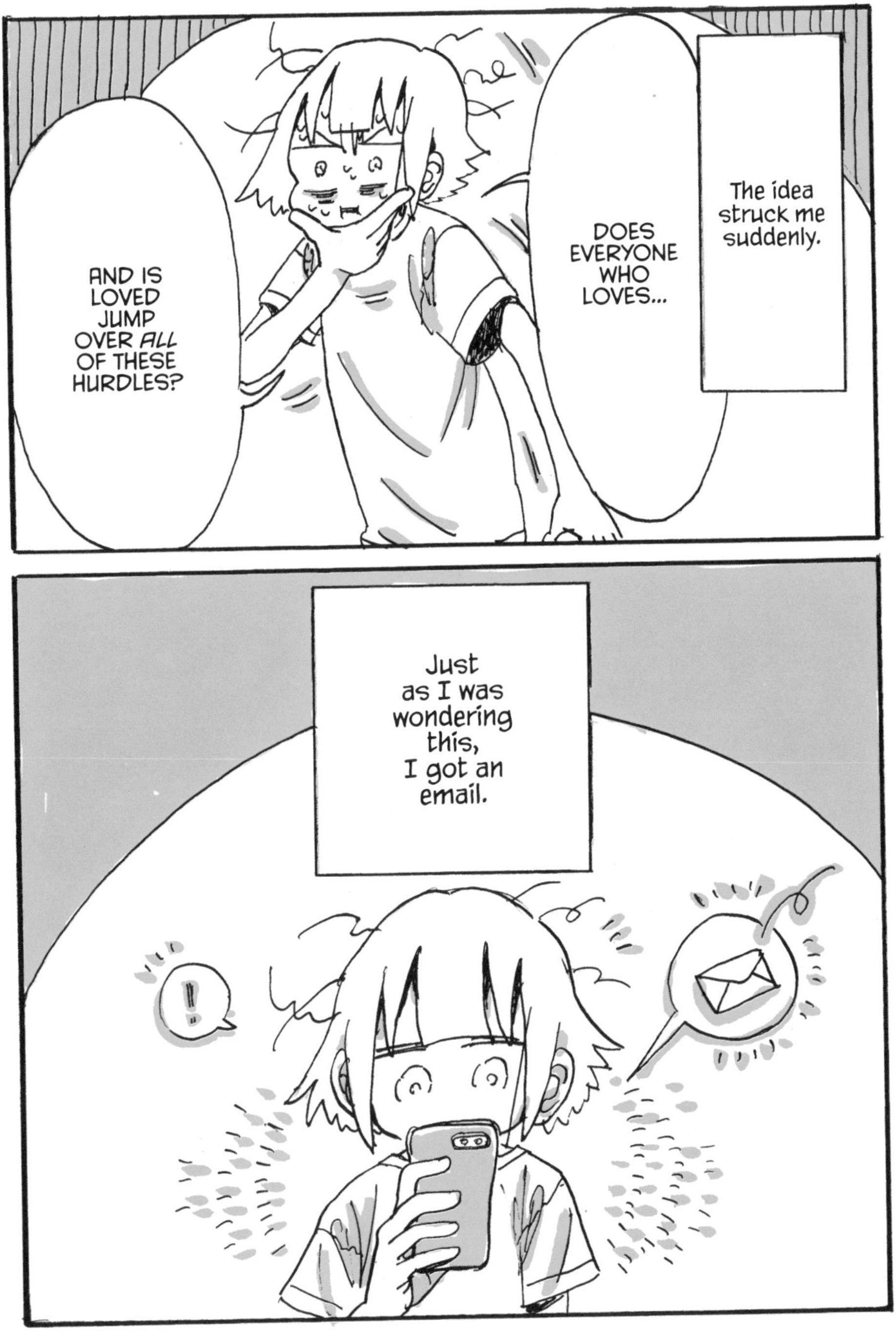
The idea struck me suddenly.
DOES EVERYONE WHO LOVES...
AND IS LOVED JUMP OVER ALL OF THESE HURDLES?
Just as I was wondering this, I got an email.
!

Chapter 5/END

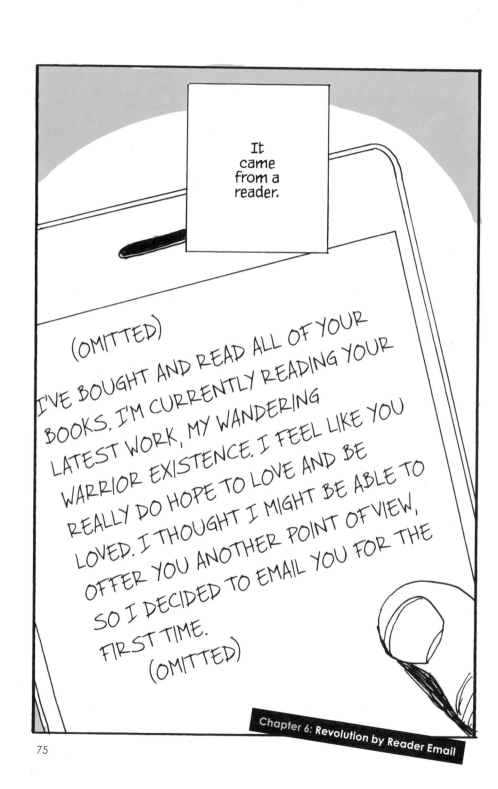

It came from a reader.

(OMITTED)
I'VE BOUGHT AND READ ALL OF YOUR BOOKS. I'M CURRENTLY READING YOUR LATEST WORK, MY WANDERING WARRIOR EXISTENCE. I FEEL LIKE YOU REALLY DO HOPE TO LOVE AND BE LOVED. I THOUGHT I MIGHT BE ABLE TO OFFER YOU ANOTHER POINT OF VIEW, SO I DECIDED TO EMAIL YOU FOR THE FIRST TIME.
(OMITTED)

Chapter 6: Revolution by Reader Email

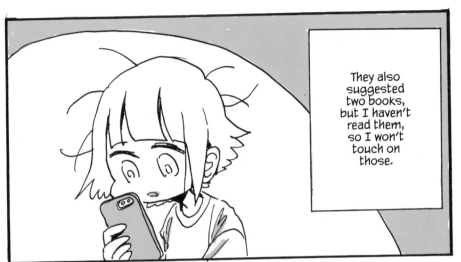

They also suggested two books, but I haven't read them, so I won't touch on those.

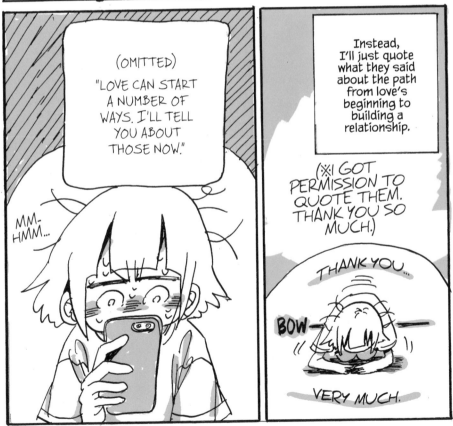

(OMITTED)

"LOVE CAN START A NUMBER OF WAYS. I'LL TELL YOU ABOUT THOSE NOW."

MM-HMM...

Instead, I'll just quote what they said about the path from love's beginning to building a relationship.

(※I GOT PERMISSION TO QUOTE THEM. THANK YOU SO MUCH.)

THANK YOU...

BOW

VERY MUCH.

INSTEAD, BOTH PEOPLE FEEL LIKE THEY WANT TO TALK MORE WITH THE OTHER PERSON, TO SHARE A BOND OF SOME KIND. IT'S NOT TILL LATER THAT THEY REALIZE THEIR MEETING WAS FATE. THIS HAPPENS A LOT IN REALITY.

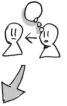

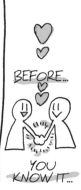

BEFORE...

YOU KNOW IT...

① A FATEFUL ENCOUNTER DOESN'T ALWAYS START WITH ROMANTIC FEELINGS.

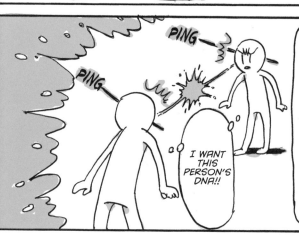

PING

PING

I WANT THIS PERSON'S DNA!!

② MUTUAL LOVE AT FIRST SIGHT IS WHEN BOTH PEOPLE'S GENES INSTINCTIVELY SEEK EACH OTHER OUT TO PRODUCE SUPERIOR OFFSPRING.

(OMITTED)

IN OTHER WORDS, ONE PERSON FALLING FOR ANOTHER BECOMES AN EMOTIONAL TRIGGER.

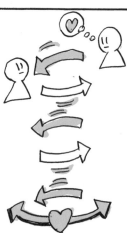

③ HOWEVER, MOST OF THE WORLD'S ROMANCES OCCUR WHEN ONE PERSON FALLS FOR ANOTHER. SPENDING TIME TOGETHER STIRS THE OTHER PERSON'S EMOTIONS, AND THE FEELINGS BECOME MUTUAL.

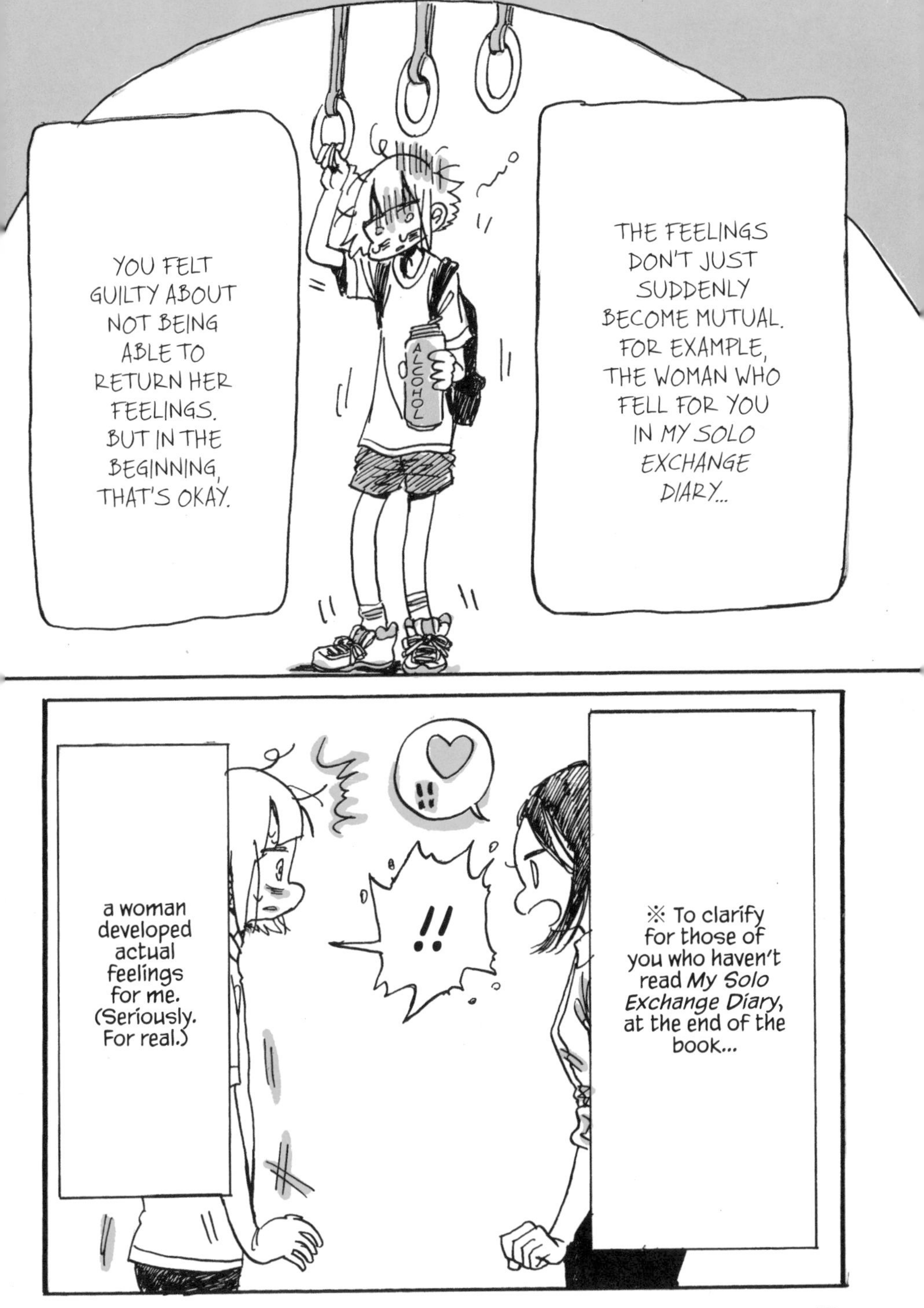
YOU FELT GUILTY ABOUT NOT BEING ABLE TO RETURN HER FEELINGS. BUT IN THE BEGINNING, THAT'S OKAY.
ALCOHOL
THE FEELINGS DON'T JUST SUDDENLY BECOME MUTUAL. FOR EXAMPLE, THE WOMAN WHO FELL FOR YOU IN *MY SOLO EXCHANGE DIARY*...
※ To clarify for those of you who haven't read *My Solo Exchange Diary*, at the end of the book...
!!
!!
a woman developed actual feelings for me. (Seriously. For real.)

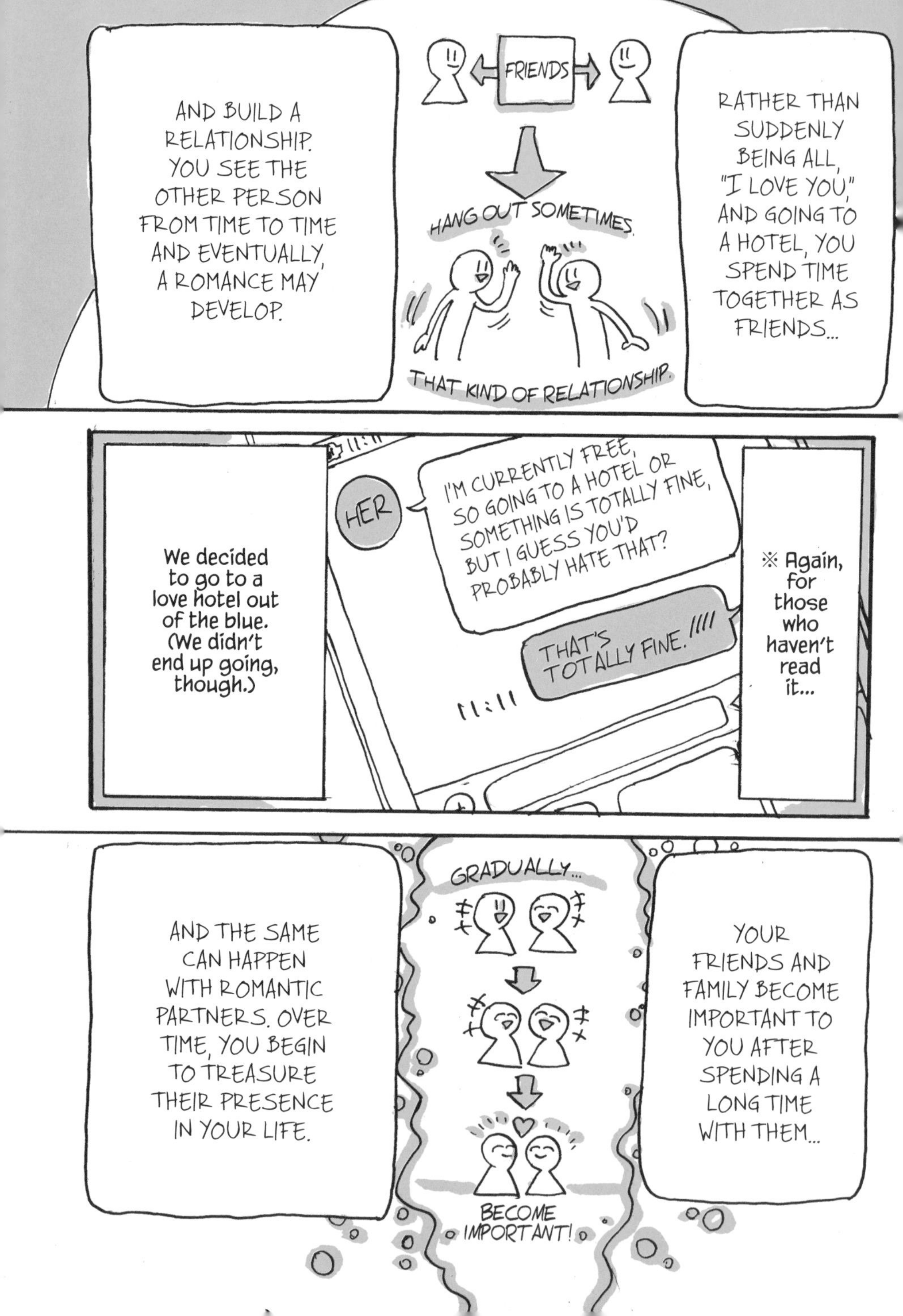
RATHER THAN SUDDENLY BEING ALL, "I LOVE YOU," AND GOING TO A HOTEL, YOU SPEND TIME TOGETHER AS FRIENDS...
FRIENDS
HANG OUT SOMETIMES.
THAT KIND OF RELATIONSHIP.
AND BUILD A RELATIONSHIP. YOU SEE THE OTHER PERSON FROM TIME TO TIME AND EVENTUALLY, A ROMANCE MAY DEVELOP.
※ Again, for those who haven't read it...
HER
I'M CURRENTLY FREE, SO GOING TO A HOTEL OR SOMETHING IS TOTALLY FINE, BUT I GUESS YOU'D PROBABLY HATE THAT?
THAT'S TOTALLY FINE.
11:11
We decided to go to a love hotel out of the blue. (We didn't end up going, though.)
YOUR FRIENDS AND FAMILY BECOME IMPORTANT TO YOU AFTER SPENDING A LONG TIME WITH THEM...
GRADUALLY...
BECOME IMPORTANT!
AND THE SAME CAN HAPPEN WITH ROMANTIC PARTNERS. OVER TIME, YOU BEGIN TO TREASURE THEIR PRESENCE IN YOUR LIFE.

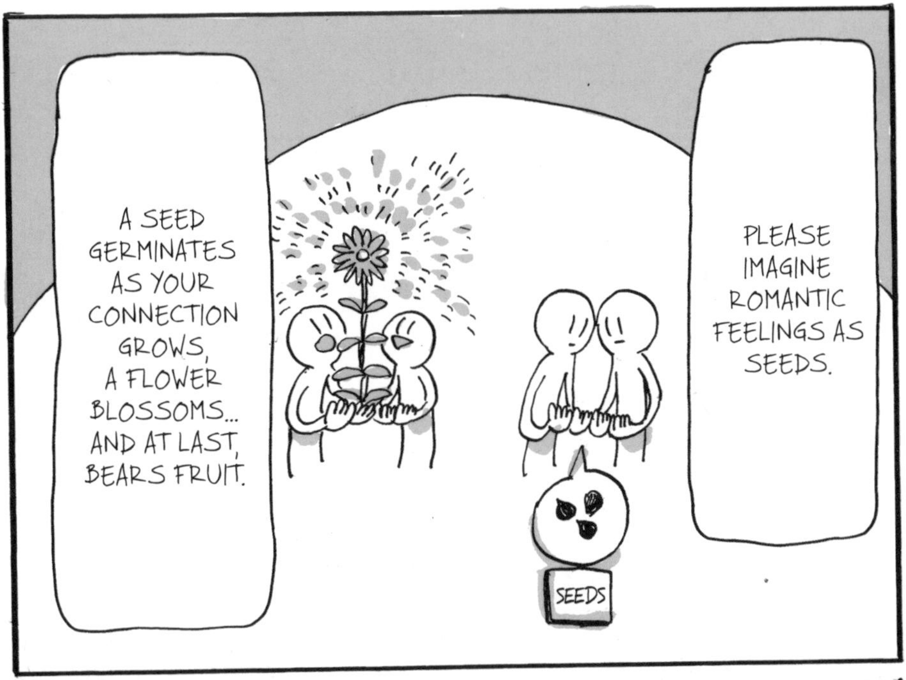
PLEASE IMAGINE ROMANTIC FEELINGS AS SEEDS.
A SEED GERMINATES AS YOUR CONNECTION GROWS, A FLOWER BLOSSOMS... AND AT LAST, BEARS FRUIT.
SEEDS

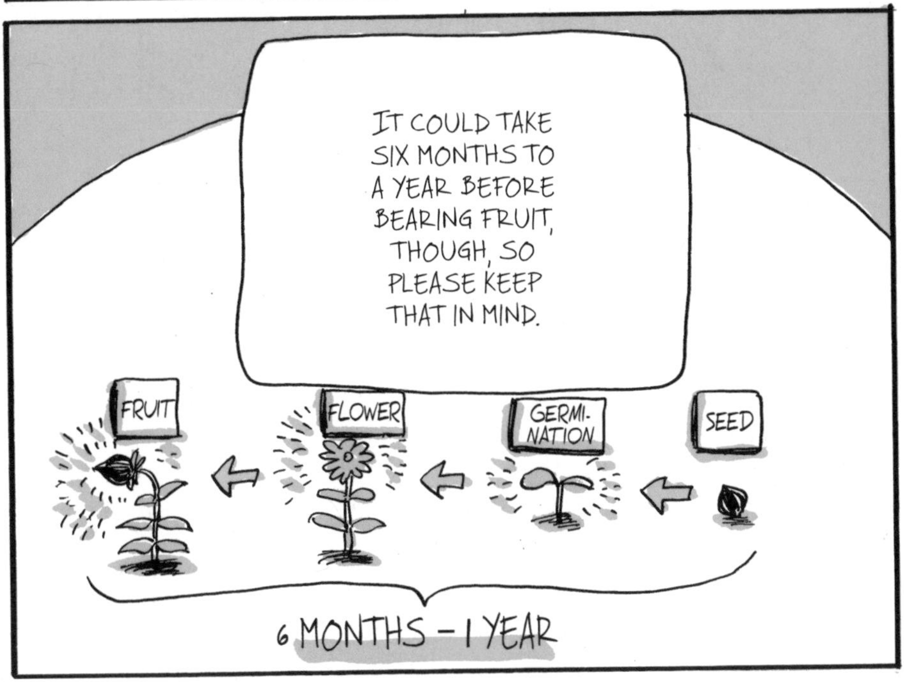
IT COULD TAKE SIX MONTHS TO A YEAR BEFORE BEARING FRUIT, THOUGH, SO PLEASE KEEP THAT IN MIND.
SEED
GERMI-NATION
FLOWER
FRUIT
6 MONTHS – 1 YEAR

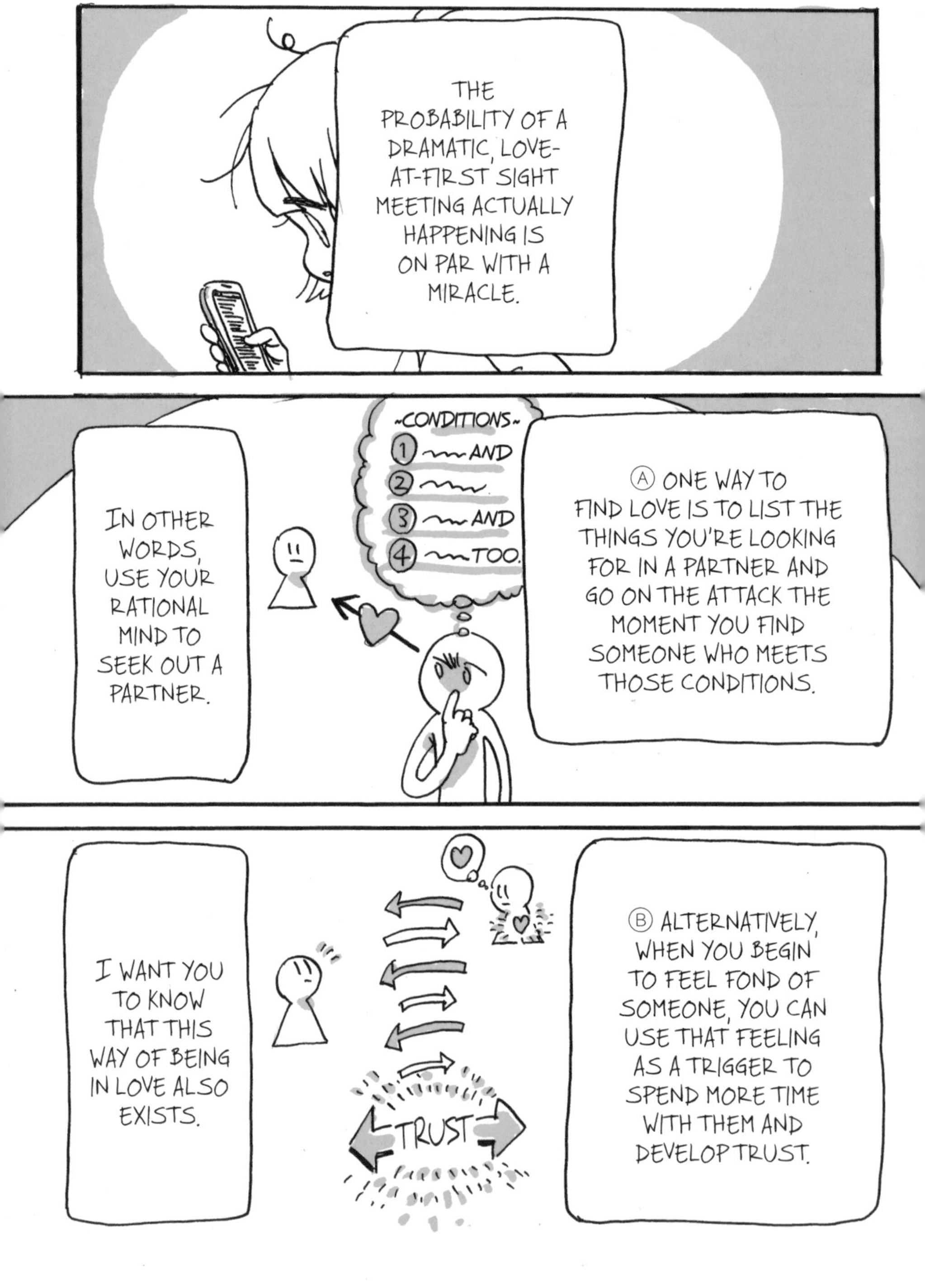
THE PROBABILITY OF A DRAMATIC, LOVE-AT-FIRST SIGHT MEETING ACTUALLY HAPPENING IS ON PAR WITH A MIRACLE.
Ⓐ ONE WAY TO FIND LOVE IS TO LIST THE THINGS YOU'RE LOOKING FOR IN A PARTNER AND GO ON THE ATTACK THE MOMENT YOU FIND SOMEONE WHO MEETS THOSE CONDITIONS.
~CONDITIONS~
1 AND
2
3 AND
4 TOO.
IN OTHER WORDS, USE YOUR RATIONAL MIND TO SEEK OUT A PARTNER.
Ⓑ ALTERNATIVELY, WHEN YOU BEGIN TO FEEL FOND OF SOMEONE, YOU CAN USE THAT FEELING AS A TRIGGER TO SPEND MORE TIME WITH THEM AND DEVELOP TRUST.
TRUST
I WANT YOU TO KNOW THAT THIS WAY OF BEING IN LOVE ALSO EXISTS.

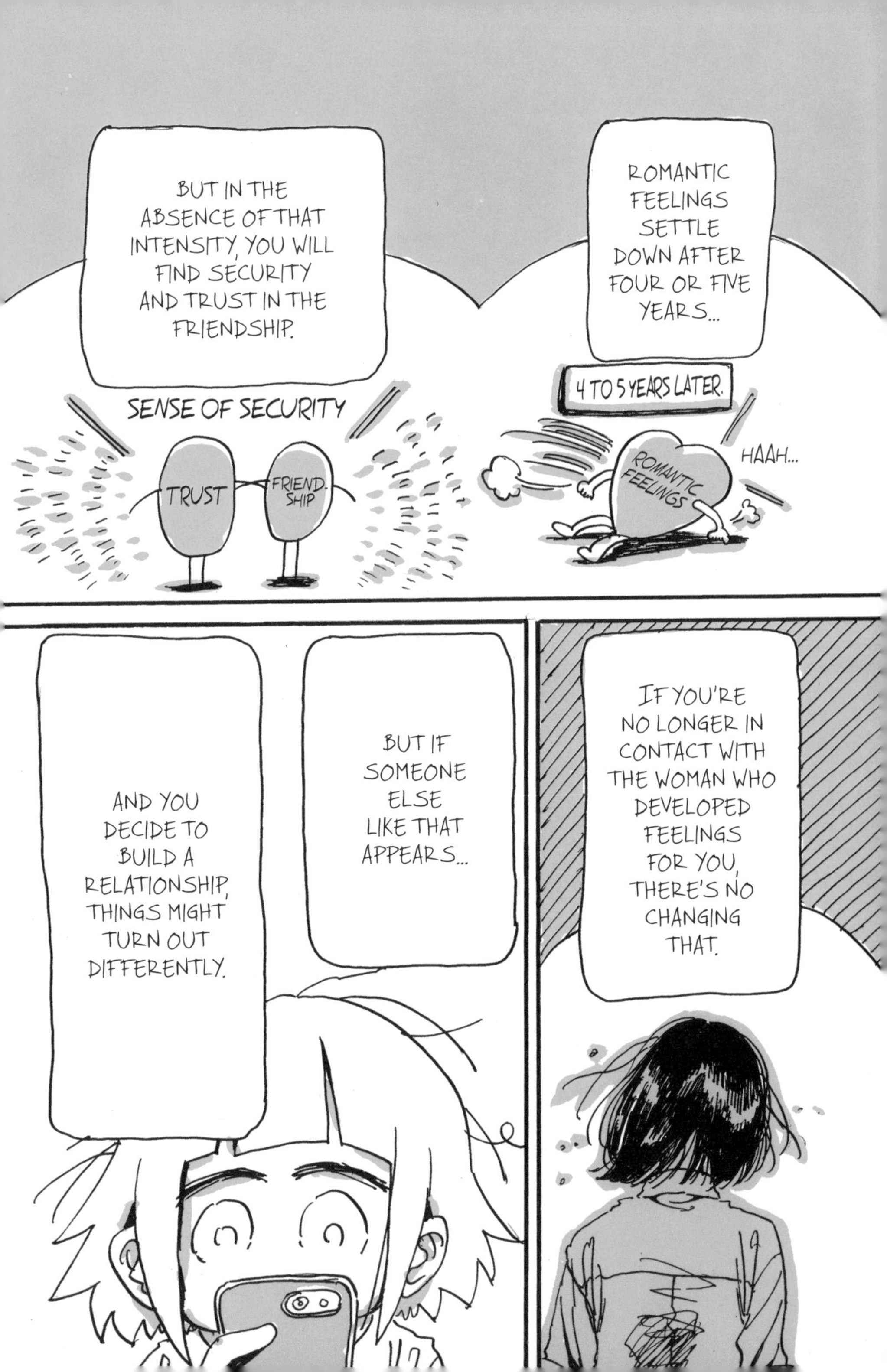
ROMANTIC FEELINGS SETTLE DOWN AFTER FOUR OR FIVE YEARS...
4 TO 5 YEARS LATER.
ROMANTIC FEELINGS
HAAH...
BUT IN THE ABSENCE OF THAT INTENSITY, YOU WILL FIND SECURITY AND TRUST IN THE FRIENDSHIP.
SENSE OF SECURITY
TRUST
FRIENDSHIP
IF YOU'RE NO LONGER IN CONTACT WITH THE WOMAN WHO DEVELOPED FEELINGS FOR YOU, THERE'S NO CHANGING THAT.
BUT IF SOMEONE ELSE LIKE THAT APPEARS...
AND YOU DECIDE TO BUILD A RELATIONSHIP, THINGS MIGHT TURN OUT DIFFERENTLY.

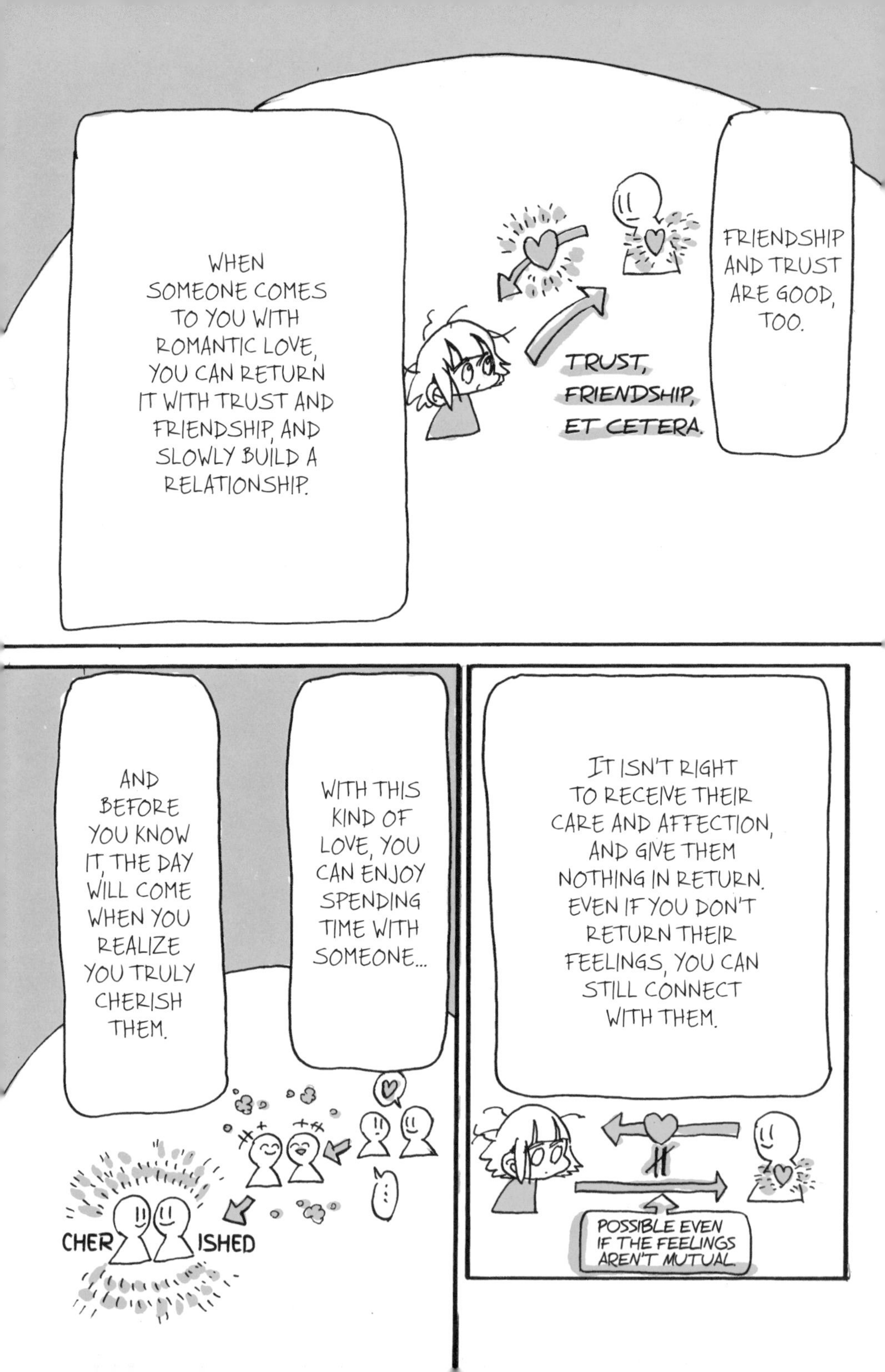
FRIENDSHIP AND TRUST ARE GOOD, TOO.
TRUST, FRIENDSHIP, ET CETERA.
WHEN SOMEONE COMES TO YOU WITH ROMANTIC LOVE, YOU CAN RETURN IT WITH TRUST AND FRIENDSHIP, AND SLOWLY BUILD A RELATIONSHIP.
IT ISN'T RIGHT TO RECEIVE THEIR CARE AND AFFECTION, AND GIVE THEM NOTHING IN RETURN. EVEN IF YOU DON'T RETURN THEIR FEELINGS, YOU CAN STILL CONNECT WITH THEM.
POSSIBLE EVEN IF THE FEELINGS AREN'T MUTUAL.
WITH THIS KIND OF LOVE, YOU CAN ENJOY SPENDING TIME WITH SOMEONE...
AND BEFORE YOU KNOW IT, THE DAY WILL COME WHEN YOU REALIZE YOU TRULY CHERISH THEM.
CHER ISHED

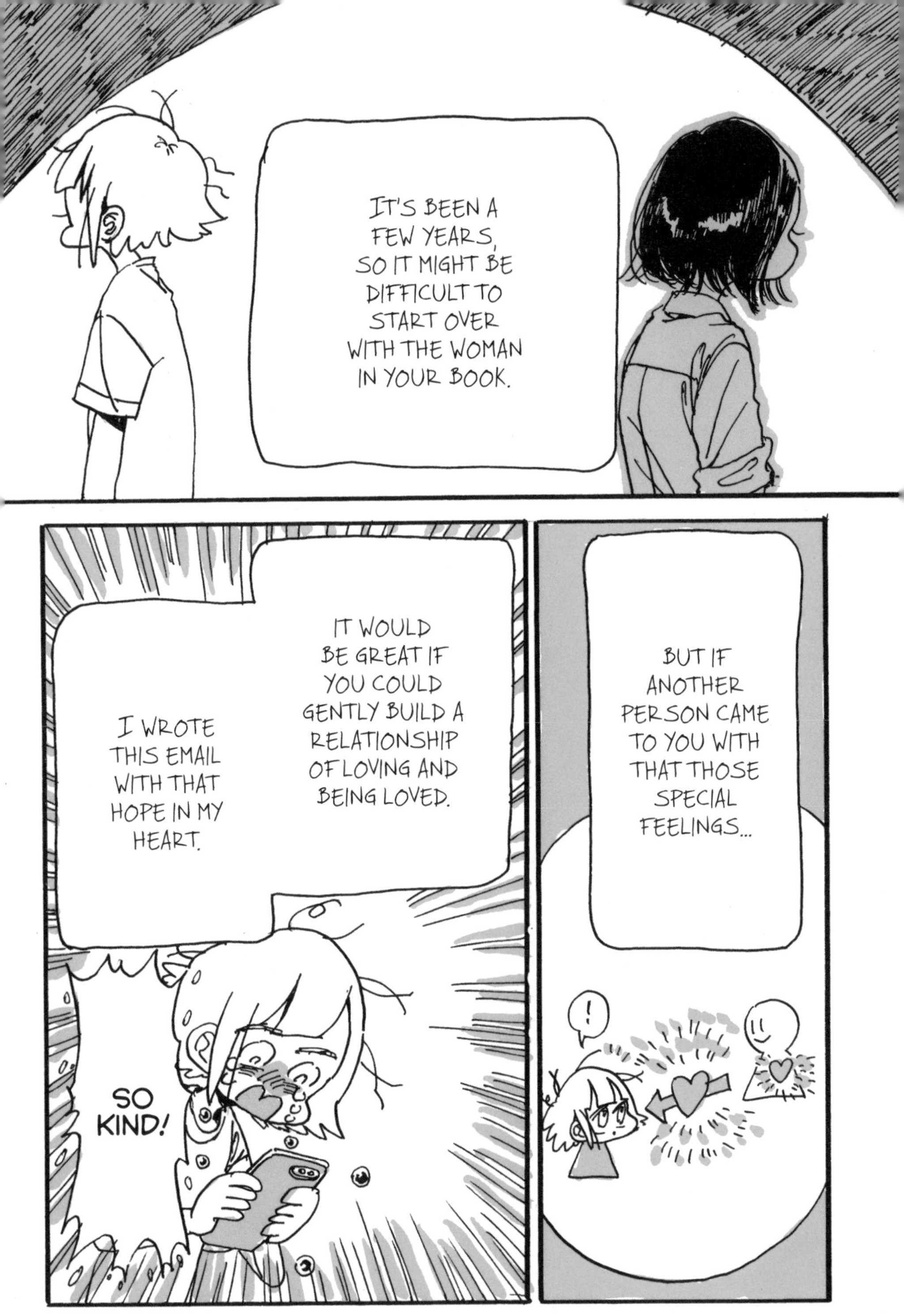
IT'S BEEN A FEW YEARS, SO IT MIGHT BE DIFFICULT TO START OVER WITH THE WOMAN IN YOUR BOOK.
BUT IF ANOTHER PERSON CAME TO YOU WITH THAT THOSE SPECIAL FEELINGS...
!
IT WOULD BE GREAT IF YOU COULD GENTLY BUILD A RELATIONSHIP OF LOVING AND BEING LOVED.
I WROTE THIS EMAIL WITH THAT HOPE IN MY HEART.
SO KIND!

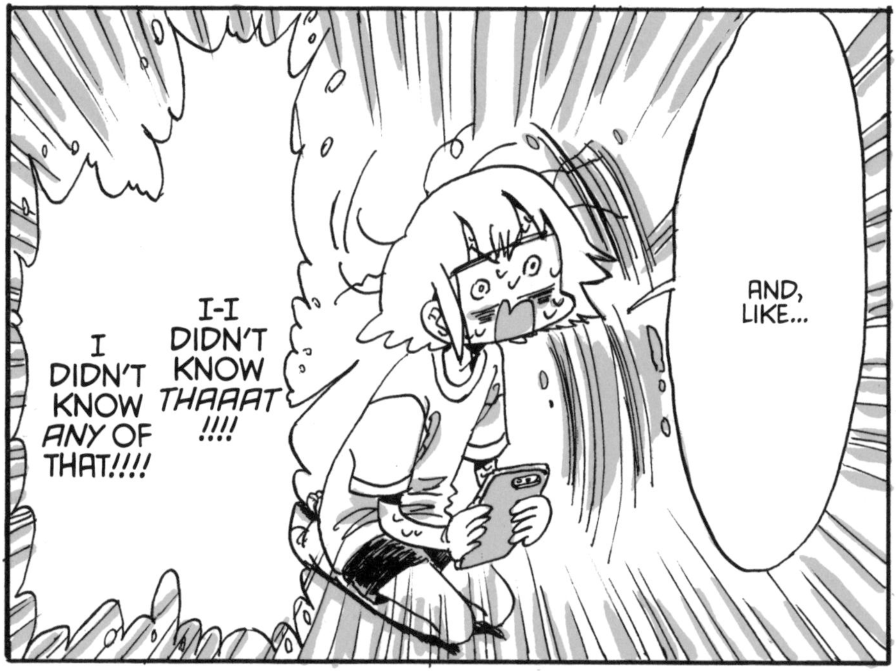
AND, LIKE...
I-I DIDN'T KNOW *THAAAT* !!!!
I DIDN'T KNOW *ANY* OF THAT!!!!

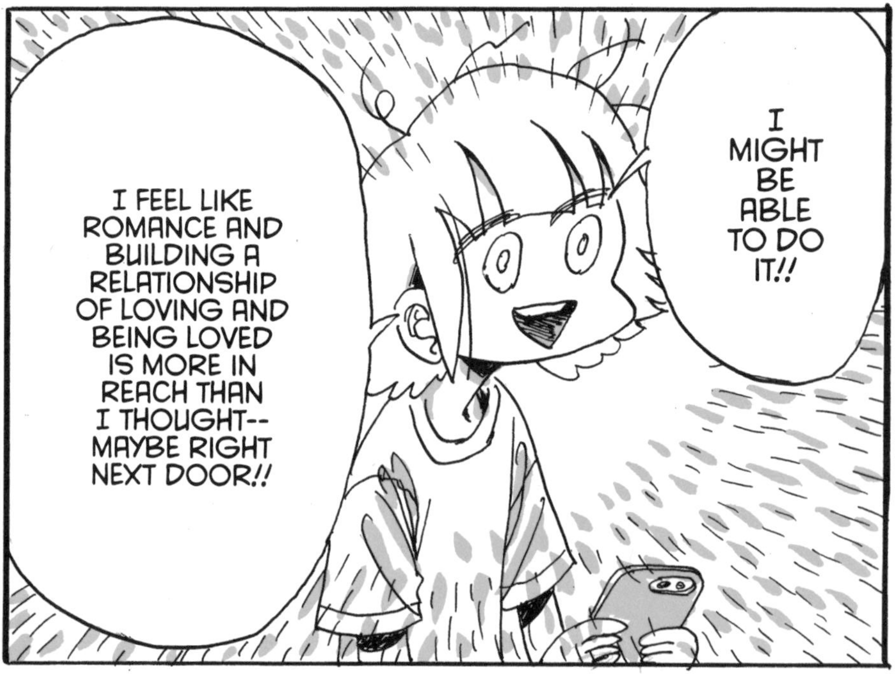
I MIGHT BE ABLE TO DO IT!!
I FEEL LIKE ROMANCE AND BUILDING A RELATIONSHIP OF LOVING AND BEING LOVED IS MORE IN REACH THAN I THOUGHT-- MAYBE RIGHT NEXT DOOR!!

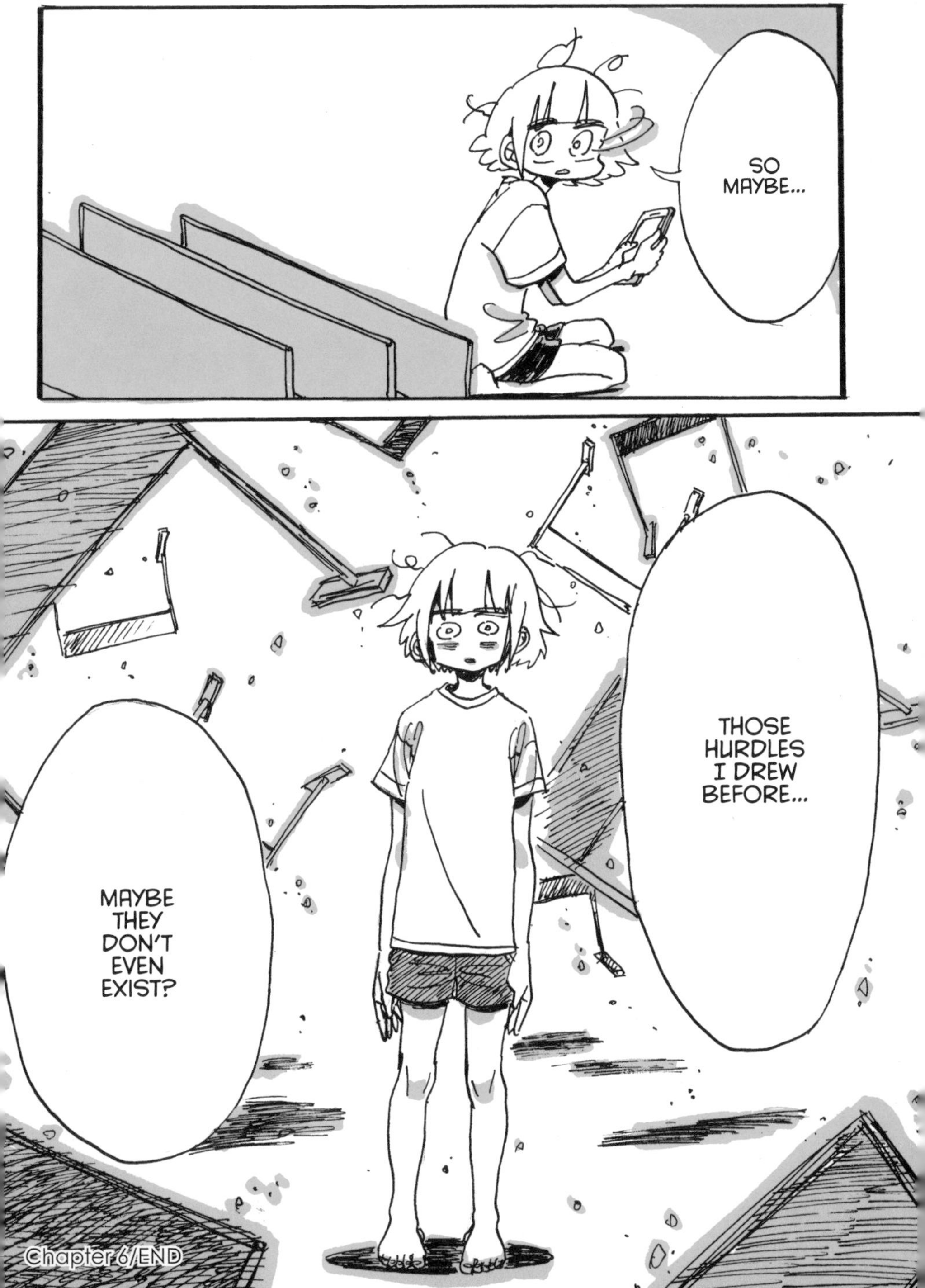
SO MAYBE...
THOSE HURDLES I DREW BEFORE...
MAYBE THEY DON'T EVEN EXIST?
Chapter 6/END

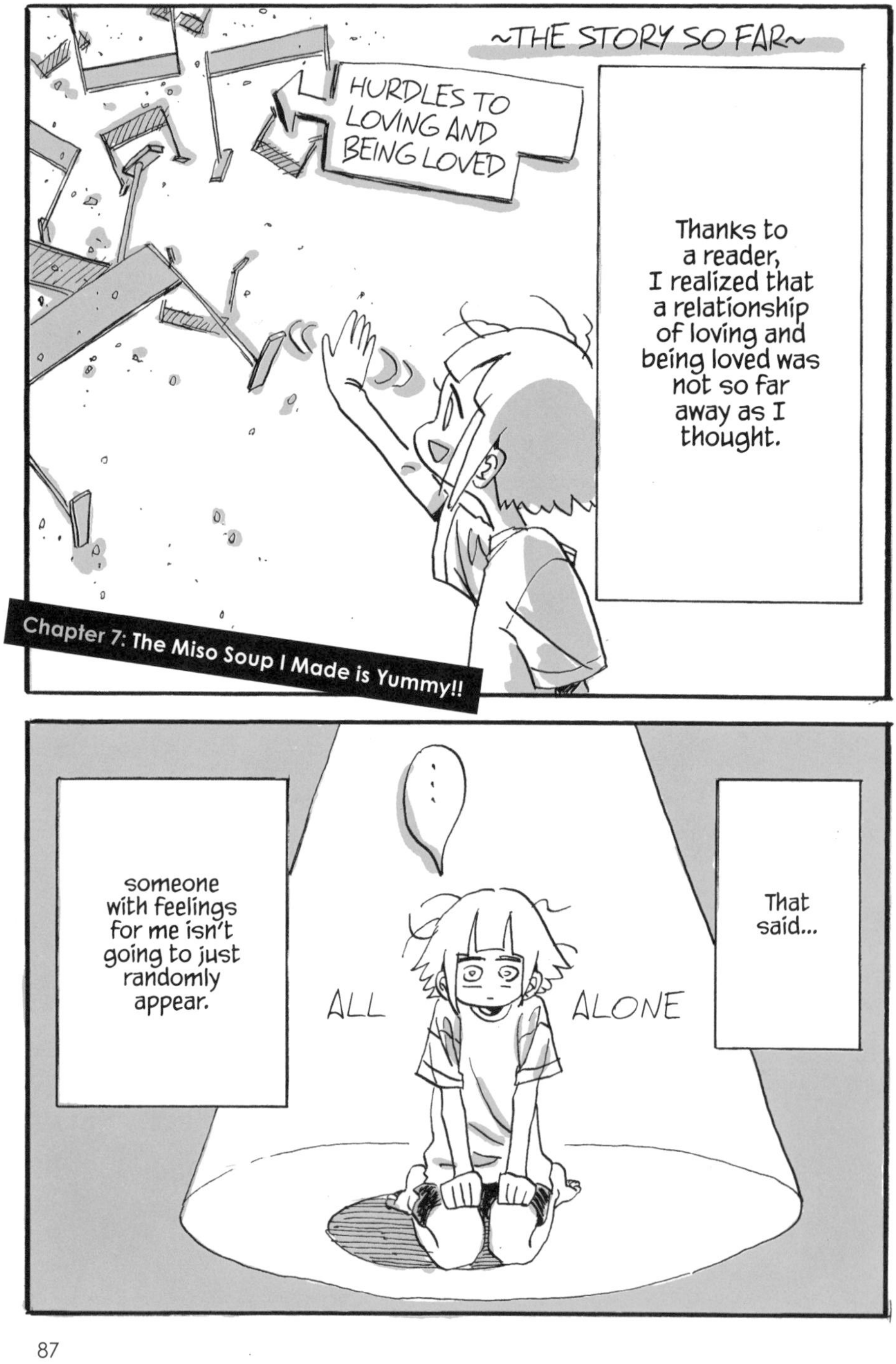
~THE STORY SO FAR~
Thanks to a reader, I realized that a relationship of loving and being loved was not so far away as I thought.
HURDLES TO LOVING AND BEING LOVED
Chapter 7: The Miso Soup I Made is Yummy!!
That said...
ALONE
...
ALL
someone with feelings for me isn't going to just randomly appear.

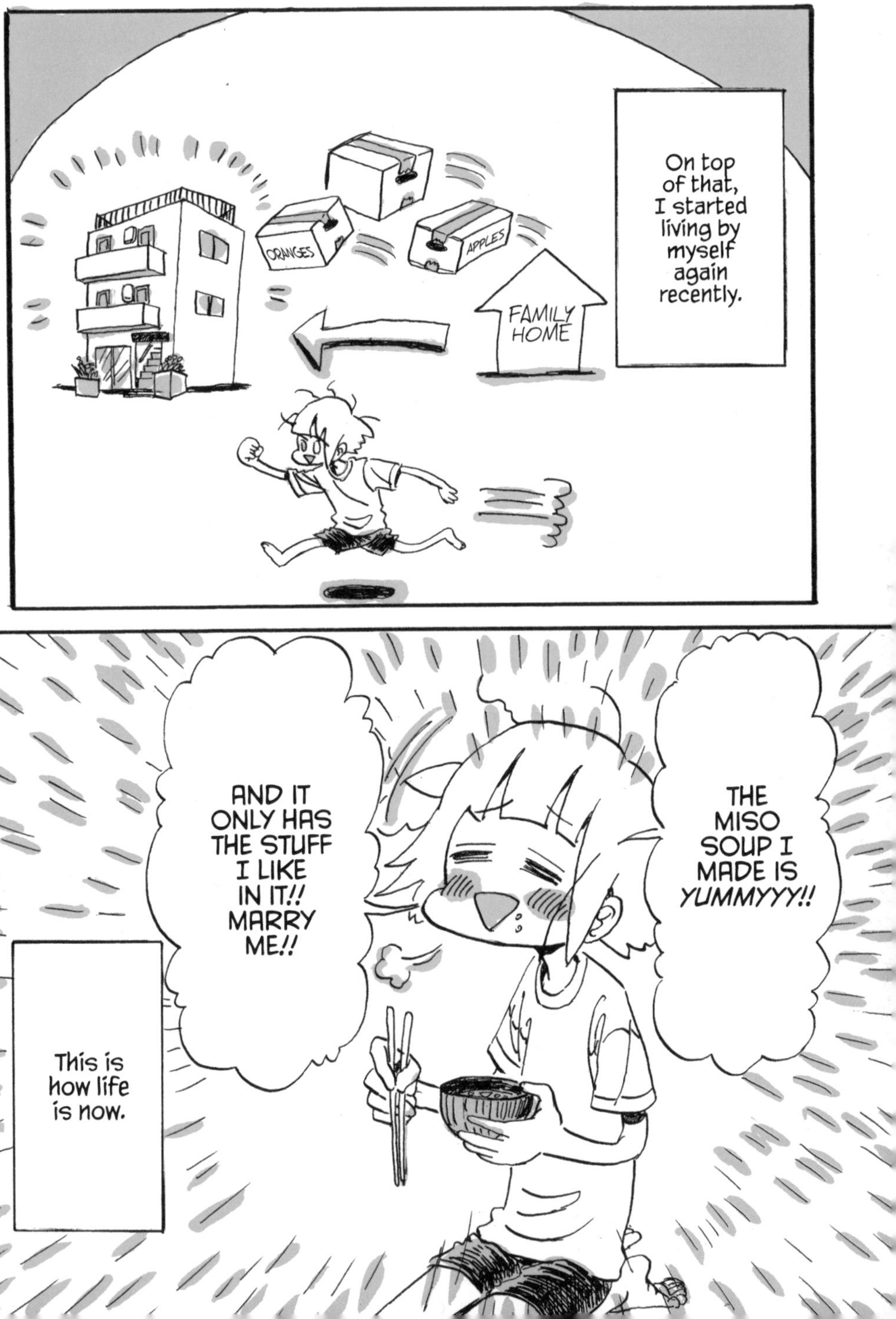

On top of that, I started living by myself again recently.
FAMILY HOME
APPLES
ORANGES
THE MISO SOUP I MADE IS *YUMMYYY!!*
AND IT ONLY HAS THE STUFF I LIKE IN IT!! MARRY ME!!
This is how life is now.

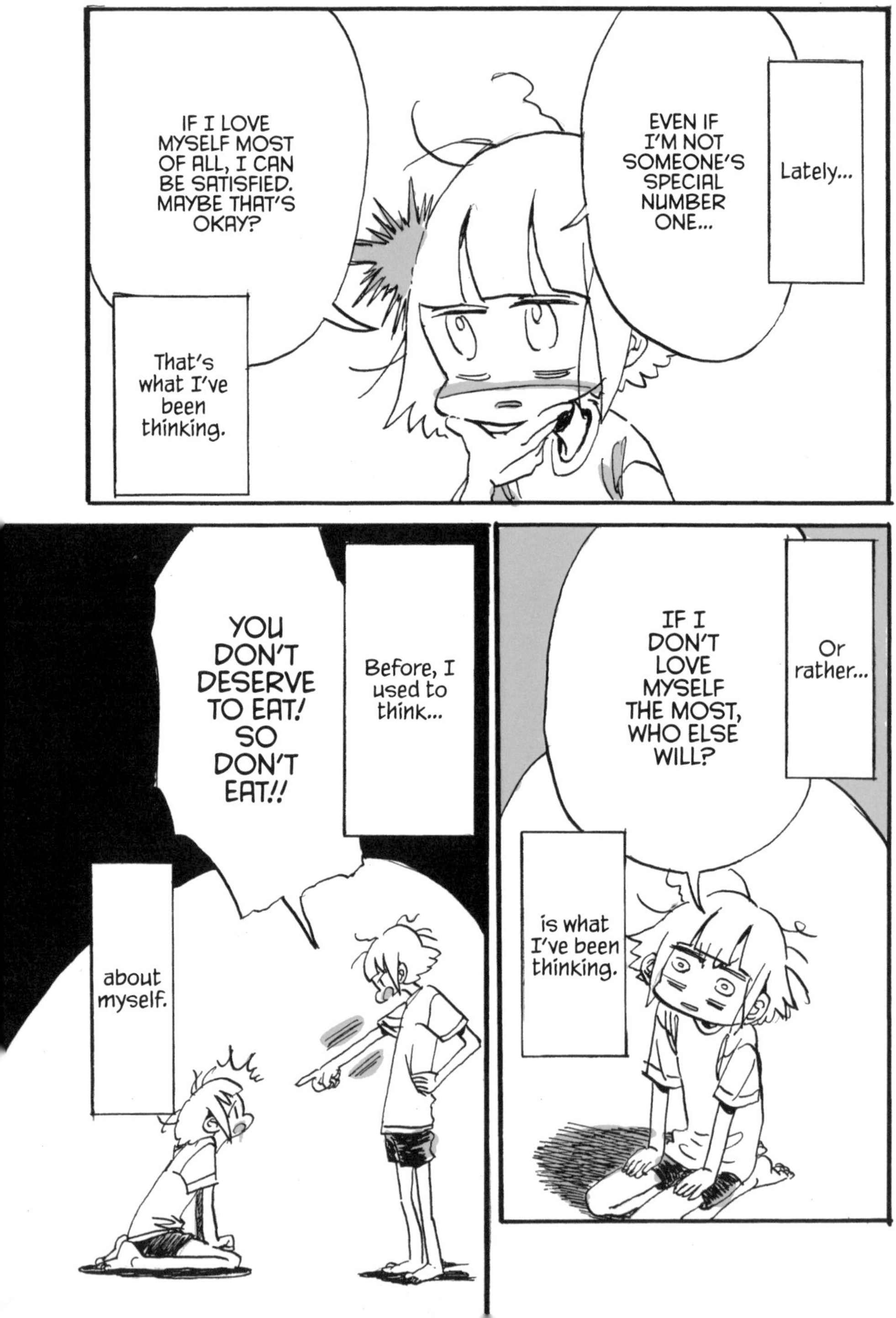
Lately...
EVEN IF I'M NOT SOMEONE'S SPECIAL NUMBER ONE...
IF I LOVE MYSELF MOST OF ALL, I CAN BE SATISFIED. MAYBE THAT'S OKAY?
That's what I've been thinking.
Or rather...
IF I DON'T LOVE MYSELF THE MOST, WHO ELSE WILL?
is what I've been thinking.
Before, I used to think...
YOU DON'T DESERVE TO EAT! SO DON'T EAT!!
about myself.

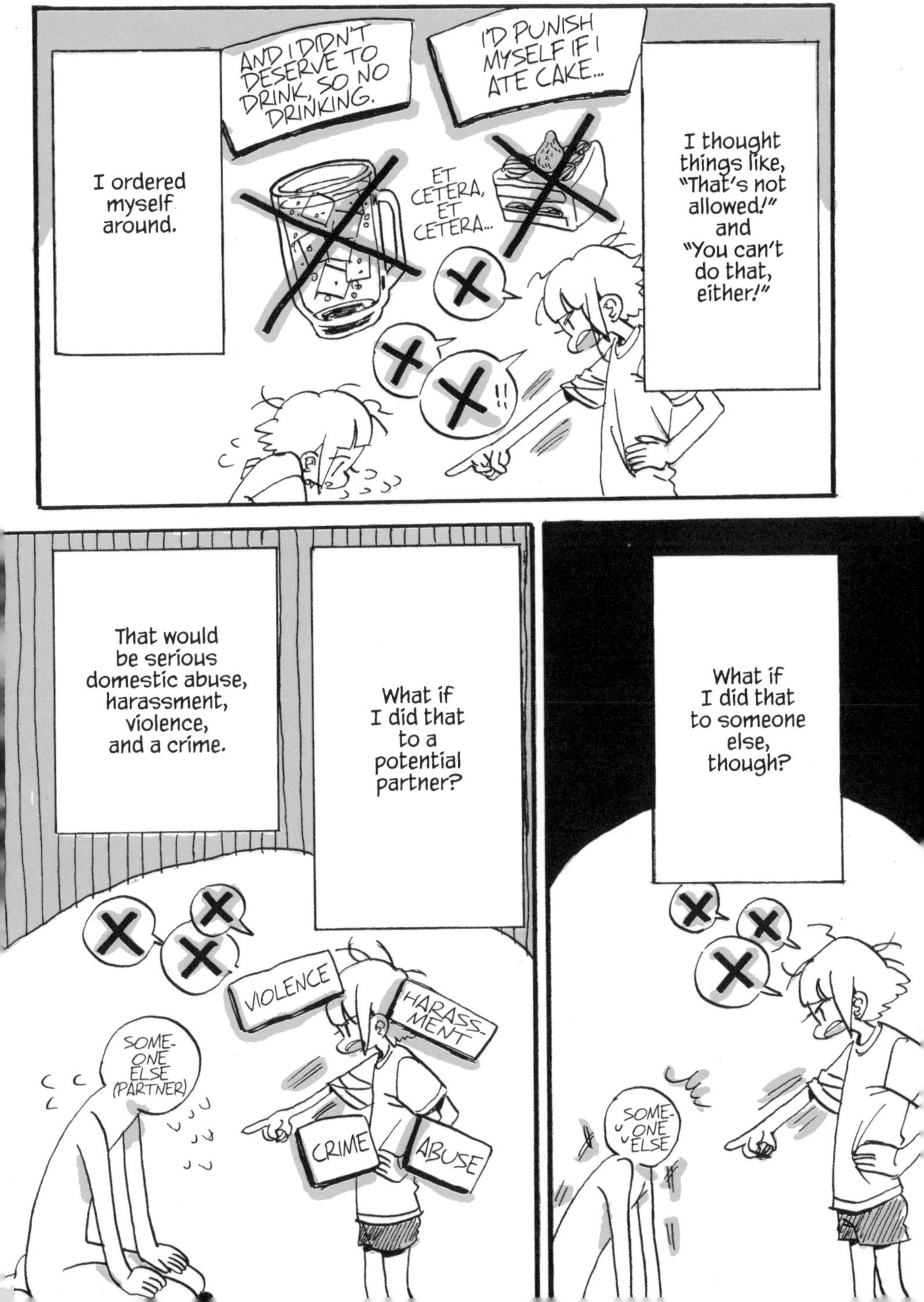
I thought things like, "That's not allowed!" and "You can't do that, either!"
I'D PUNISH MYSELF IF I ATE CAKE...
AND I DIDN'T DESERVE TO DRINK, SO NO DRINKING.
ET CETERA, ET CETERA...
!!
I ordered myself around.
What if I did that to someone else, though?
SOME-ONE ELSE
What if I did that to a potential partner?
That would be serious domestic abuse, harassment, violence, and a crime.
HARASS-MENT
VIOLENCE
ABUSE
CRIME
SOME-ONE ELSE (PARTNER)

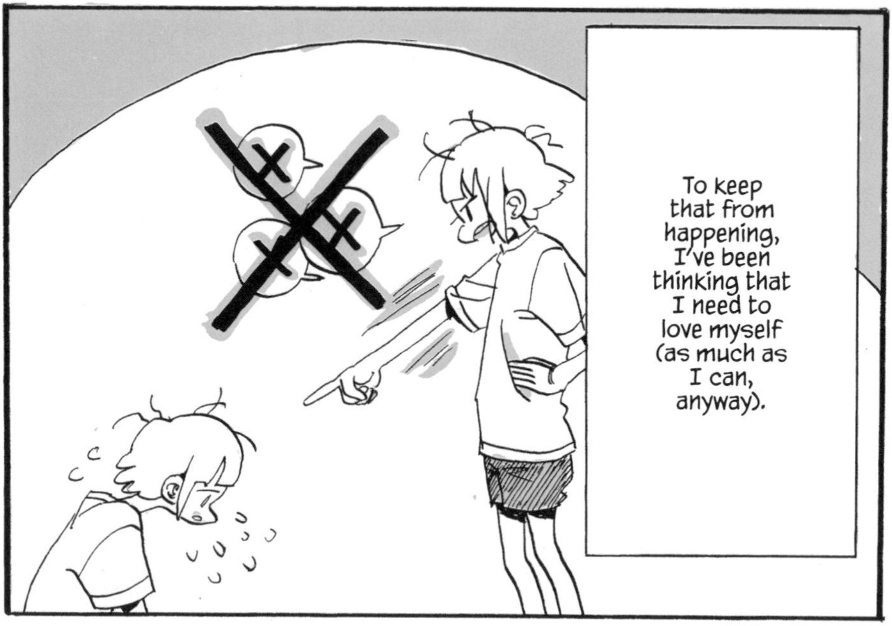
To keep that from happening, I've been thinking that I need to love myself (as much as I can, anyway).

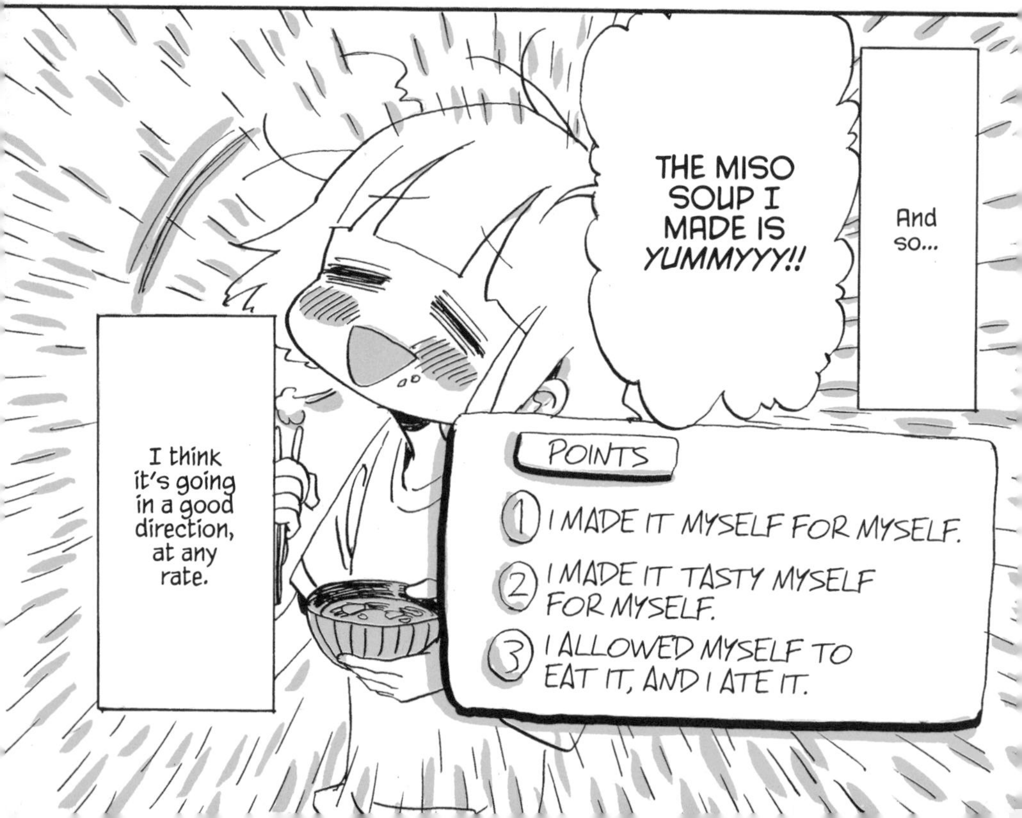
And so...
THE MISO SOUP I MADE IS YUMMYYY!!
POINTS
1 I MADE IT MYSELF FOR MYSELF.
2 I MADE IT TASTY MYSELF FOR MYSELF.
3 I ALLOWED MYSELF TO EAT IT, AND I ATE IT.
I think it's going in a good direction, at any rate.

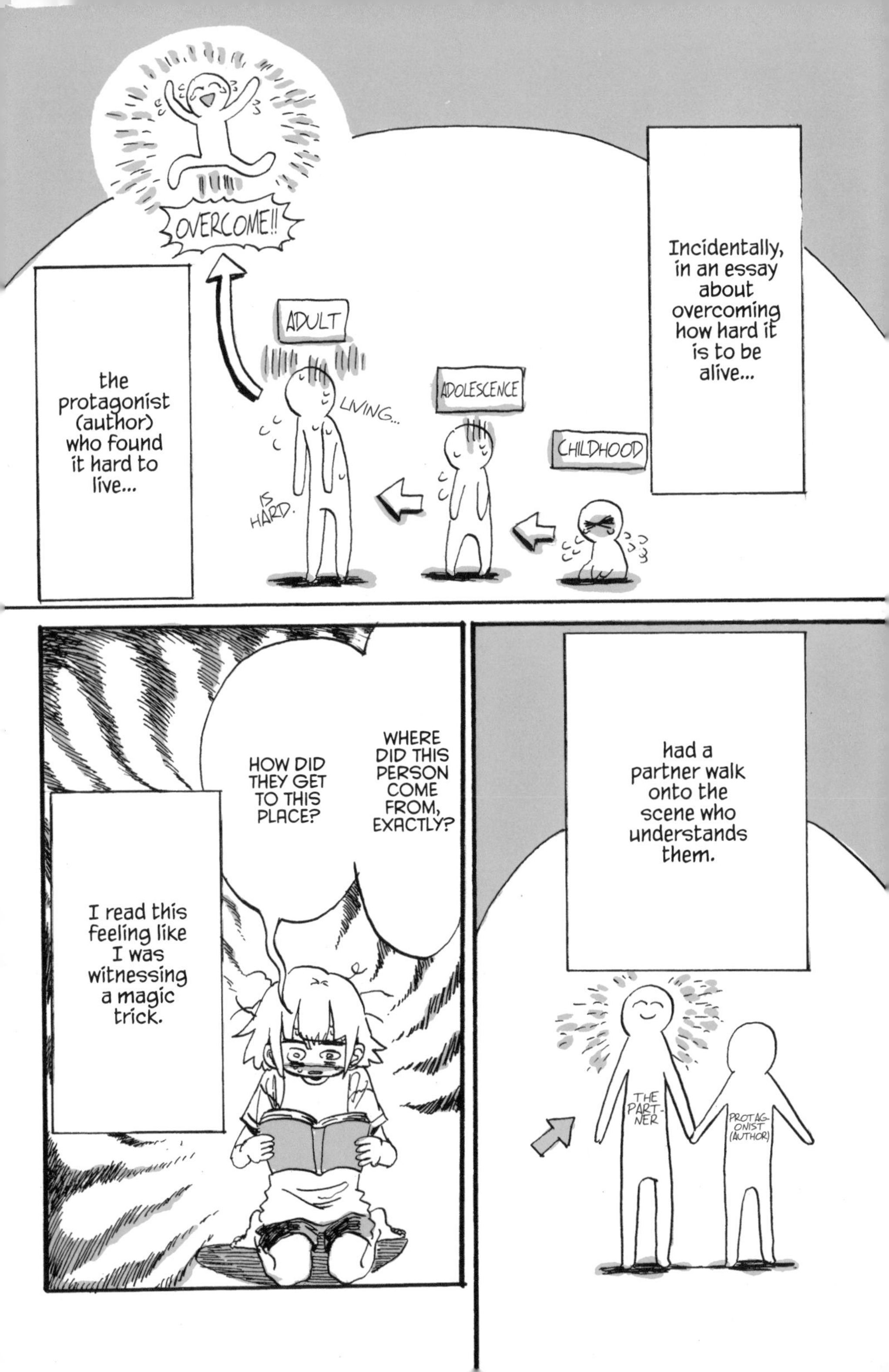
Incidentally, in an essay about overcoming how hard it is to be alive...
OVERCOME!!
CHILDHOOD
ADOLESCENCE
ADULT
LIVING... IS HARD.
the protagonist (author) who found it hard to live...
had a partner walk onto the scene who understands them.
THE PARTNER
PROTAGONIST (AUTHOR)
WHERE DID THIS PERSON COME FROM, EXACTLY?
HOW DID THEY GET TO THIS PLACE?
I read this feeling like I was witnessing a magic trick.

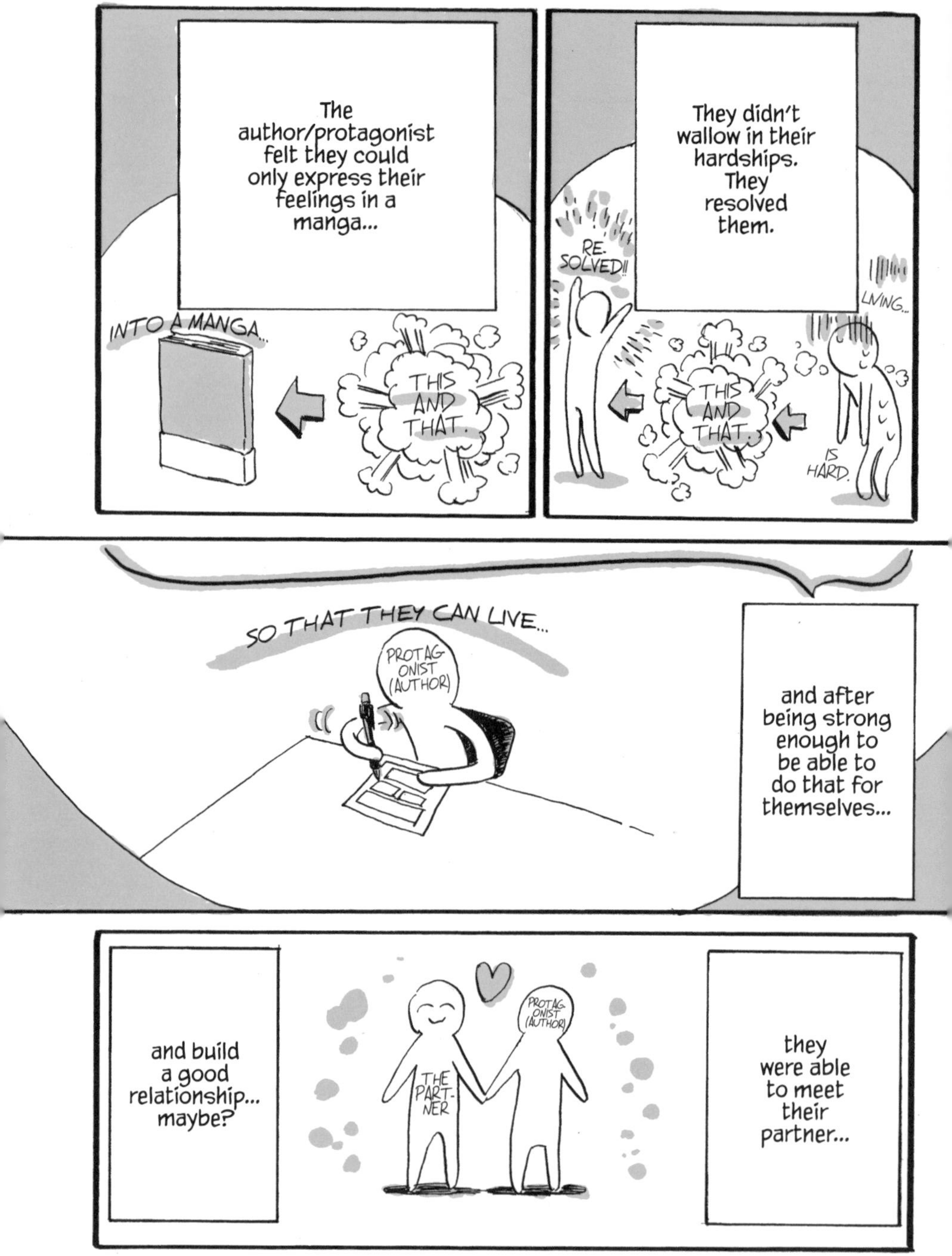
They didn't wallow in their hardships. They resolved them.
RE. SOLVED!!
LIVING...
IS HARD.
THIS AND THAT.
The author/protagonist felt they could only express their feelings in a manga...
INTO A MANGA...
THIS AND THAT.
and after being strong enough to be able to do that for themselves...
SO THAT THEY CAN LIVE...
PROTAGONIST (AUTHOR)
they were able to meet their partner...
PROTAGONIST (AUTHOR)
THE PARTNER
and build a good relationship... maybe?

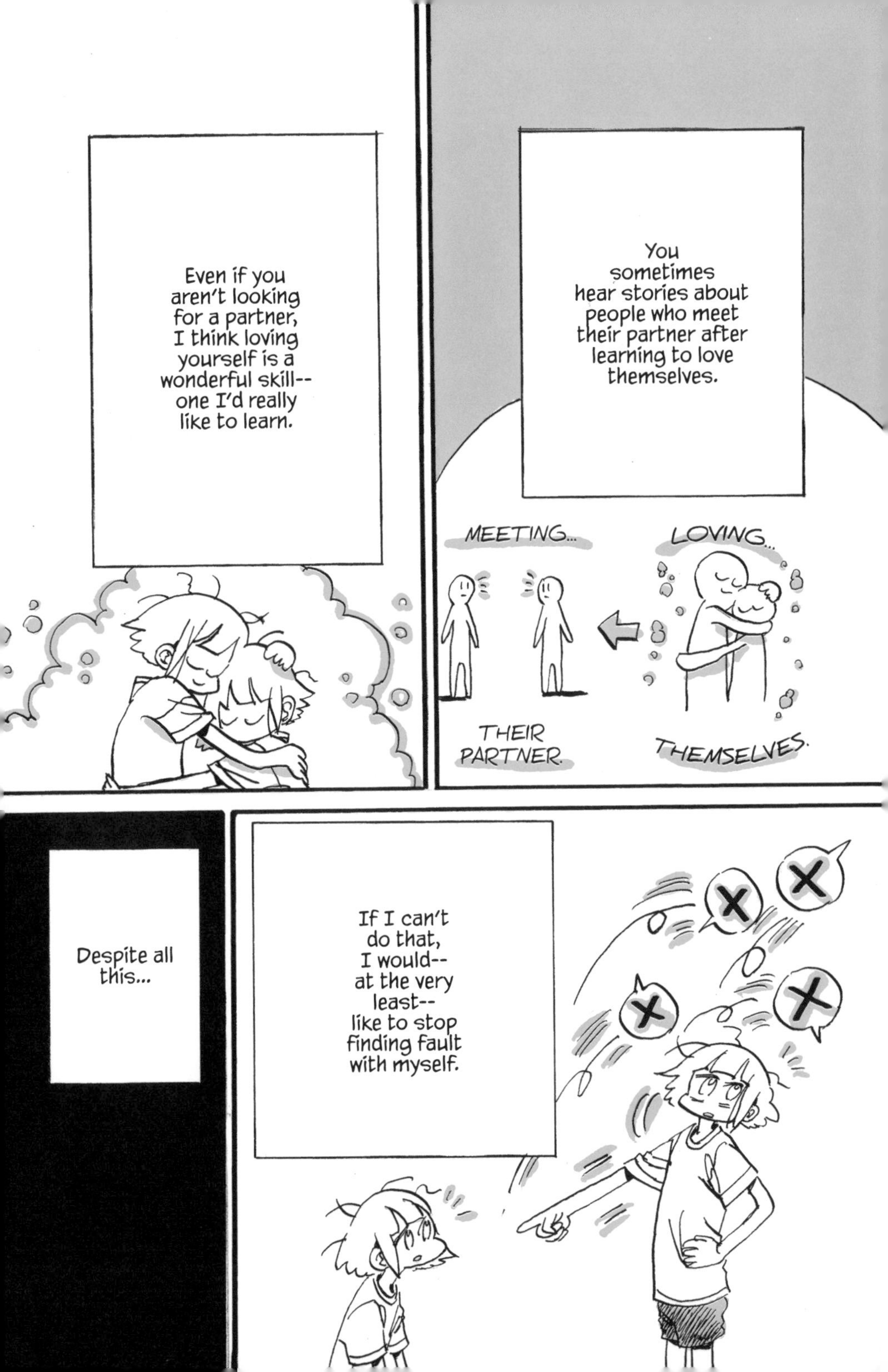
You sometimes hear stories about people who meet their partner after learning to love themselves.
LOVING...
THEMSELVES.
MEETING...
THEIR PARTNER.
Even if you aren't looking for a partner, I think loving yourself is a wonderful skill-- one I'd really like to learn.
If I can't do that, I would-- at the very least-- like to stop finding fault with myself.
Despite all this...

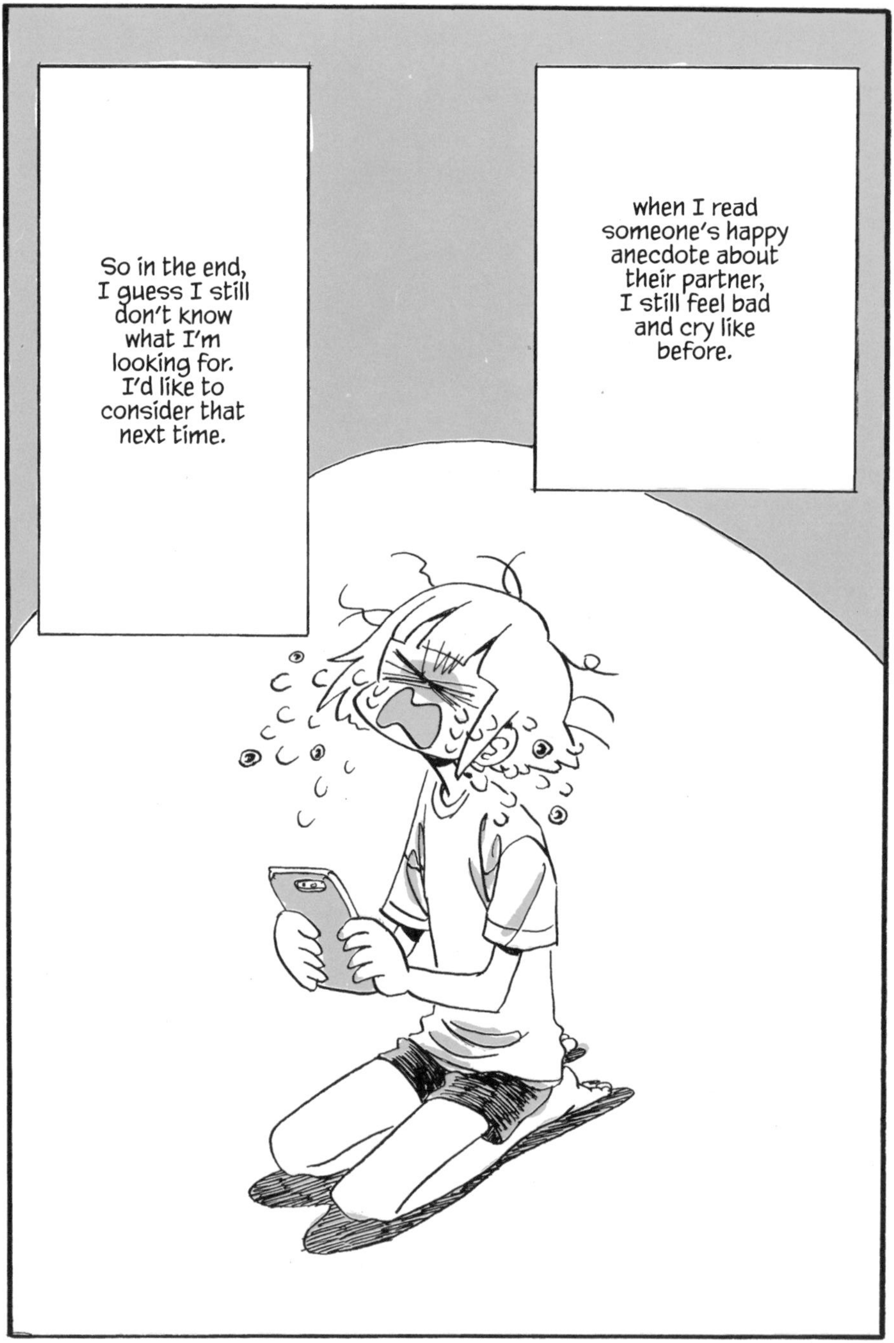
when I read someone's happy anecdote about their partner, I still feel bad and cry like before.
So in the end, I guess I still don't know what I'm looking for. I'd like to consider that next time.

Chapter 7/END

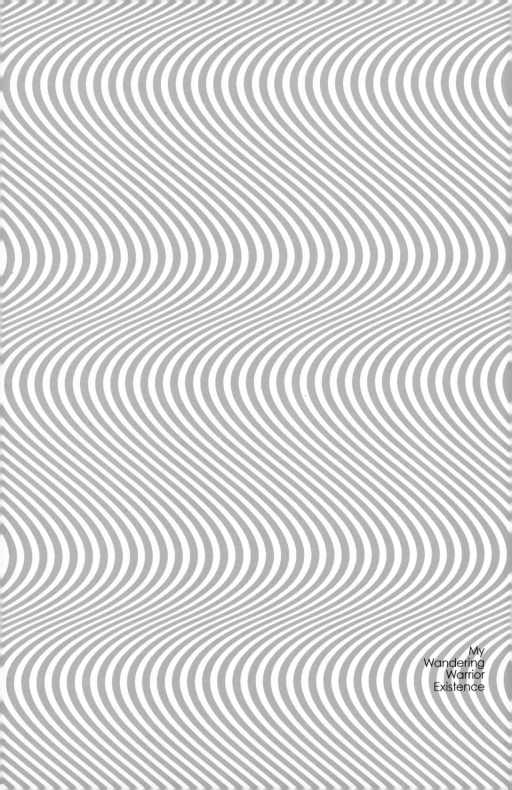

My
Wandering
Warrior
Existence

Chapter 8: Why Do Happy Moments Between Partners Shake Me Up?

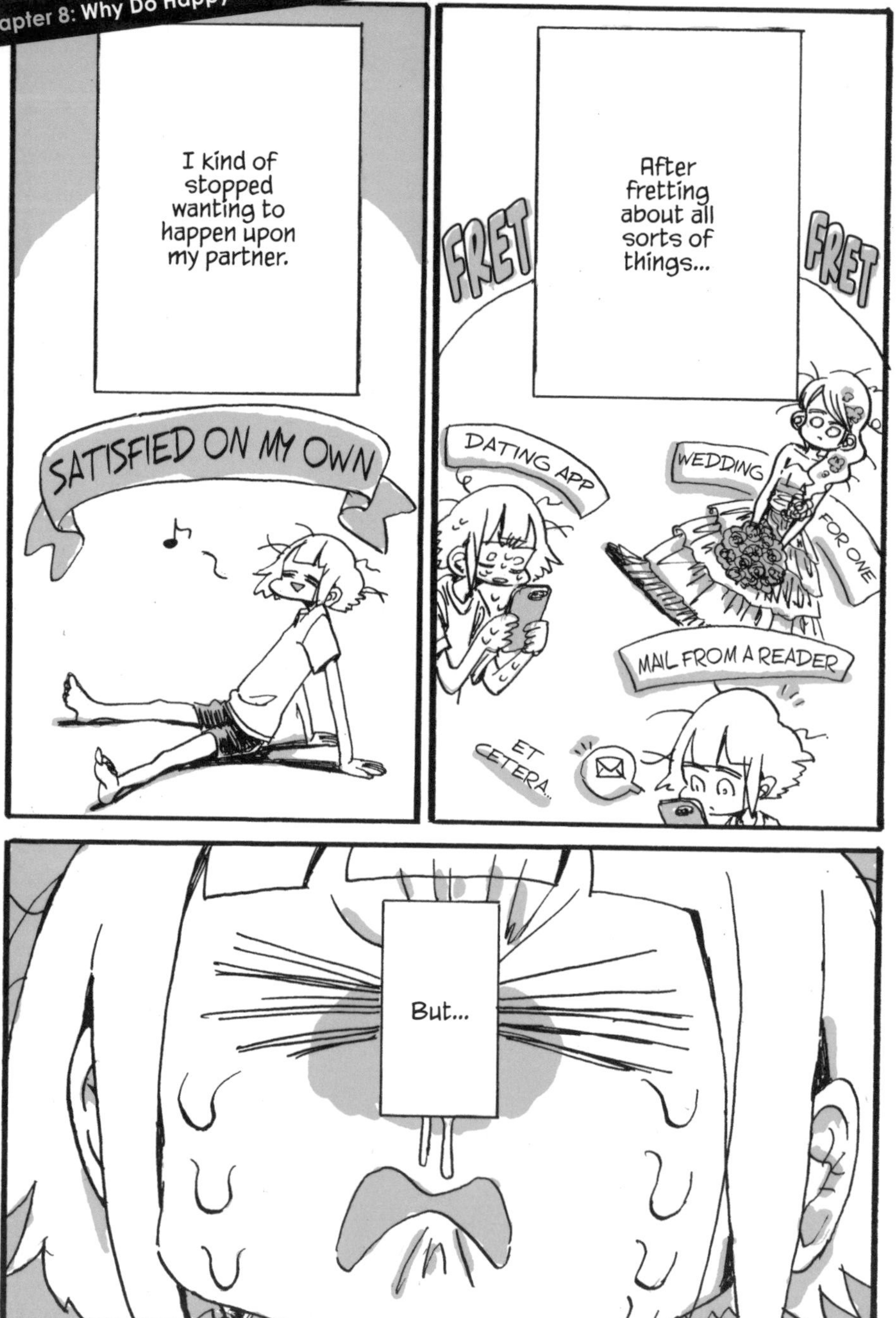
FRET
After fretting about all sorts of things...
FRET
WEDDING
FOR ONE
DATING APP
MAIL FROM A READER
ET CETERA...
I kind of stopped wanting to happen upon my partner.
SATISFIED ON MY OWN
But...

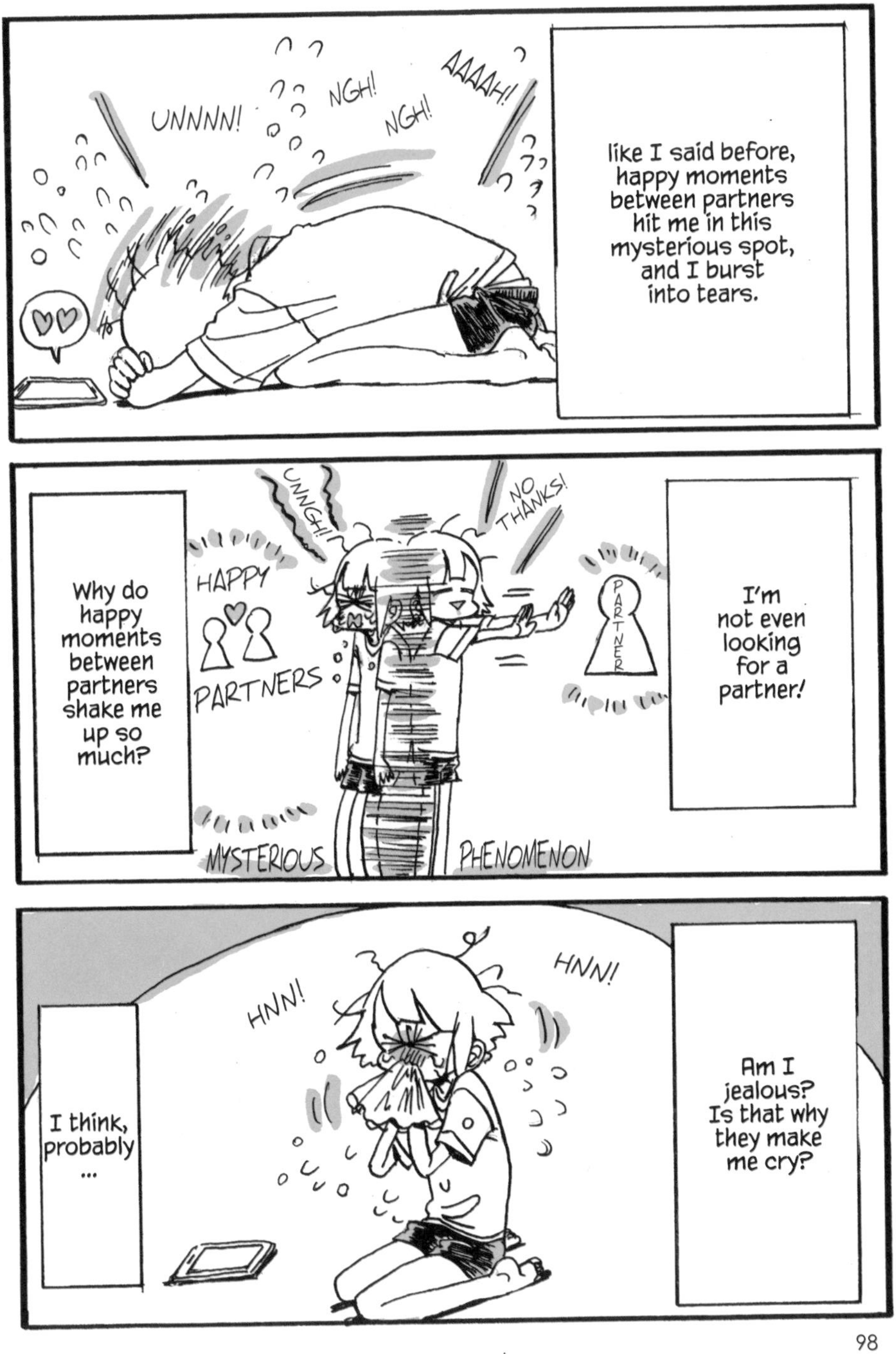

like I said before, happy moments between partners hit me in this mysterious spot, and I burst into tears.
AAAAH!
NGH!
NGH!
UNNNN!
I'm not even looking for a partner!
PARTNER
NO THANKS!
UNNGH!
HAPPY PARTNERS
Why do happy moments between partners shake me up so much?
MYSTERIOUS PHENOMENON
Am I jealous? Is that why they make me cry?
HNN!
HNN!
I think, probably ...

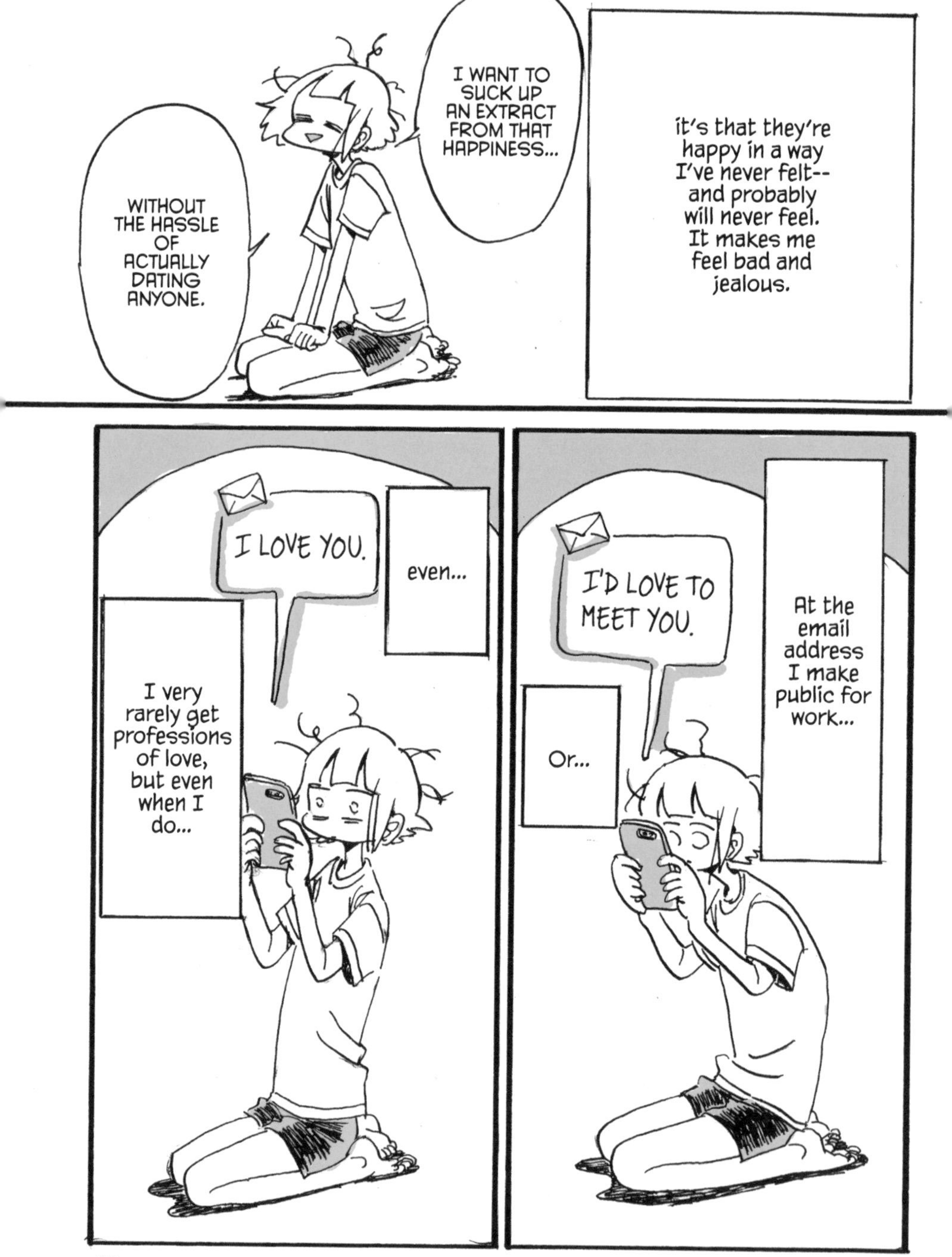
it's that they're happy in a way I've never felt-- and probably will never feel. It makes me feel bad and jealous.
I WANT TO SUCK UP AN EXTRACT FROM THAT HAPPINESS...
WITHOUT THE HASSLE OF ACTUALLY DATING ANYONE.
At the email address I make public for work...
I'D LOVE TO MEET YOU.
Or...
even...
I LOVE YOU.
I very rarely get professions of love, but even when I do...

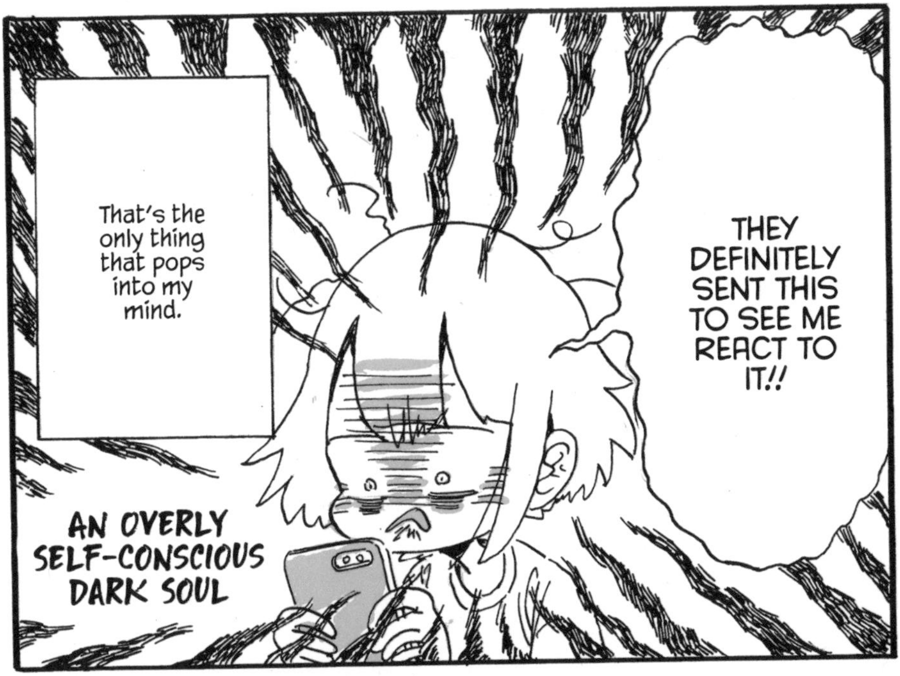
THEY DEFINITELY SENT THIS TO SEE ME REACT TO IT!!
That's the only thing that pops into my mind.
AN OVERLY SELF-CONSCIOUS DARK SOUL

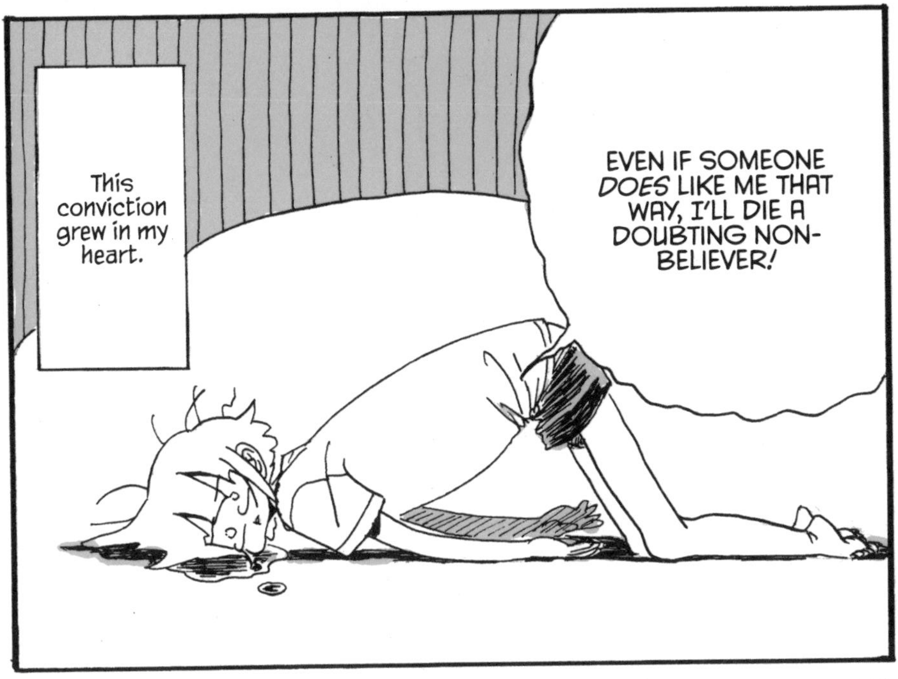
EVEN IF SOMEONE *DOES* LIKE ME THAT WAY, I'LL DIE A DOUBTING NON-BELIEVER!
This conviction grew in my heart.

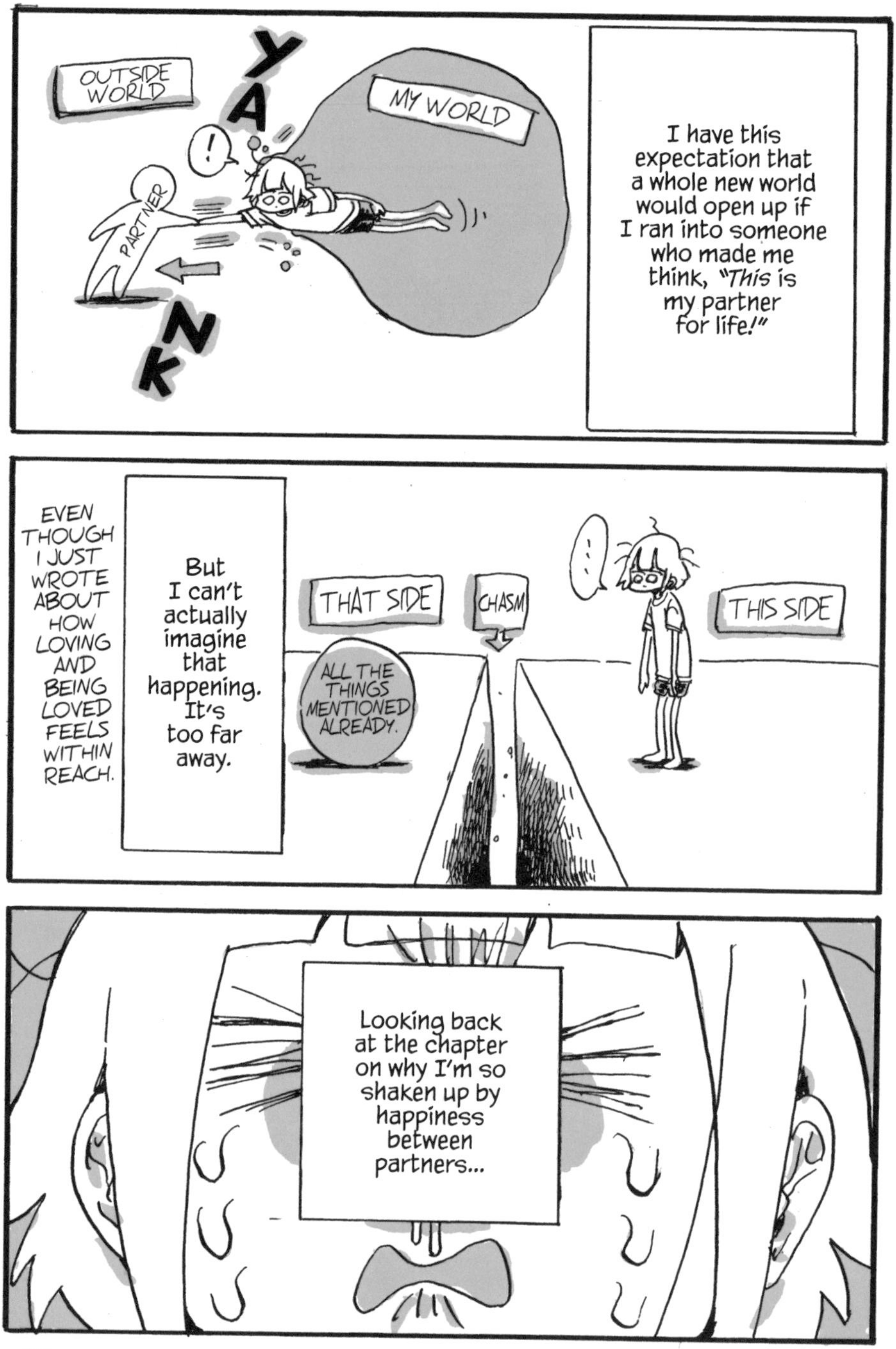

I have this expectation that a whole new world would open up if I ran into someone who made me think, "*This* is my partner for life!"
MY WORLD
YANK
OUTSIDE WORLD
!
PARTNER
THIS SIDE
...
CHASM
THAT SIDE
ALL THE THINGS MENTIONED ALREADY.
But I can't actually imagine that happening. It's too far away.
EVEN THOUGH I JUST WROTE ABOUT HOW LOVING AND BEING LOVED FEELS WITHIN REACH.
Looking back at the chapter on why I'm so shaken up by happiness between partners...

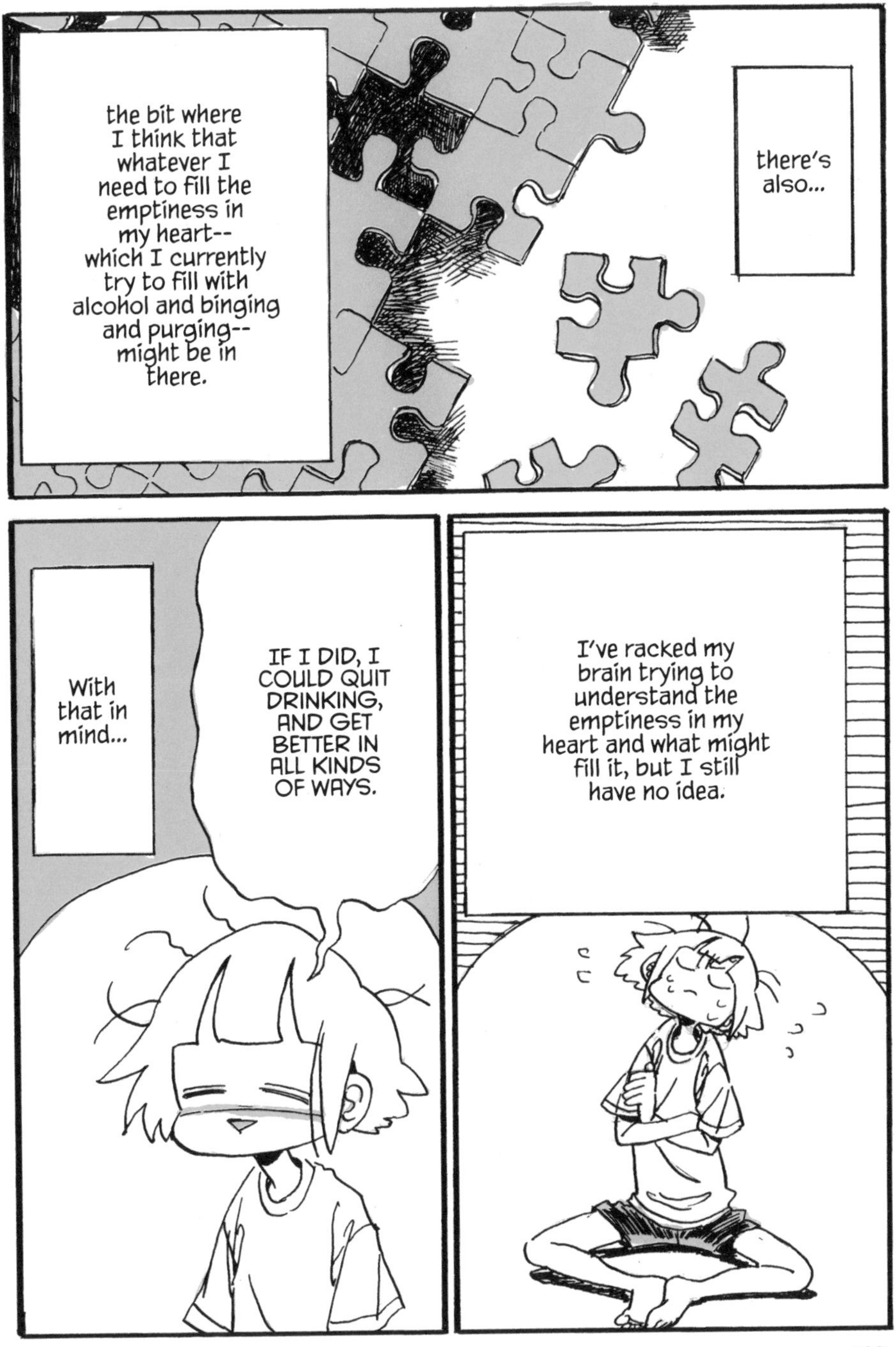
there's also...
the bit where I think that whatever I need to fill the emptiness in my heart-- which I currently try to fill with alcohol and binging and purging-- might be in there.
I've racked my brain trying to understand the emptiness in my heart and what might fill it, but I still have no idea.
IF I DID, I COULD QUIT DRINKING, AND GET BETTER IN ALL KINDS OF WAYS.
With that in mind...

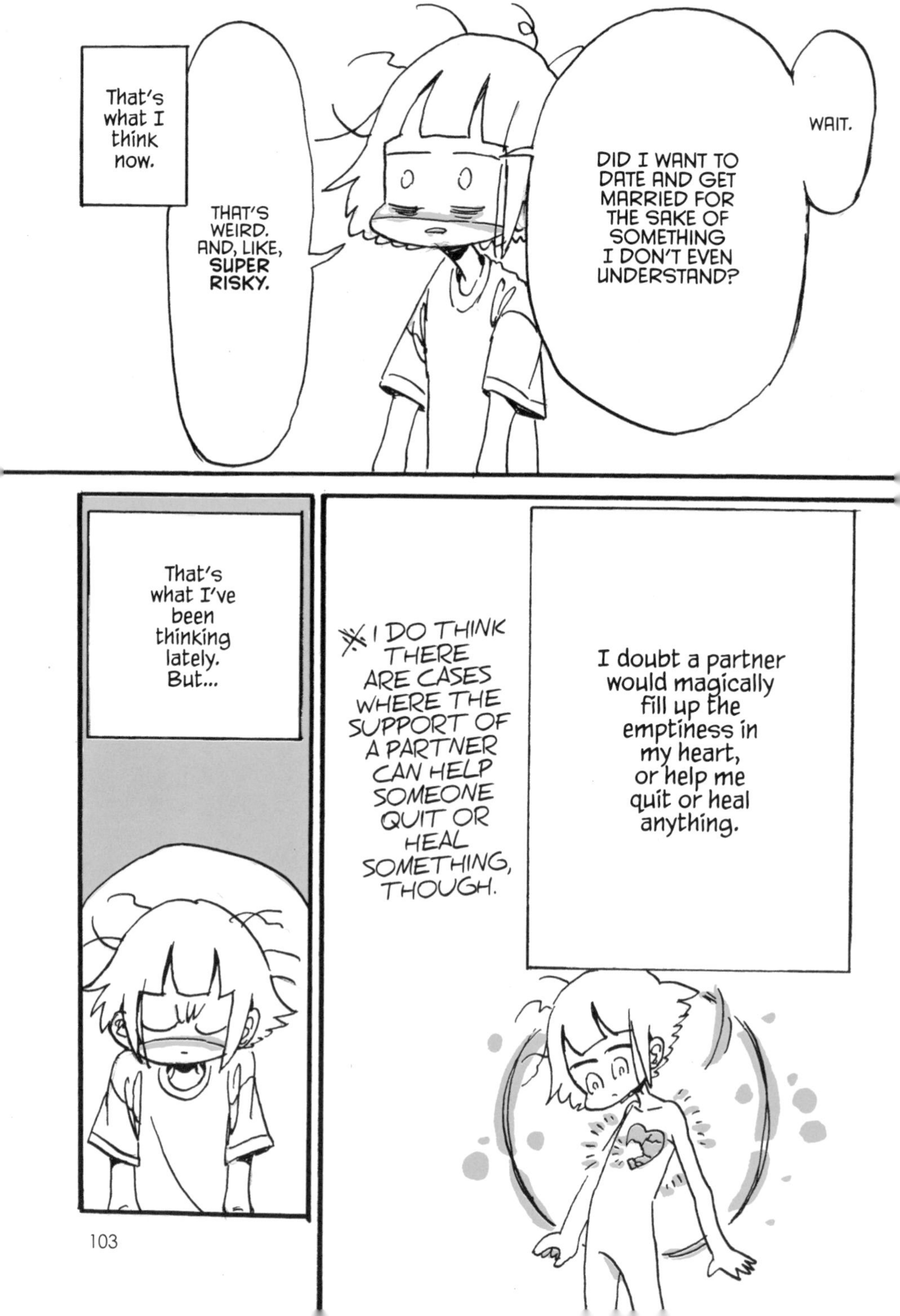
WAIT.
DID I WANT TO DATE AND GET MARRIED FOR THE SAKE OF SOMETHING I DON'T EVEN UNDERSTAND?
THAT'S WEIRD. AND, LIKE, SUPER RISKY.
That's what I think now.
I doubt a partner would magically fill up the emptiness in my heart, or help me quit or heal anything.
※ I DO THINK THERE ARE CASES WHERE THE SUPPORT OF A PARTNER CAN HELP SOMEONE QUIT OR HEAL SOMETHING, THOUGH.
That's what I've been thinking lately. But...

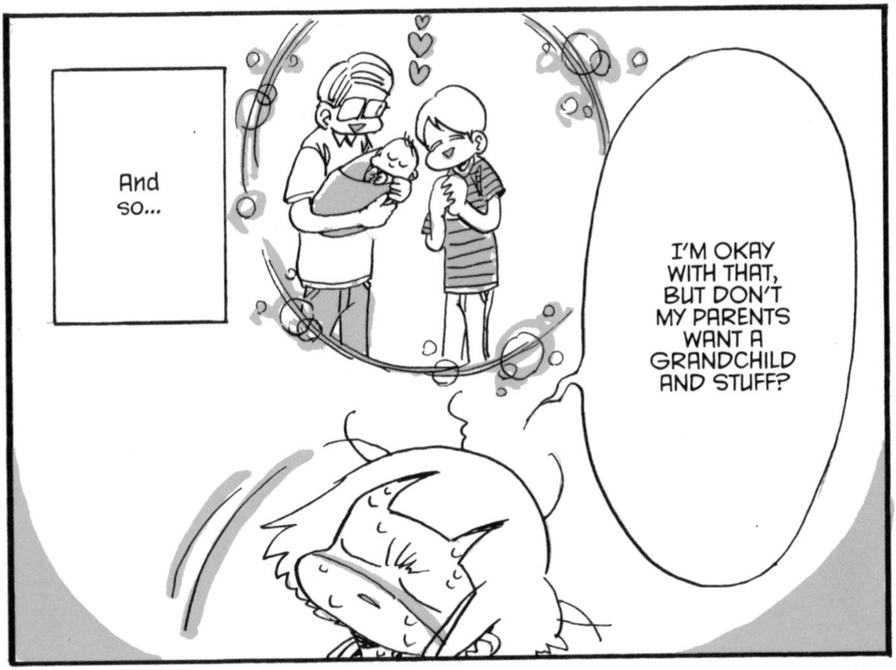
I'M OKAY WITH THAT, BUT DON'T MY PARENTS WANT A GRANDCHILD AND STUFF?
And so...

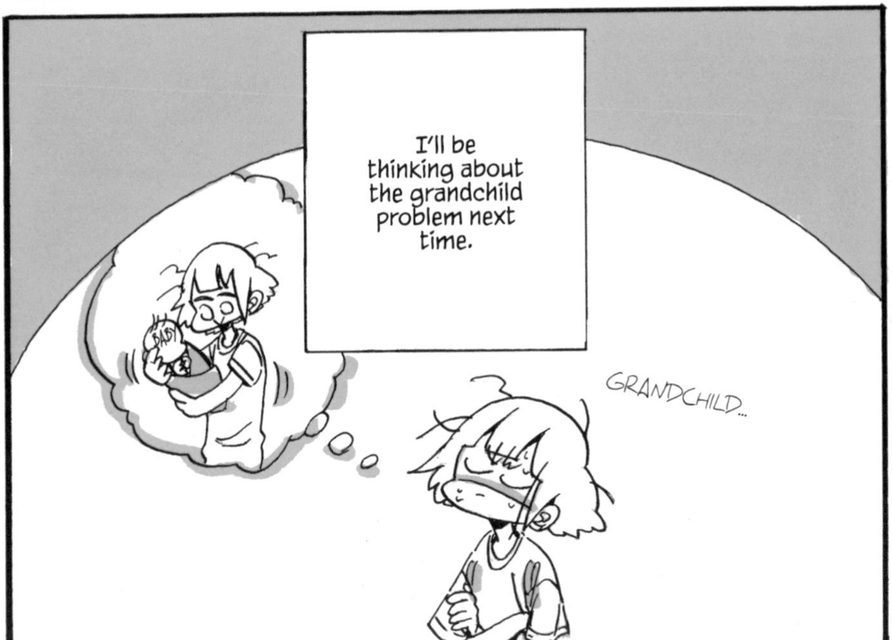
I'll be thinking about the grandchild problem next time.
GRANDCHILD...
BABY

Chapter 8/END

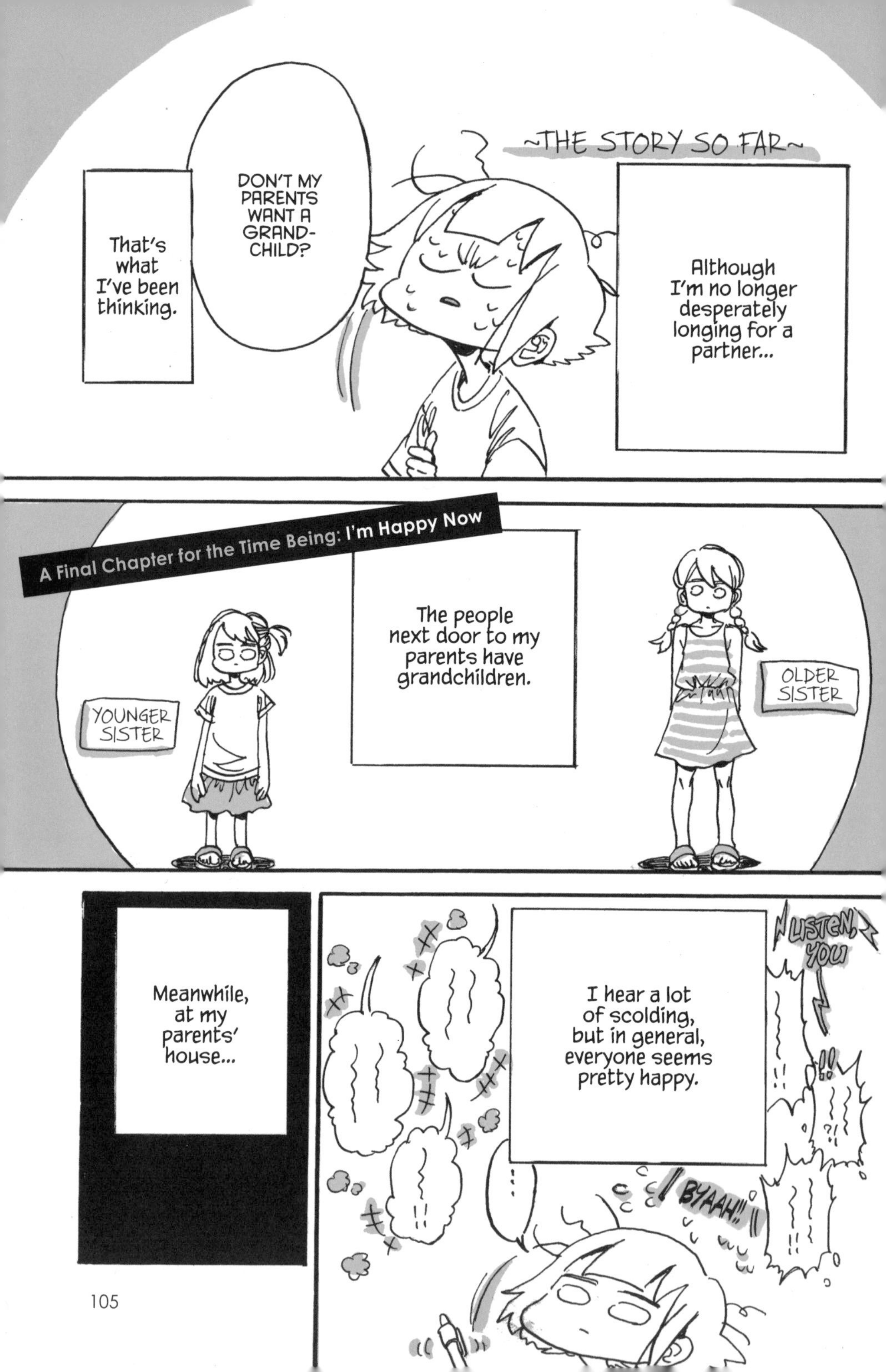
~THE STORY SO FAR~
Although I'm no longer desperately longing for a partner...
DON'T MY PARENTS WANT A GRAND-CHILD?
That's what I've been thinking.
A Final Chapter for the Time Being: I'm Happy Now
The people next door to my parents have grandchildren.
OLDER SISTER
YOUNGER SISTER
LISTEN, YOU
I hear a lot of scolding, but in general, everyone seems pretty happy.
BYAAH!!
Meanwhile, at my parents' house...

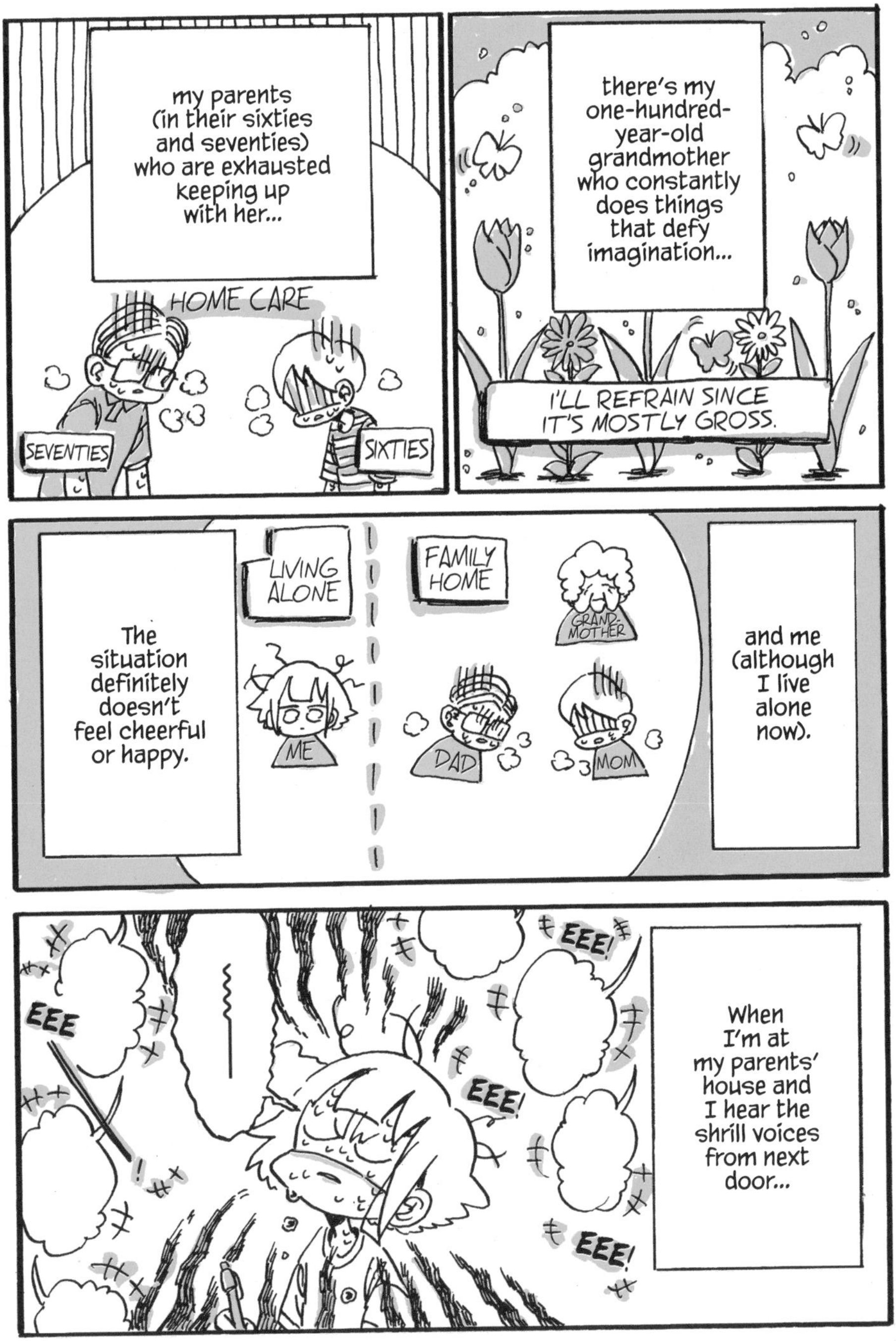
there's my one-hundred-year-old grandmother who constantly does things that defy imagination...
I'LL REFRAIN SINCE IT'S MOSTLY GROSS.
my parents (in their sixties and seventies) who are exhausted keeping up with her...
HOME CARE
SIXTIES
SEVENTIES
and me (although I live alone now).
FAMILY HOME
GRANDMOTHER
MOM
DAD
LIVING ALONE
ME
The situation definitely doesn't feel cheerful or happy.
When I'm at my parents' house and I hear the shrill voices from next door...
EEE!
EEE!
EEE!
EEE

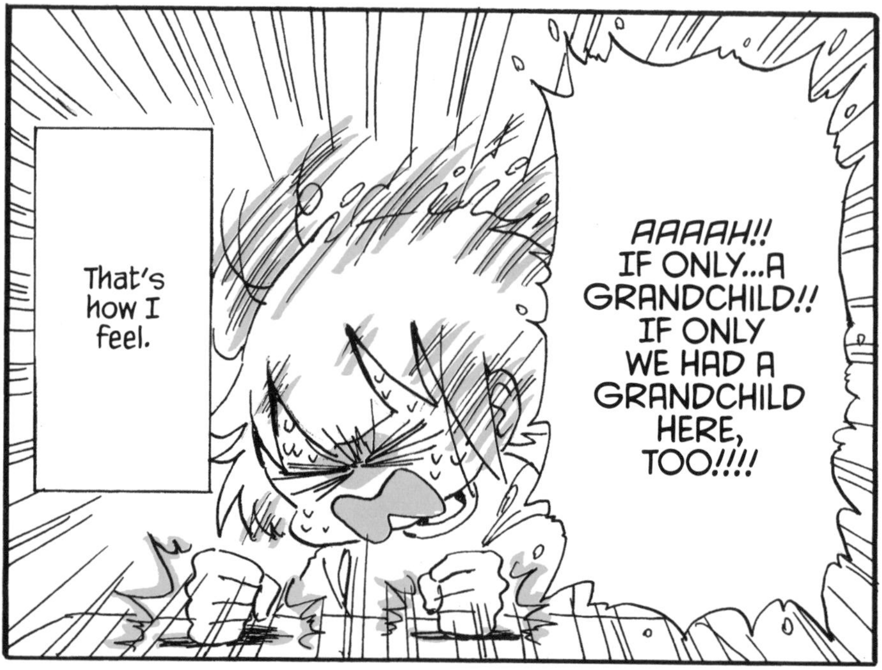
AAAAH!! IF ONLY...A GRANDCHILD!! IF ONLY WE HAD A GRANDCHILD HERE, TOO!!!!
That's how I feel.

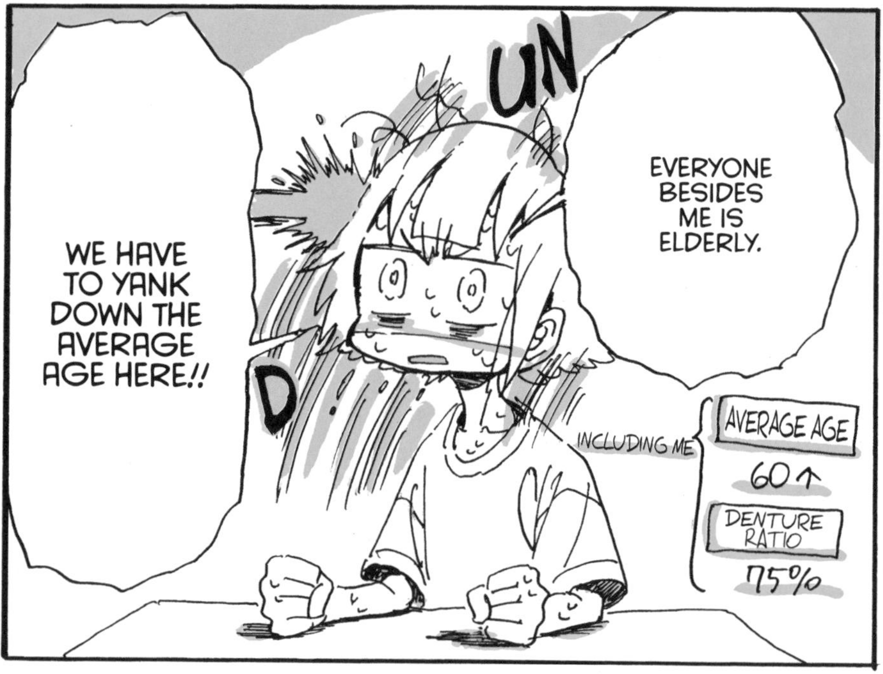
UN
EVERYONE BESIDES ME IS ELDERLY.
AVERAGE AGE
INCLUDING ME
60↑
DENTURE RATIO
75%
D
WE HAVE TO YANK DOWN THE AVERAGE AGE HERE!!

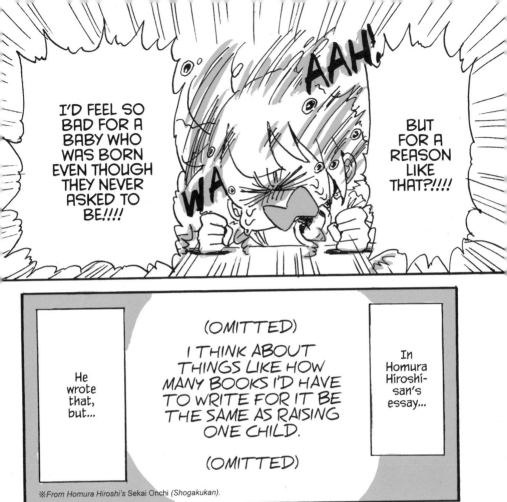

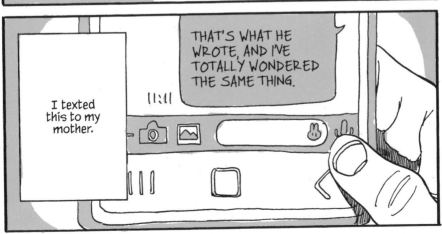

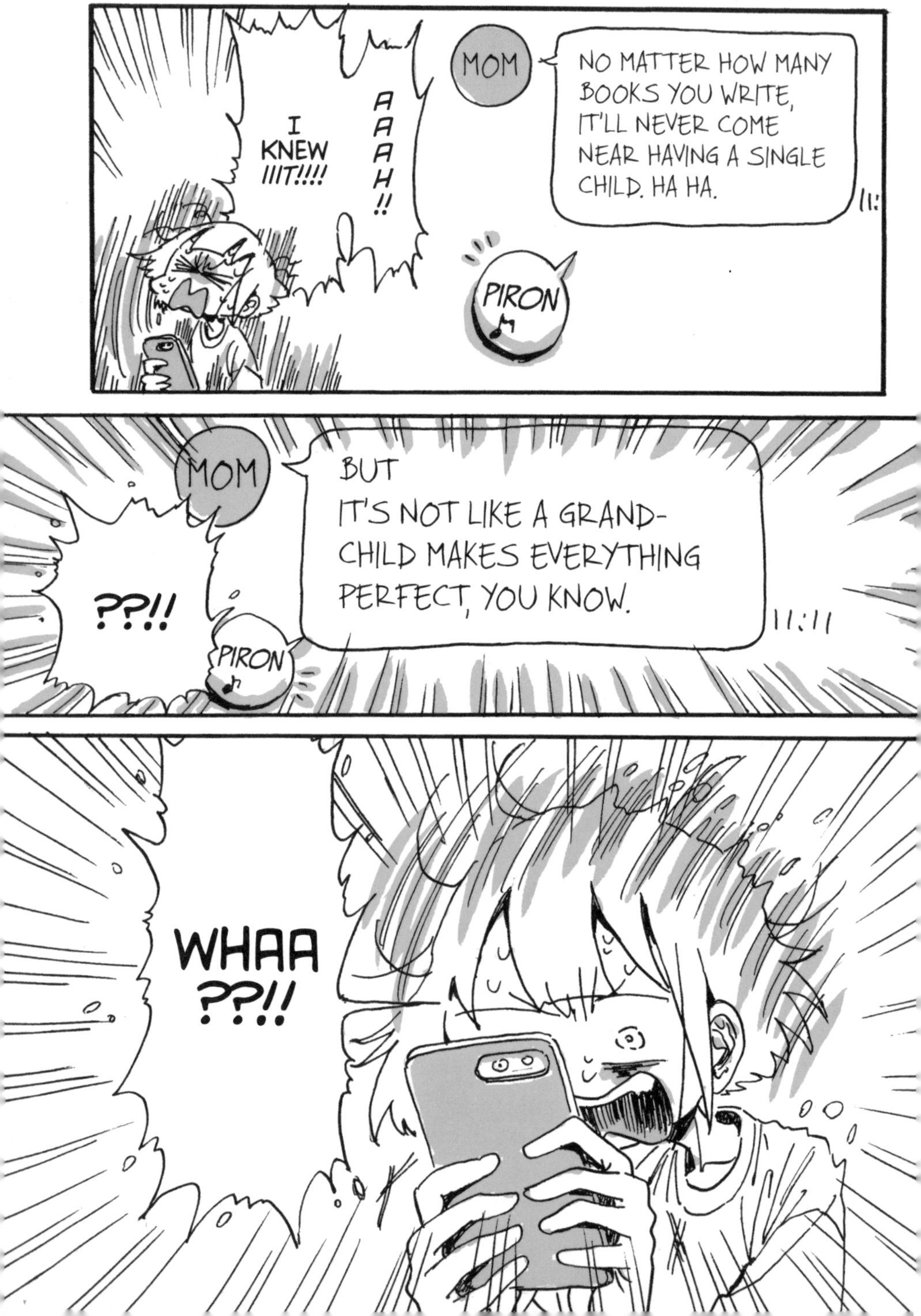
MOM
NO MATTER HOW MANY BOOKS YOU WRITE, IT'LL NEVER COME NEAR HAVING A SINGLE CHILD. HA HA.
PIRON
AAAAH!!
I KNEW IIIT!!!!
MOM
BUT IT'S NOT LIKE A GRAND-CHILD MAKES EVERYTHING PERFECT, YOU KNOW.
PIRON
??!!
WHAA ??!!

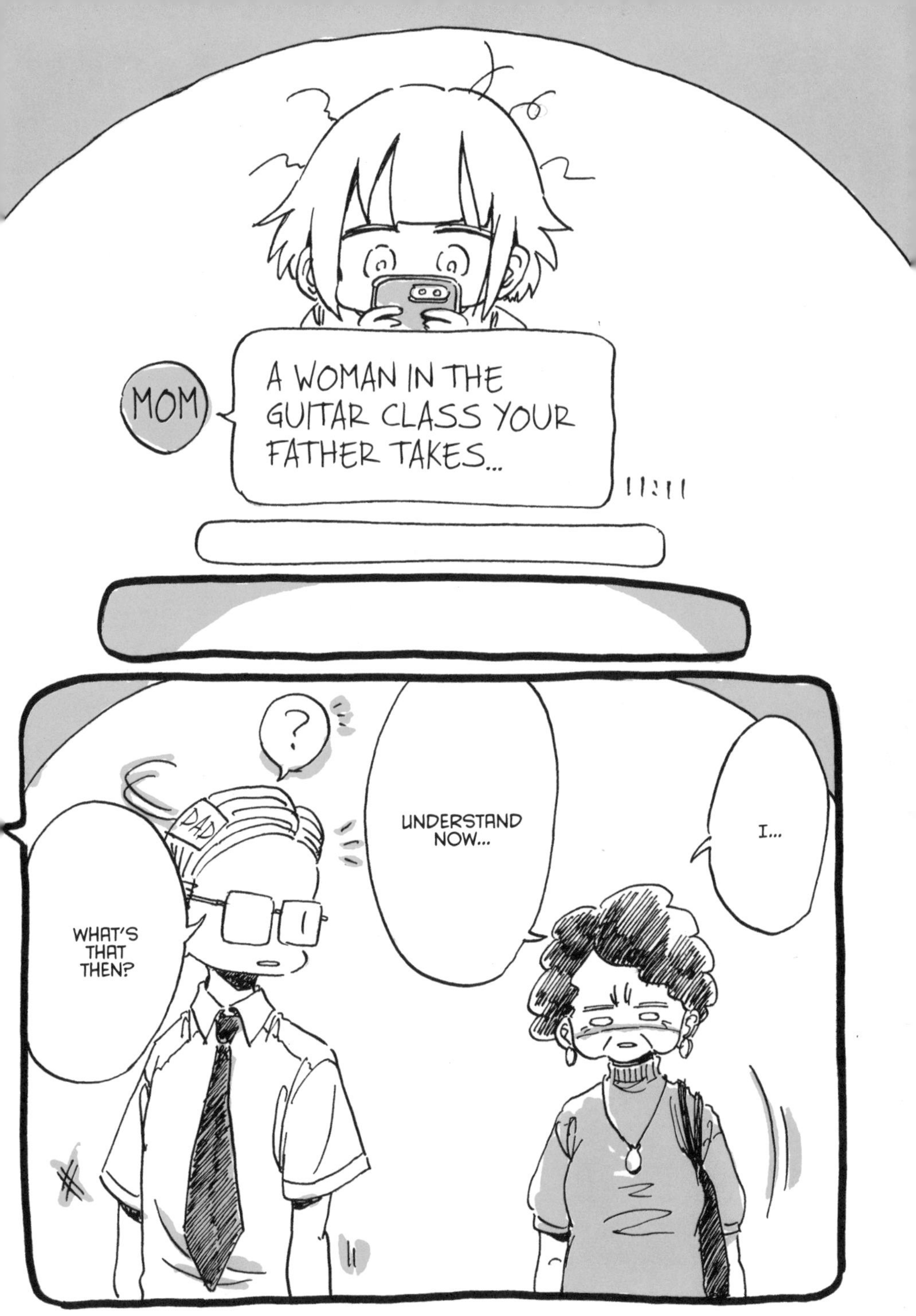
MOM
A WOMAN IN THE GUITAR CLASS YOUR FATHER TAKES...
I...
UNDERSTAND NOW...
?
DAD
WHAT'S THAT THEN?

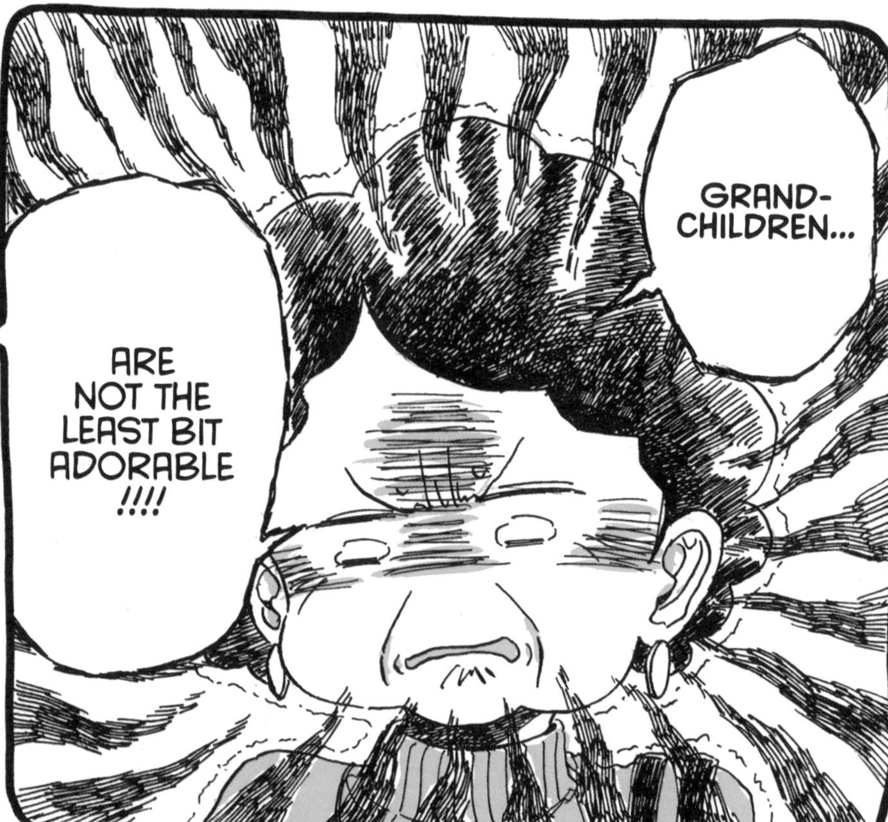
GRAND-CHILDREN...
ARE NOT THE LEAST BIT ADORABLE !!!!
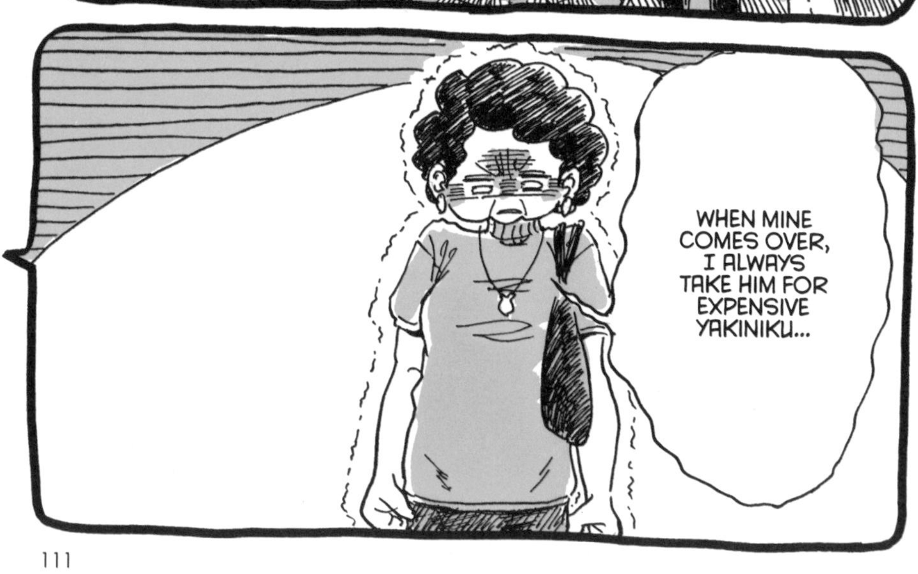
WHEN MINE COMES OVER, I ALWAYS TAKE HIM FOR EXPENSIVE YAKINIKU...

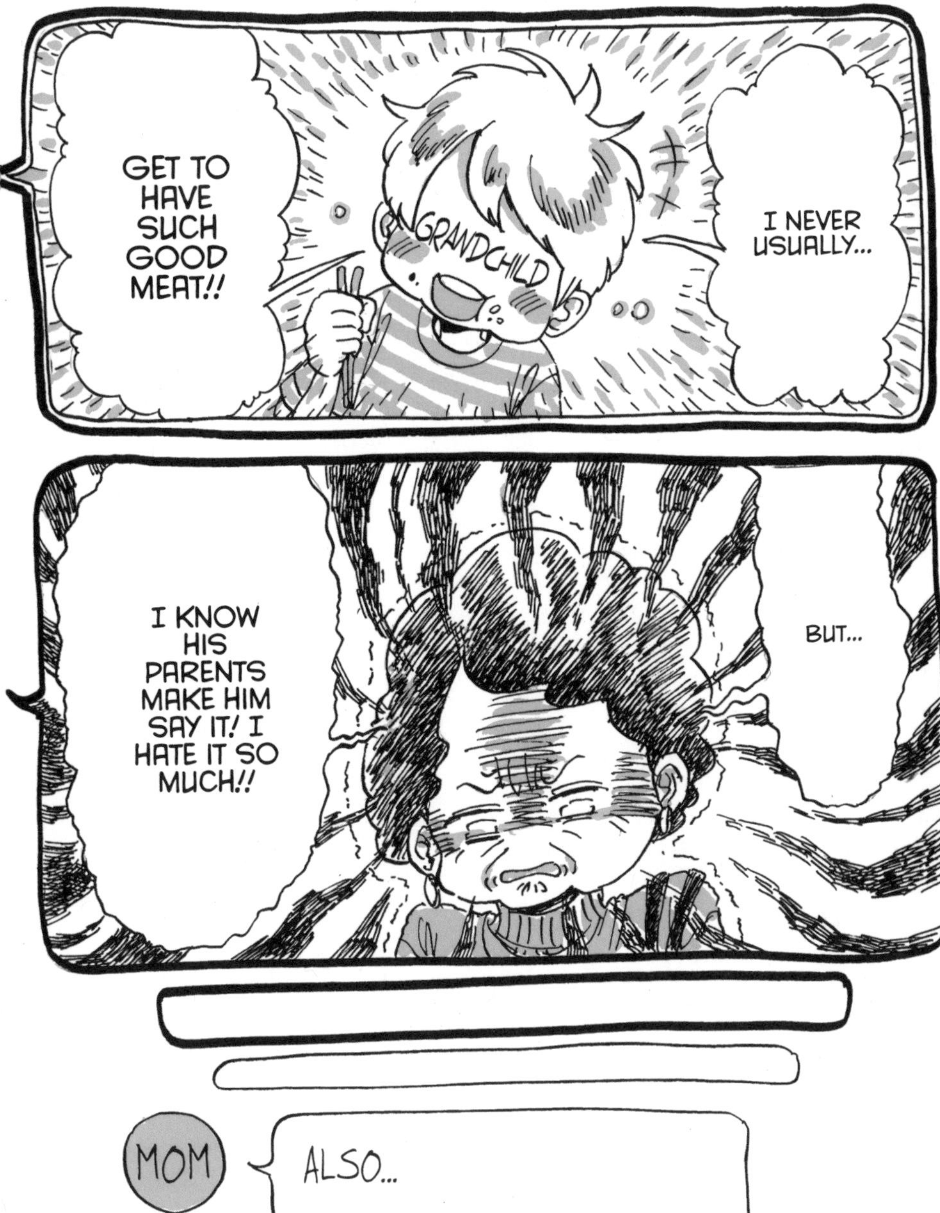
I NEVER USUALLY...
GRANDCHILD
GET TO HAVE SUCH GOOD MEAT!!
BUT...
I KNOW HIS PARENTS MAKE HIM SAY IT! I HATE IT SO MUCH!!
MOM
ALSO...
11:11

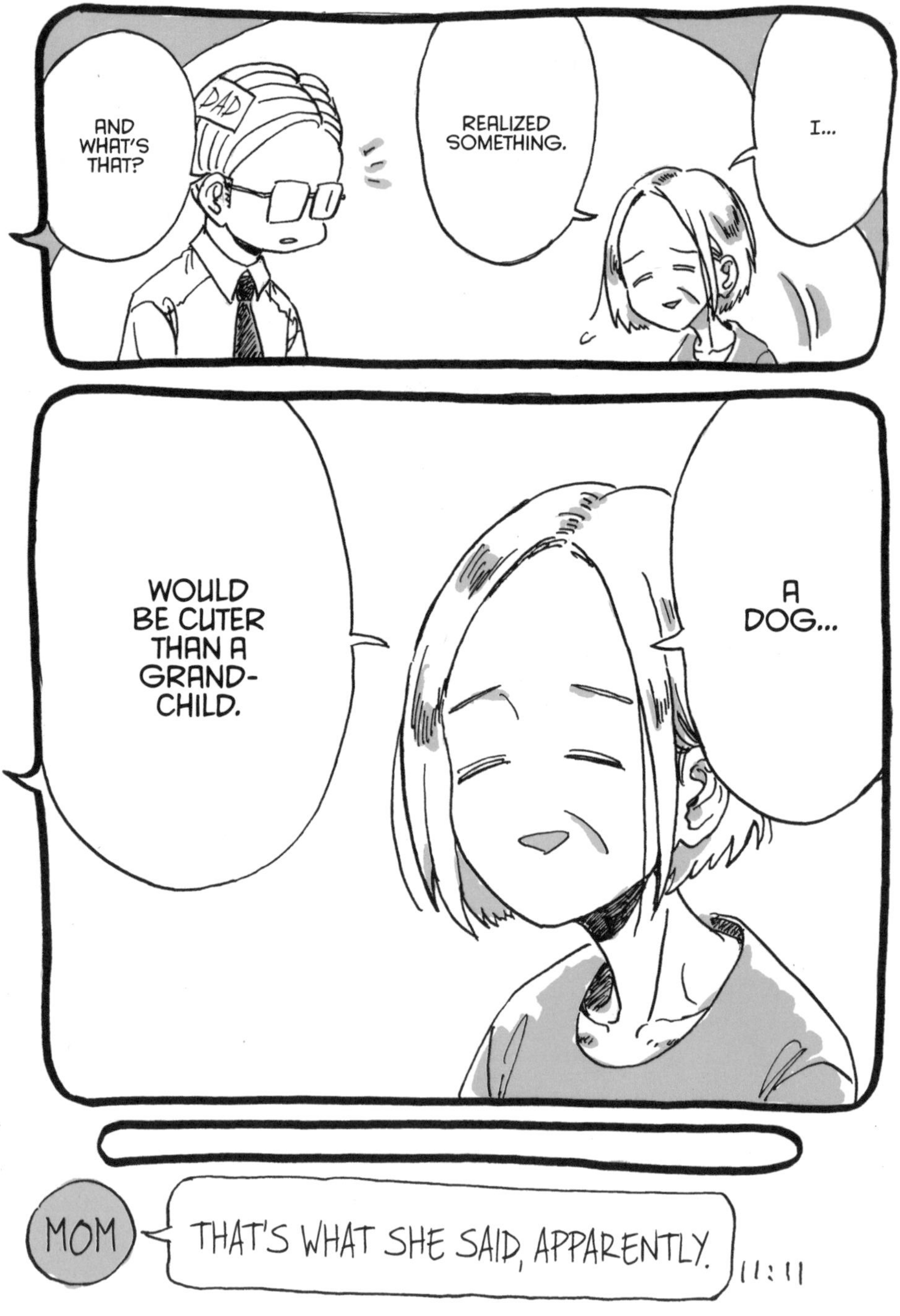
I...
REALIZED SOMETHING.
DAD
AND WHAT'S THAT?
A DOG...
WOULD BE CUTER THAN A GRAND-CHILD.
MOM
THAT'S WHAT SHE SAID, APPARENTLY.
11:11

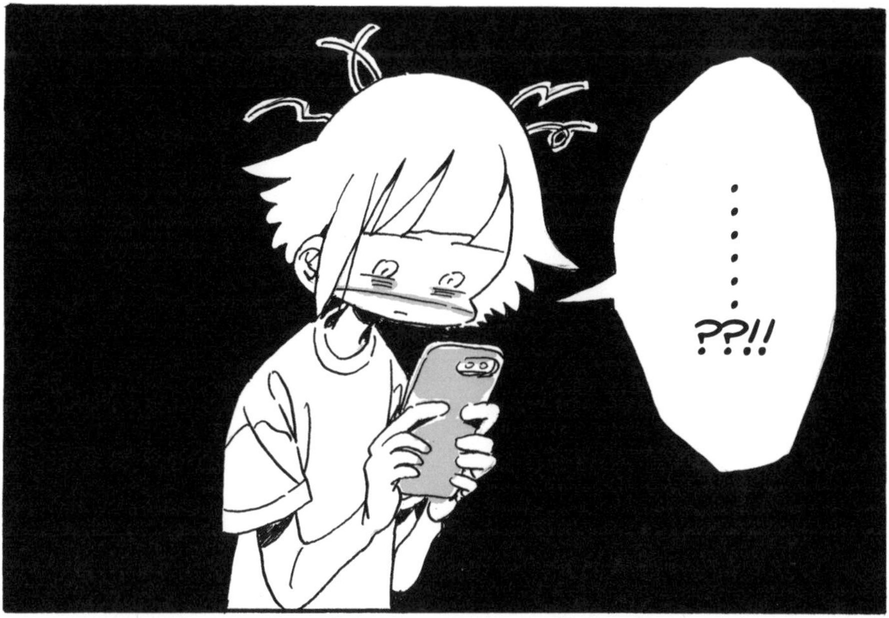
......
??!!
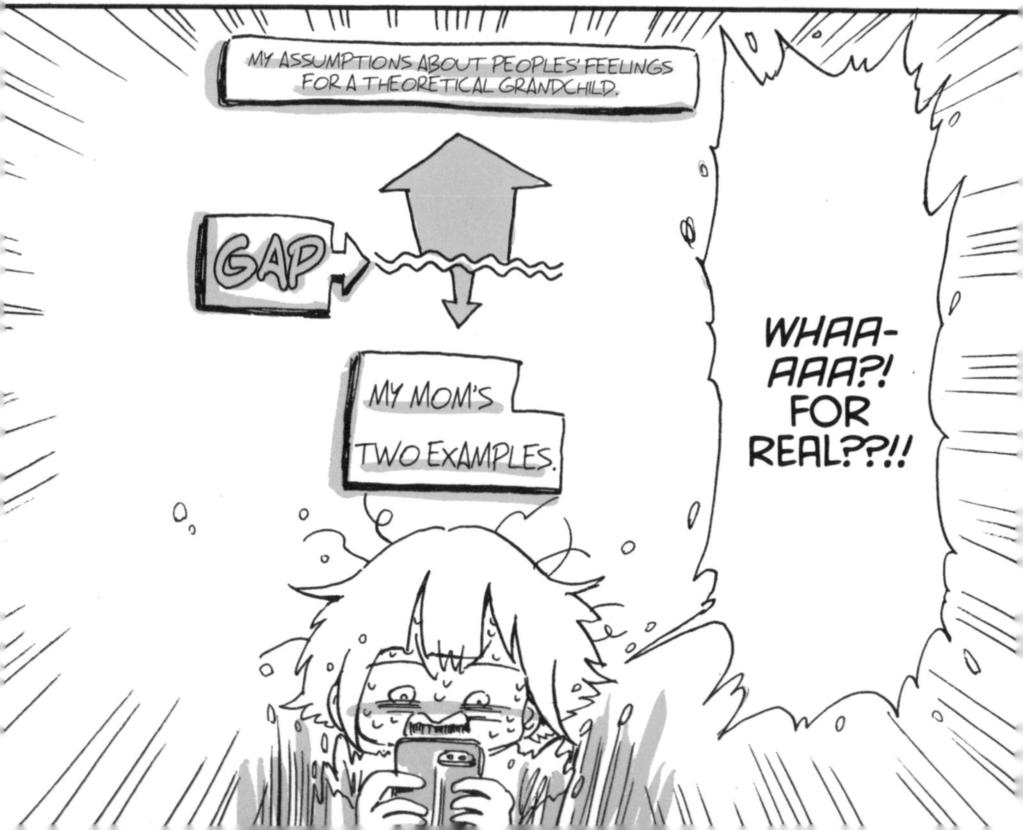
WHAA-
AAA?! FOR REAL??!!
MY ASSUMPTIONS ABOUT PEOPLES' FEELINGS FOR A THEORETICAL GRANDCHILD.
GAP
MY MOM'S TWO EXAMPLES.

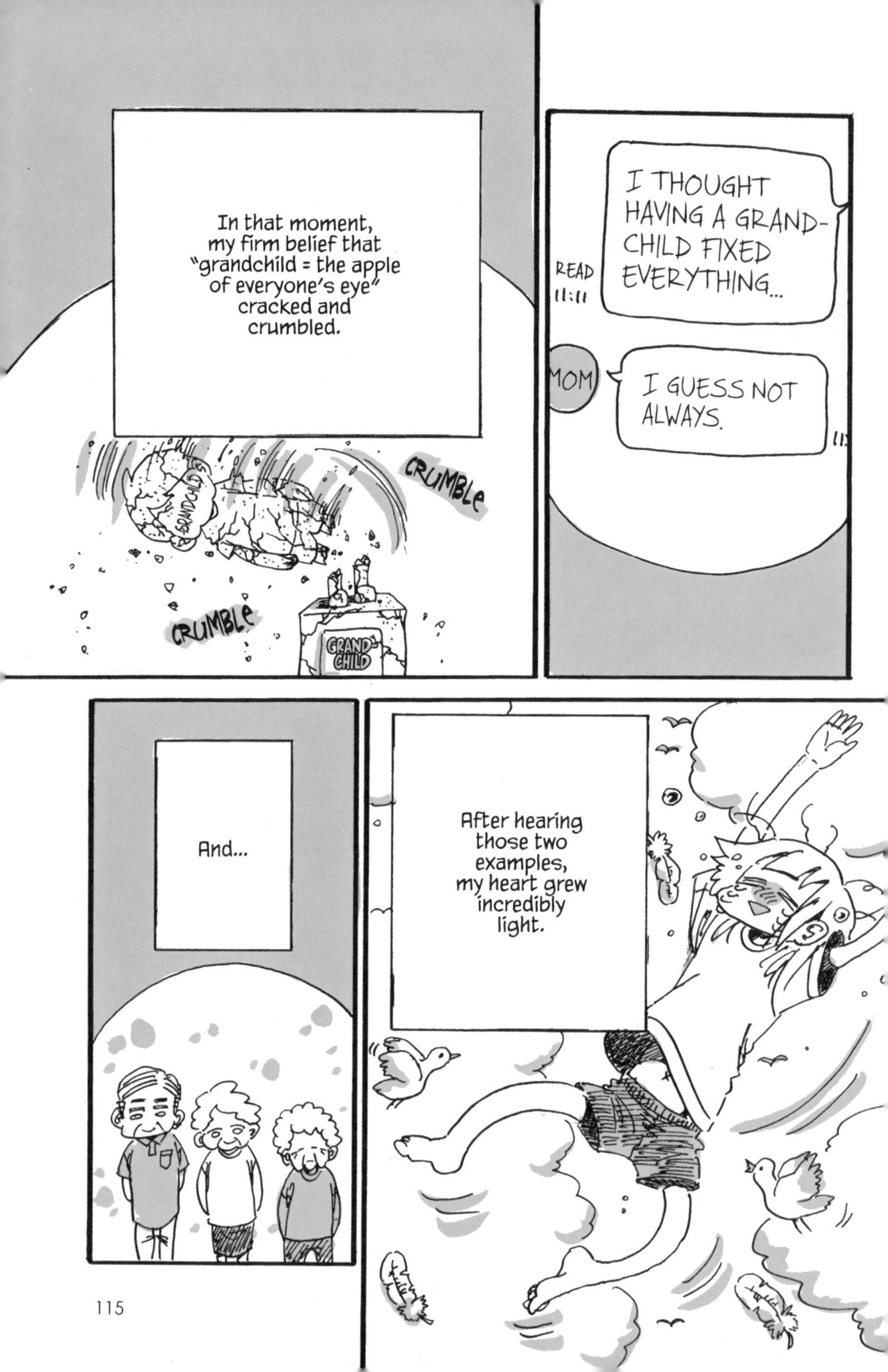
READ
11:11
I THOUGHT HAVING A GRAND-CHILD FIXED EVERYTHING...
MOM
I GUESS NOT ALWAYS.
In that moment, my firm belief that "grandchild = the apple of everyone's eye" cracked and crumbled.
GRANDCHILD
CRUMBLE
CRUMBLE
GRAND-CHILD
After hearing those two examples, my heart grew incredibly light.
And...

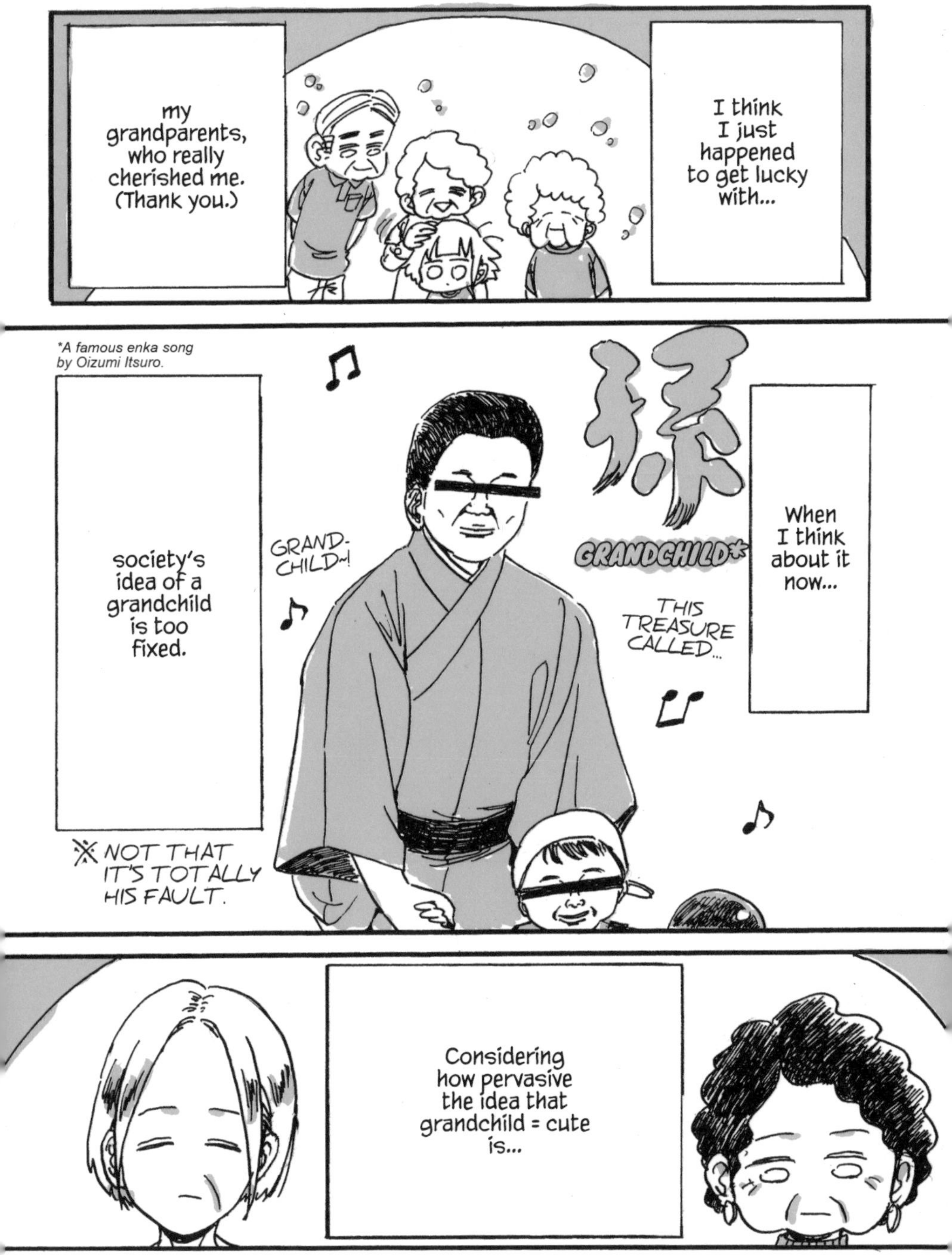
I think I just happened to get lucky with...
my grandparents, who really cherished me. (Thank you.)
When I think about it now...
THIS TREASURE CALLED...
孫
GRANDCHILD*
GRAND-CHILD~!
society's idea of a grandchild is too fixed.
※NOT THAT IT'S TOTALLY HIS FAULT.
*A famous enka song by Oizumi Itsuro.
Considering how pervasive the idea that grandchild = cute is...

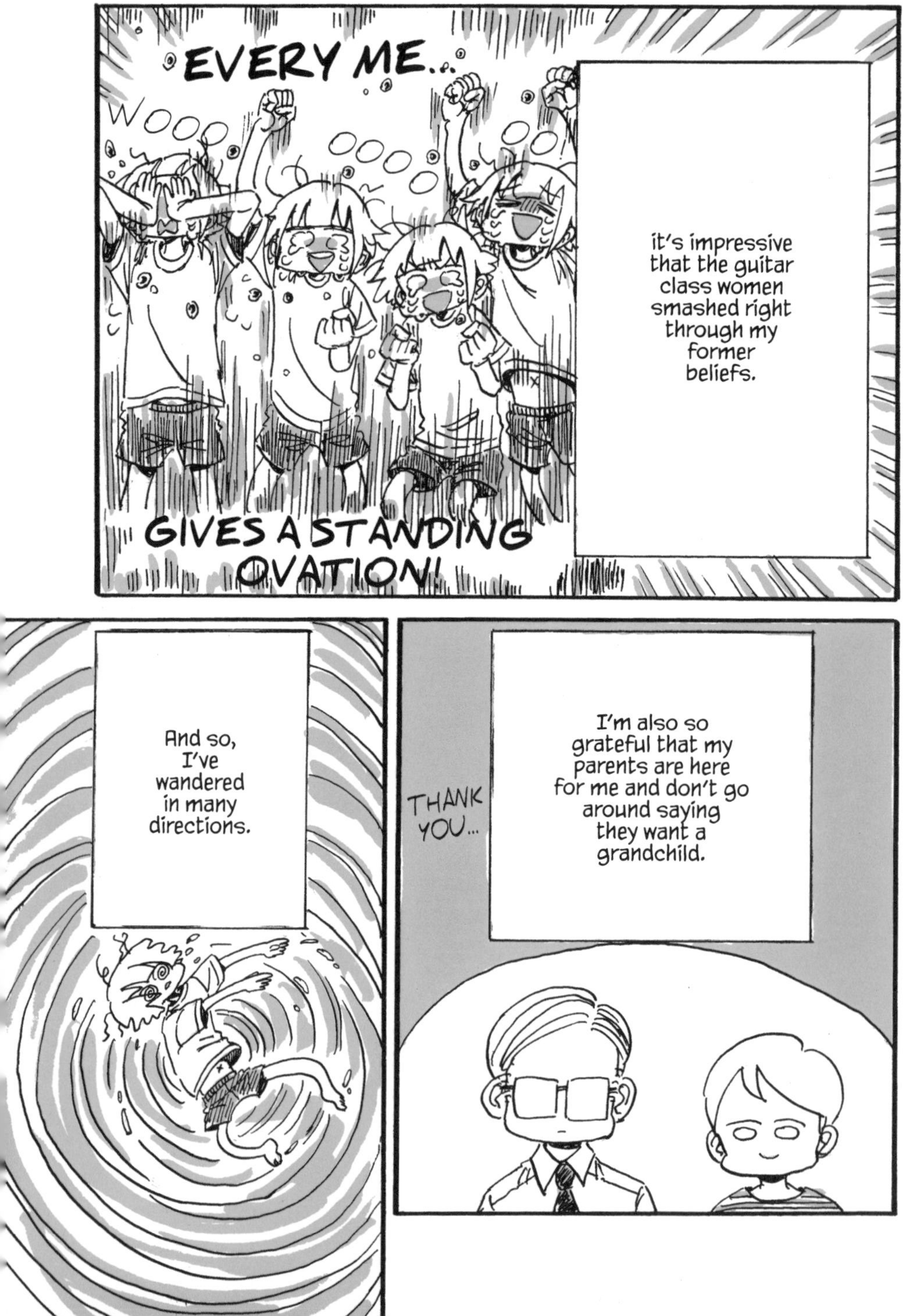
it's impressive that the guitar class women smashed right through my former beliefs.
EVERY ME...
WOOO
OOOOO
GIVES A STANDING OVATION!
I'm also so grateful that my parents are here for me and don't go around saying they want a grandchild.
THANK YOU...
And so, I've wandered in many directions.

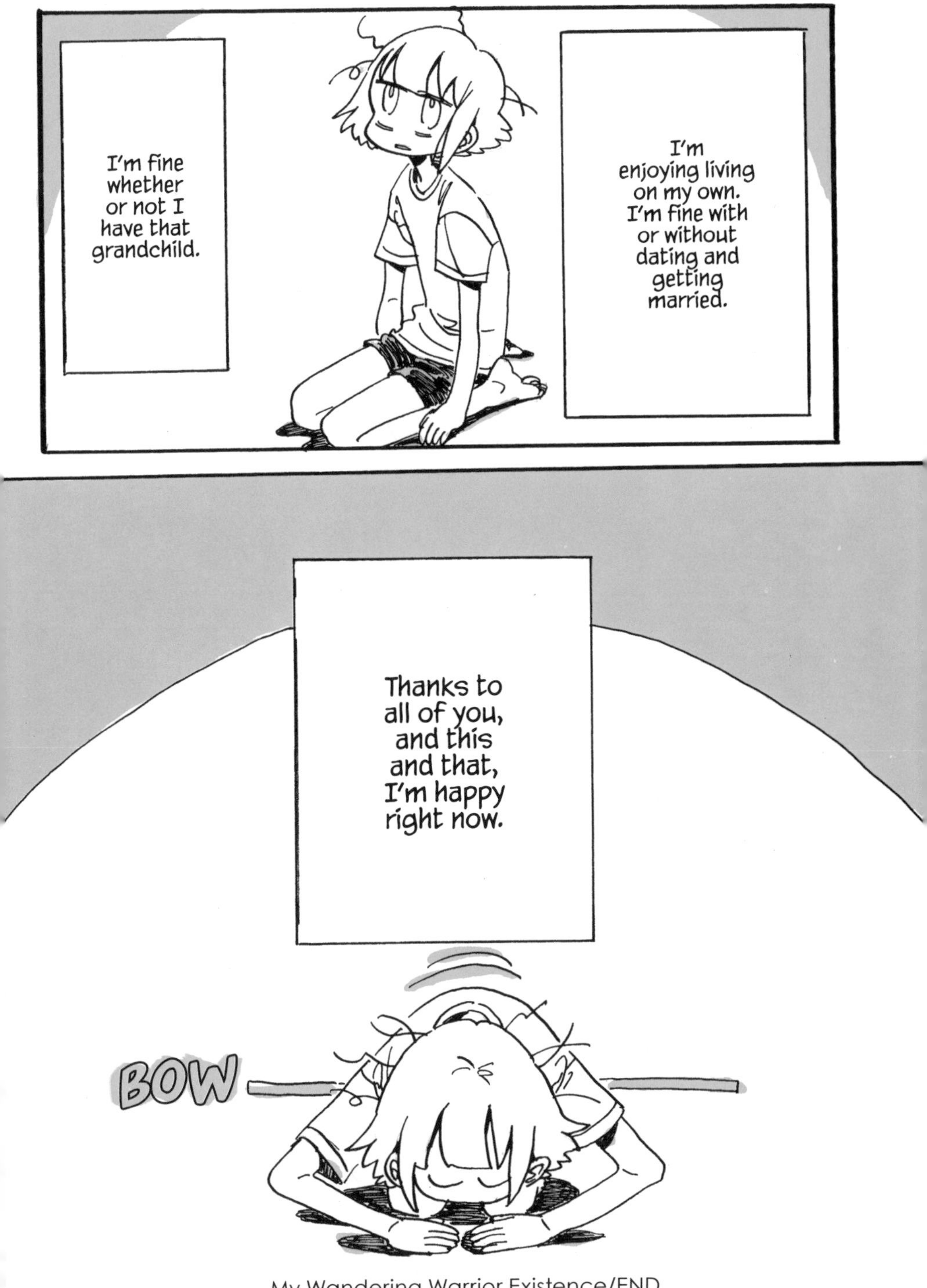
I'm enjoying living on my own. I'm fine with or without dating and getting married.
I'm fine whether or not I have that grandchild.
Thanks to all of you, and this and that, I'm happy right now.
BOW

My Wandering Warrior Existence/END

My
Wandering
Warrior
Existence

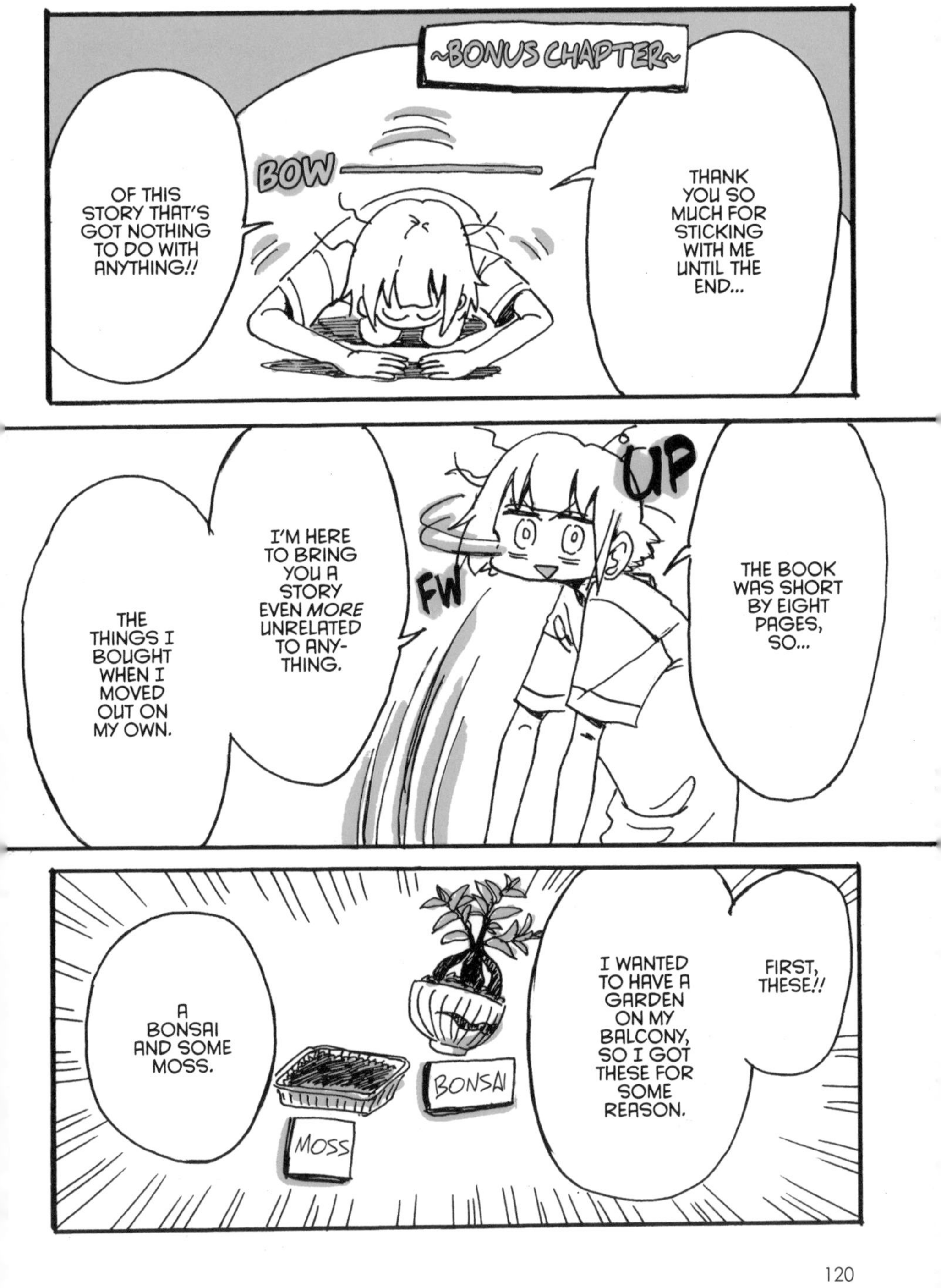
~BONUS CHAPTER~
THANK YOU SO MUCH FOR STICKING WITH ME UNTIL THE END...
BOW
OF THIS STORY THAT'S GOT NOTHING TO DO WITH ANYTHING!!
THE BOOK WAS SHORT BY EIGHT PAGES, SO...
UP
FW
I'M HERE TO BRING YOU A STORY EVEN *MORE* UNRELATED TO ANY-THING.
THE THINGS I BOUGHT WHEN I MOVED OUT ON MY OWN.
FIRST, THESE!!
I WANTED TO HAVE A GARDEN ON MY BALCONY, SO I GOT THESE FOR SOME REASON.
BONSAI
MOSS
A BONSAI AND SOME MOSS.

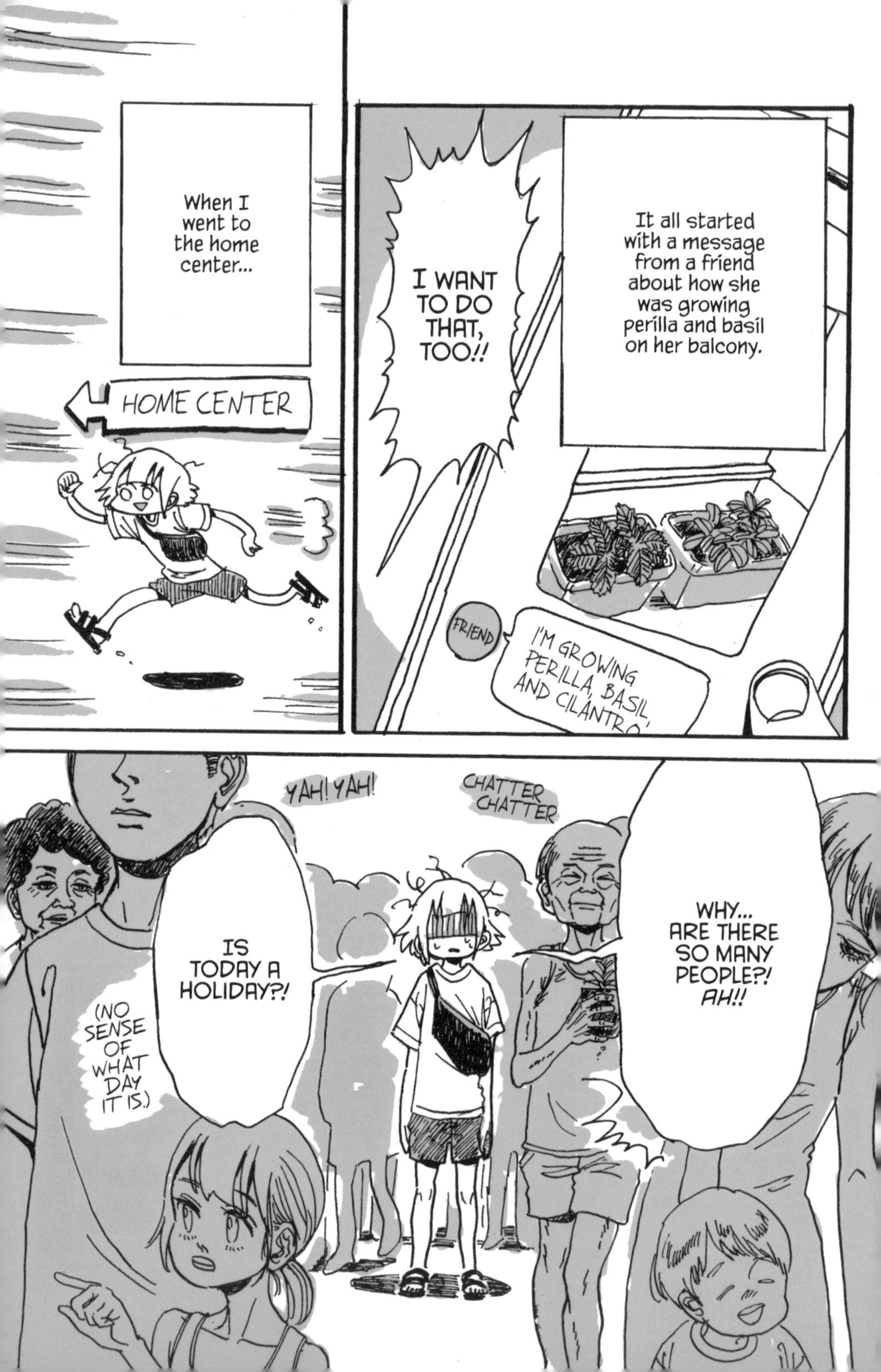
It all started with a message from a friend about how she was growing perilla and basil on her balcony.
I WANT TO DO THAT, TOO!!
FRIEND
I'M GROWING PERILLA, BASIL, AND CILANTRO,
When I went to the home center...
HOME CENTER
WHY... ARE THERE SO MANY PEOPLE?! AH!!
CHATTER CHATTER
YAH! YAH!
IS TODAY A HOLIDAY?!
(NO SENSE OF WHAT DAY IT IS.)

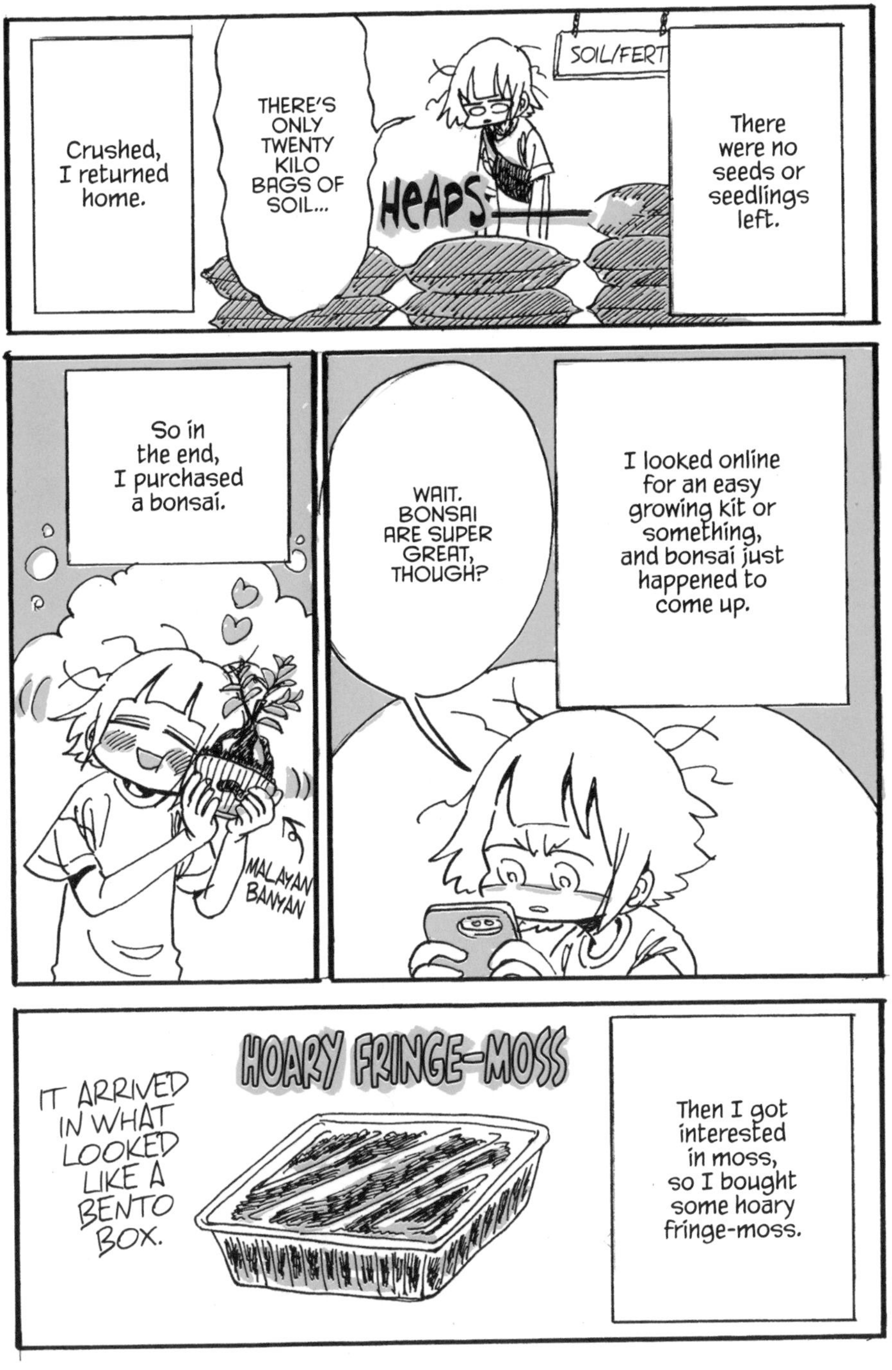
There were no seeds or seedlings left.
SOIL/FERT
HEAPS
THERE'S ONLY TWENTY KILO BAGS OF SOIL...
Crushed, I returned home.
I looked online for an easy growing kit or something, and bonsai just happened to come up.
WAIT. BONSAI ARE SUPER GREAT, THOUGH?
So in the end, I purchased a bonsai.
MALAYAN BANYAN
Then I got interested in moss, so I bought some hoary fringe-moss.
HOARY FRINGE-MOSS
IT ARRIVED IN WHAT LOOKED LIKE A BENTO BOX.

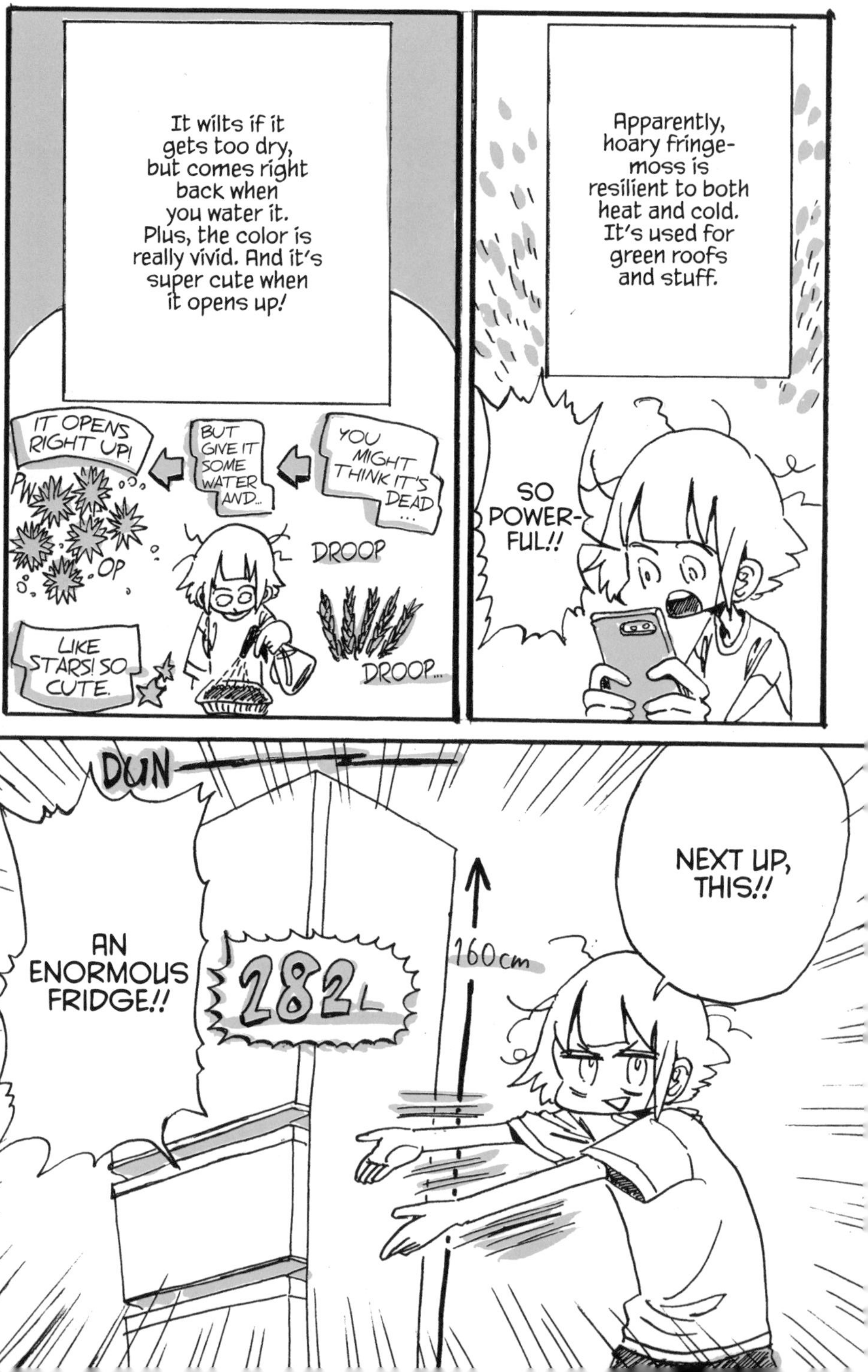
Apparently, hoary fringe-moss is resilient to both heat and cold. It's used for green roofs and stuff.
SO POWER-FUL!!
It wilts if it gets too dry, but comes right back when you water it. Plus, the color is really vivid. And it's super cute when it opens up!
YOU MIGHT THINK IT'S DEAD...
BUT GIVE IT SOME WATER AND...
IT OPENS RIGHT UP!
PWOP
LIKE STARS! SO CUTE.
DROOP
DROOP...
NEXT UP, THIS!!
DUN
AN ENORMOUS FRIDGE!!
282L
160cm

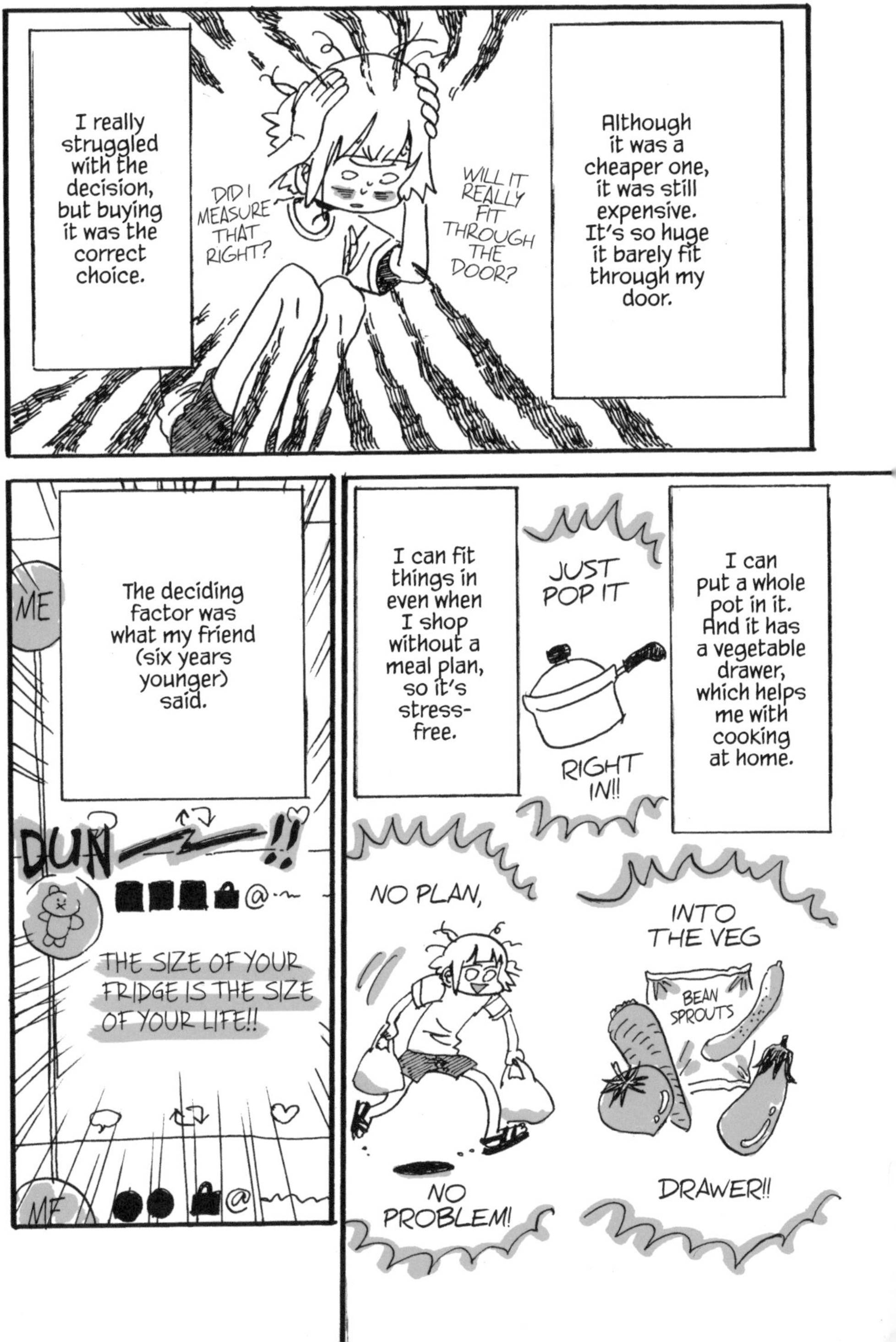
Although it was a cheaper one, it was still expensive. It's so huge it barely fit through my door.
WILL IT REALLY FIT THROUGH THE DOOR?
DID I MEASURE THAT RIGHT?
I really struggled with the decision, but buying it was the correct choice.
I can put a whole pot in it. And it has a vegetable drawer, which helps me with cooking at home.
JUST POP IT
RIGHT IN!!
I can fit things in even when I shop without a meal plan, so it's stress-free.
INTO THE VEG
BEAN SPROUTS
DRAWER!!
NO PLAN,
NO PROBLEM!
The deciding factor was what my friend (six years younger) said.
ME
DUN—!!
[redacted]@
THE SIZE OF YOUR FRIDGE IS THE SIZE OF YOUR LIFE!!
ME
[redacted]@

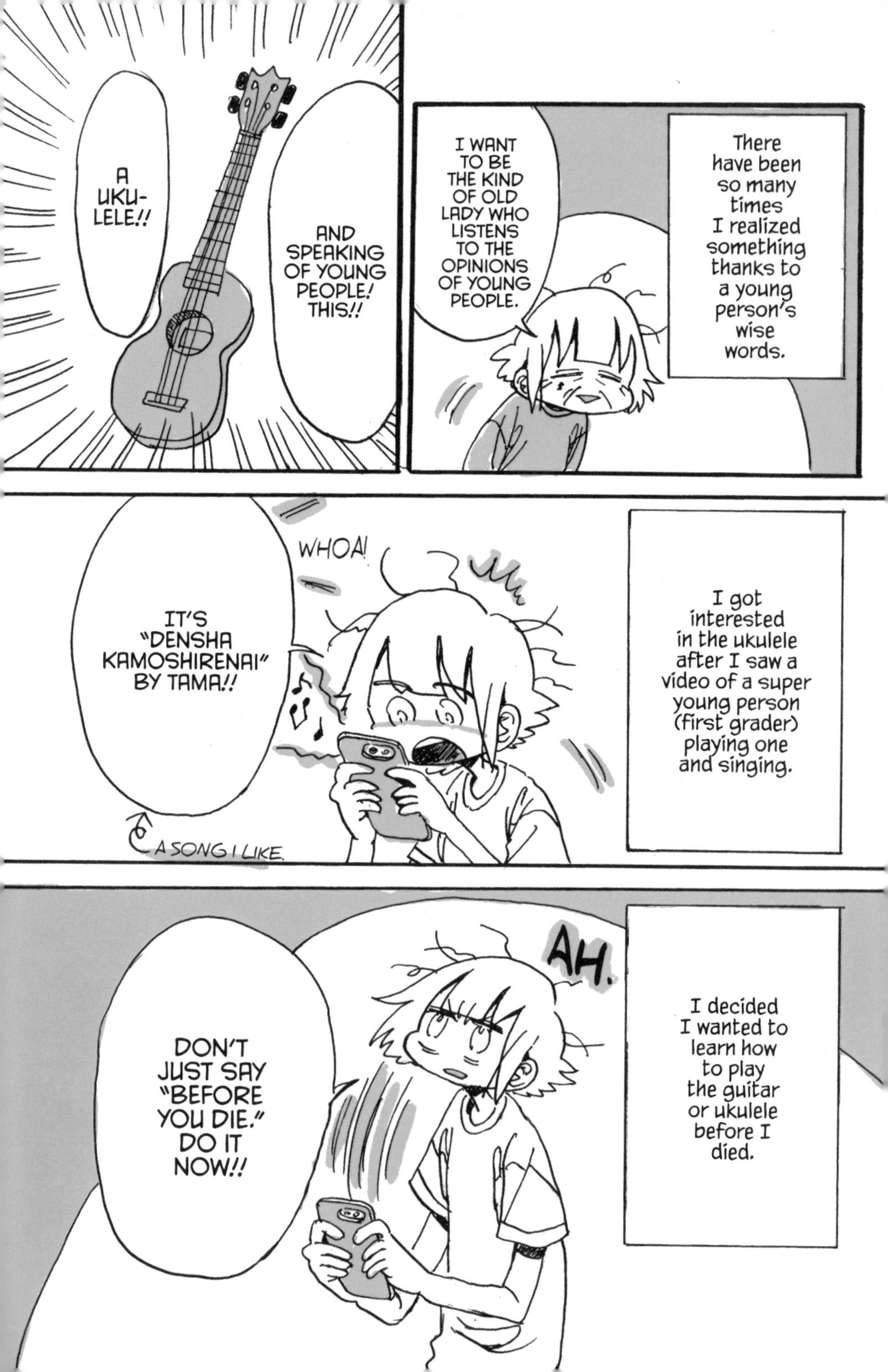
There have been so many times I realized something thanks to a young person's wise words.
I WANT TO BE THE KIND OF OLD LADY WHO LISTENS TO THE OPINIONS OF YOUNG PEOPLE.
AND SPEAKING OF YOUNG PEOPLE! THIS!!
A UKU-LELE!!
I got interested in the ukulele after I saw a video of a super young person (first grader) playing one and singing.
WHOA!
IT'S "DENSHA KAMOSHIRENAI" BY TAMA!!
A SONG I LIKE.
I decided I wanted to learn how to play the guitar or ukulele before I died.
AH.
DON'T JUST SAY "BEFORE YOU DIE." DO IT NOW!!

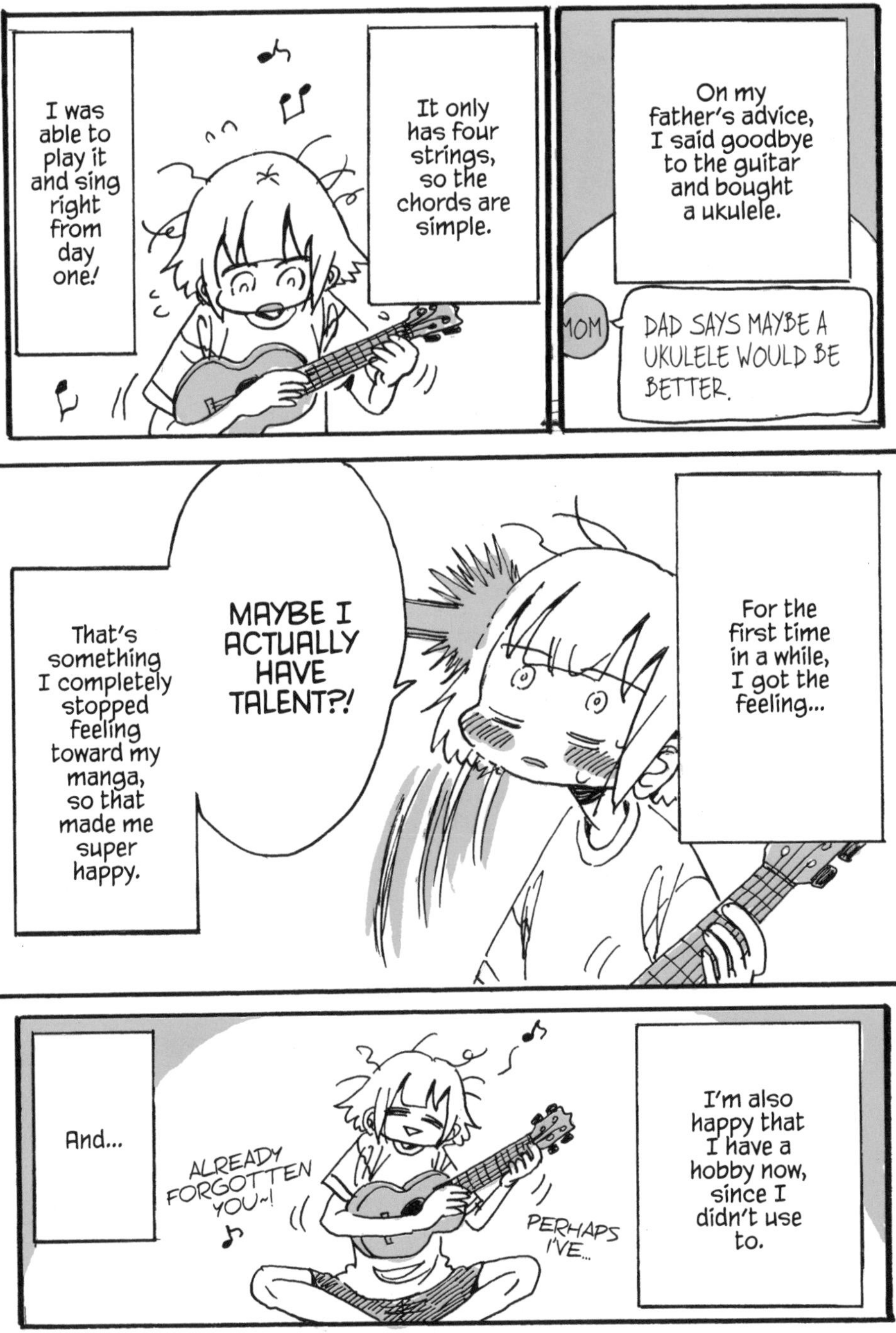
On my father's advice, I said goodbye to the guitar and bought a ukulele.
MOM
DAD SAYS MAYBE A UKULELE WOULD BE BETTER.
It only has four strings, so the chords are simple.
I was able to play it and sing right from day one!
For the first time in a while, I got the feeling...
MAYBE I ACTUALLY HAVE TALENT?!
That's something I completely stopped feeling toward my manga, so that made me super happy.
I'm also happy that I have a hobby now, since I didn't use to.
PERHAPS I'VE...
ALREADY FORGOTTEN YOU~!
And...

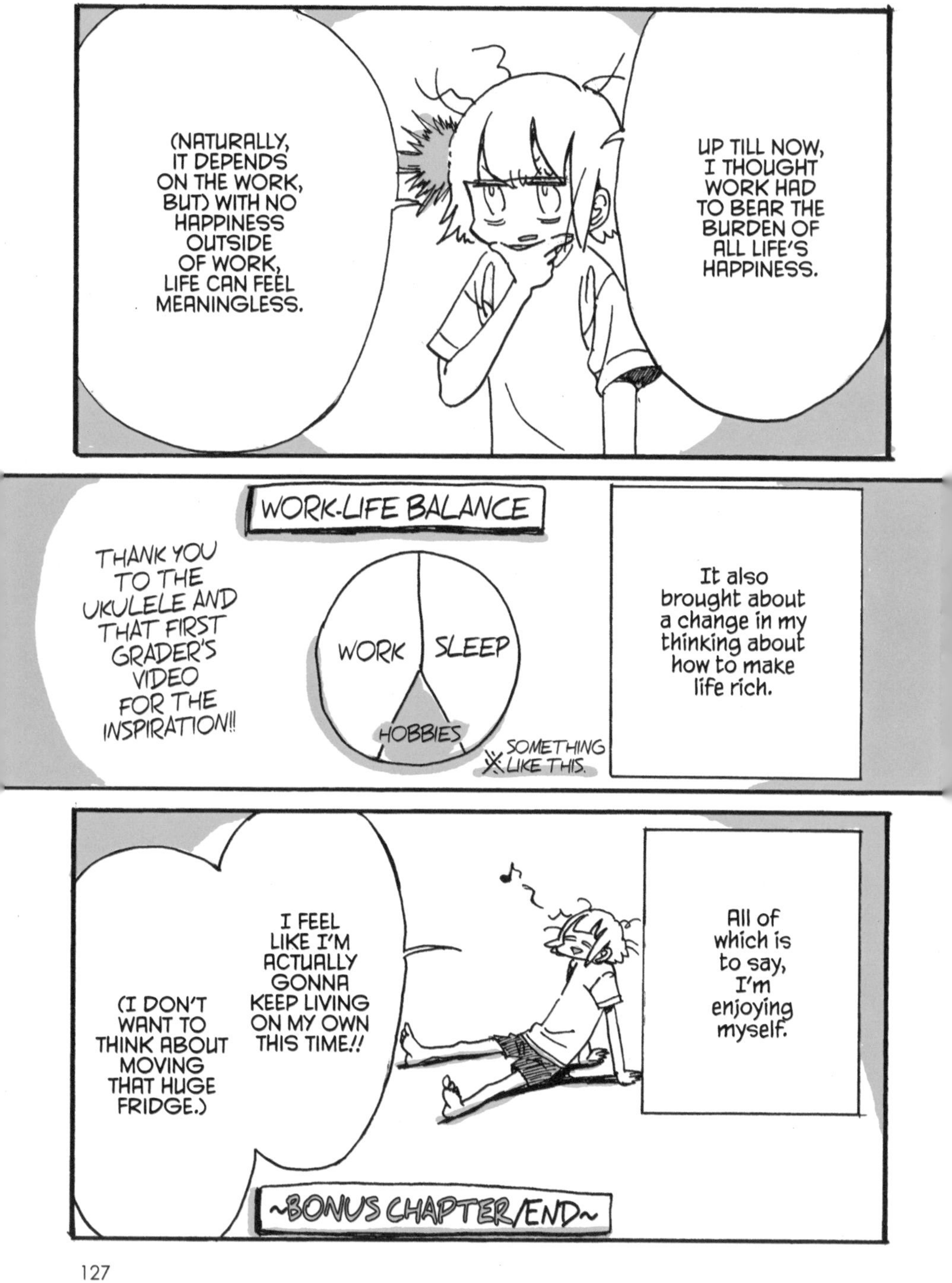
UP TILL NOW, I THOUGHT WORK HAD TO BEAR THE BURDEN OF ALL LIFE'S HAPPINESS.
(NATURALLY, IT DEPENDS ON THE WORK, BUT) WITH NO HAPPINESS OUTSIDE OF WORK, LIFE CAN FEEL MEANINGLESS.
It also brought about a change in my thinking about how to make life rich.
WORK-LIFE BALANCE
WORK
SLEEP
HOBBIES
※SOMETHING LIKE THIS.
THANK YOU TO THE UKULELE AND THAT FIRST GRADER'S VIDEO FOR THE INSPIRATION!!
All of which is to say, I'm enjoying myself.
I FEEL LIKE I'M ACTUALLY GONNA KEEP LIVING ON MY OWN THIS TIME!!
(I DON'T WANT TO THINK ABOUT MOVING THAT HUGE FRIDGE.)
~BONUS CHAPTER/END~

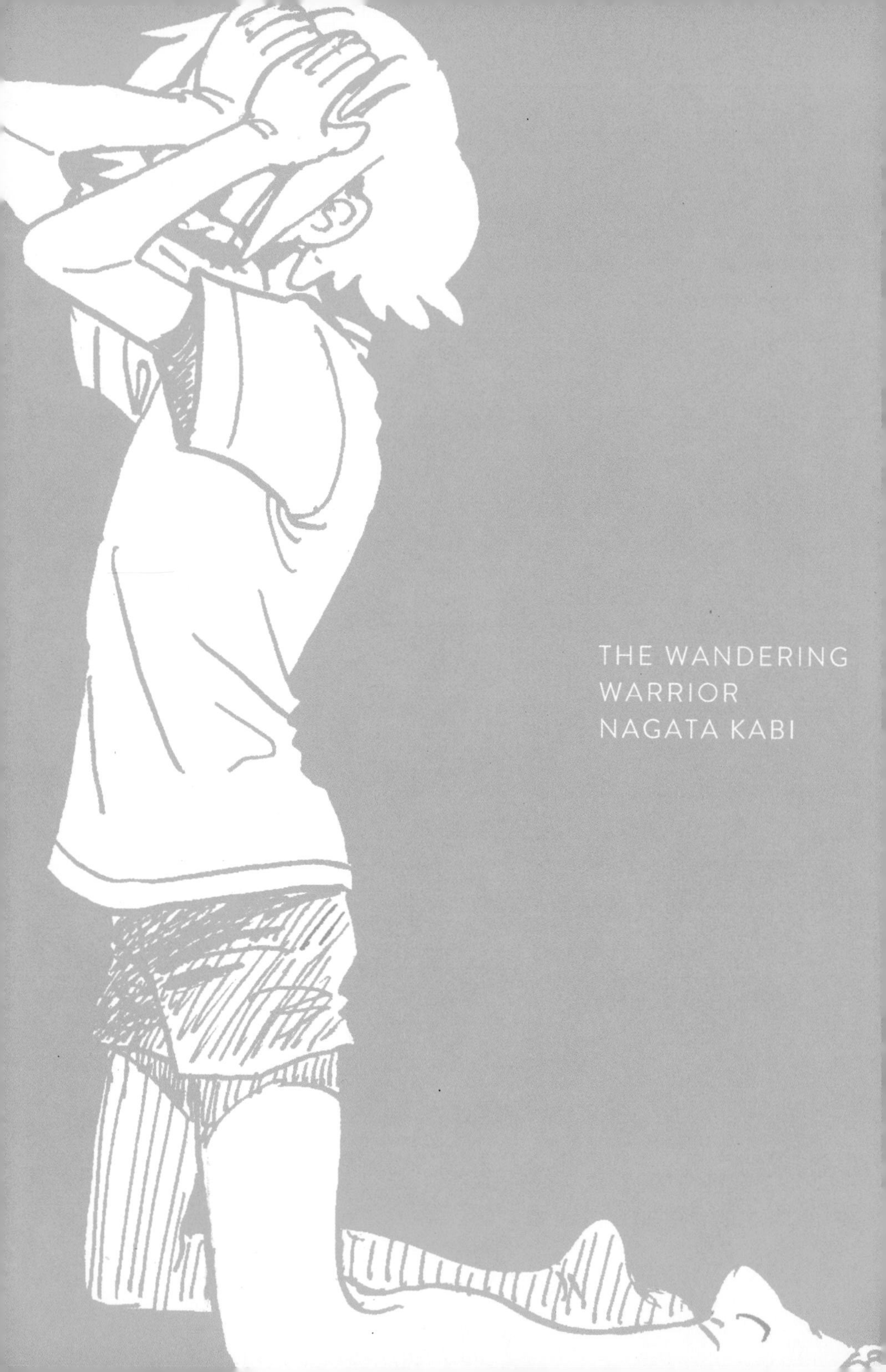

THE WANDERING WARRIOR

NAGATA KABI

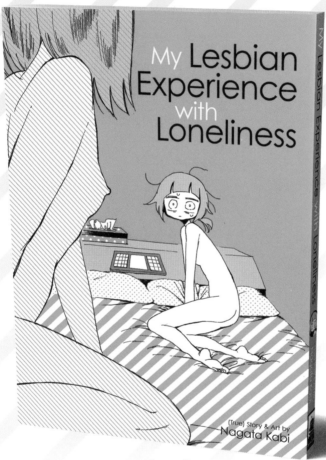

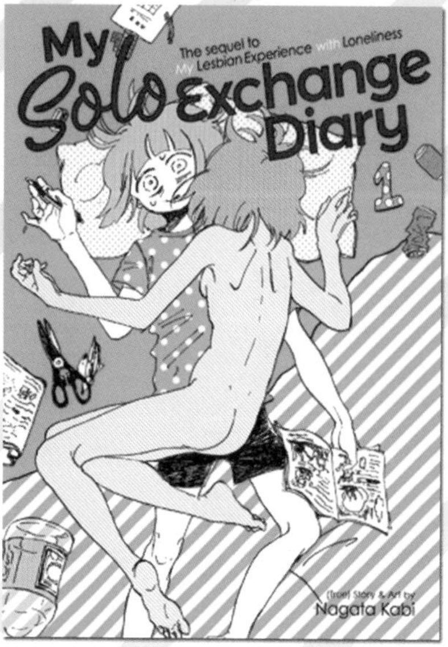
My Solo Exchange Diary
The sequel to My Lesbian Experience with Loneliness
1
(True) Story & Art by
Nagata Kabi

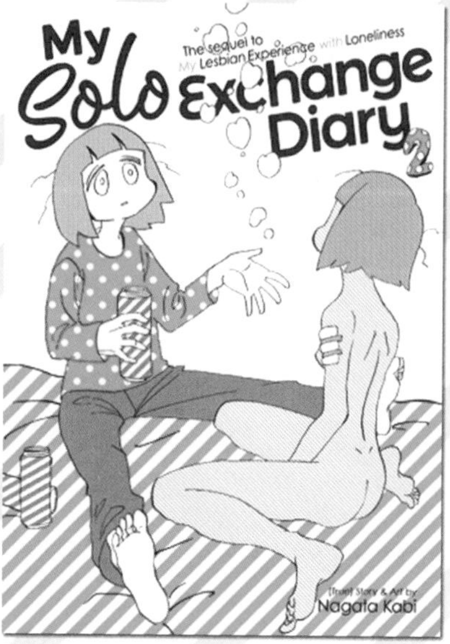
My Solo Exchange Diary
The sequel to My Lesbian Experience with Loneliness
2
(True) Story & Art by
Nagata Kabi

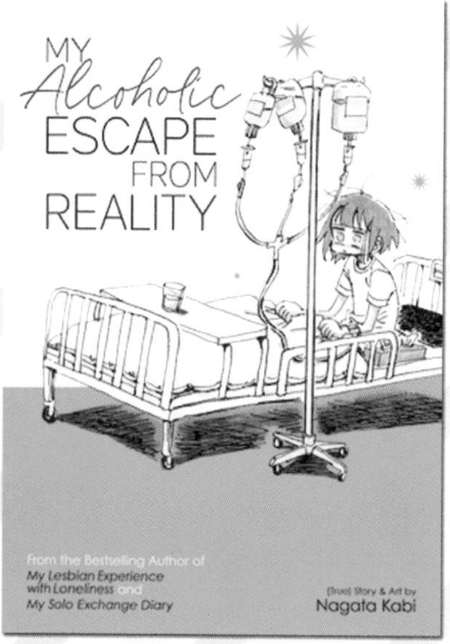
MY Alcoholic ESCAPE FROM REALITY
From the Bestselling Author of My Lesbian Experience with Loneliness and My Solo Exchange Diary
(True) Story & Art by
Nagata Kabi

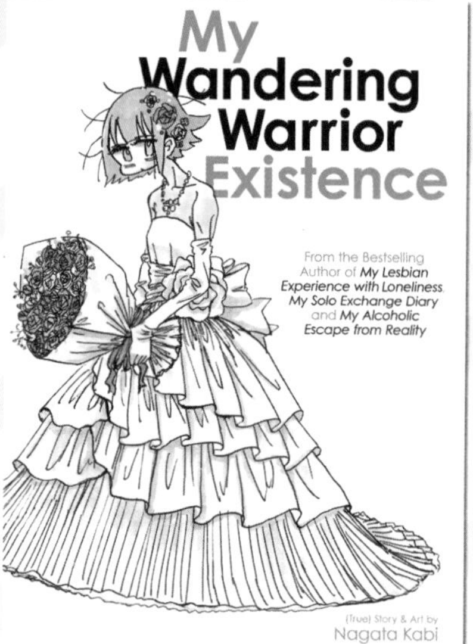
My Wandering Warrior Existence
From the Bestselling Author of My Lesbian Experience with Loneliness, My Solo Exchange Diary and My Alcoholic Escape from Reality
(True) Story & Art by
Nagata Kabi

My Solo Exchange Diary Vol. 1
ISBN: 978-1-626928-89-3

My Solo Exchange Diary Vol. 2
ISBN: 978-1-626929-99-9

My Alcoholic Escape from Reality
ISBN: 978-1-64505-999-8

My Wandering Warrior Existence
ISBN: 978-1-64827-882-2

The Works of

SEVEN SEAS ENTERTAINMENT PRESENTS

My Wandering Warrior Existence

(true) story & art by **NAGATA KABI**

TRANSLATION
Jocelyne Allen

LETTERING
Karis Page

COVER DESIGN
Nicky Lim

PROOFREADING
Danielle King
B. Lillian Martin

COPY EDITOR
Dawn Davis

SENIOR EDITOR
Jenn Grunigen

PREPRESS TECHNICIAN
Melanie Ujimori

PRINT MANAGER
Rhiannon Rasmussen-Silverstein

PRODUCTION MANAGER
Lissa Pattillo

EDITOR-IN-CHIEF
Julie Davis

ASSOCIATE PUBLISHER
Adam Arnold

PUBLISHER
Jason DeAngelis

First published by Futabasha Publishers Ltd., in 2020
English version published by Seven Seas Entertainment, LLC.

Seven Seas press and purchase enquiries can be sent to Marketing Manager Lianne Sentar at press@gomanga.com. Information regarding the distribution and purchase of digital editions is available from Digital Manager CK Russell at digital@gomanga.com.

ISBN: 978-1-64827-882-2
Printed in Canada
First Printing: March 2022
10 9 8 7 6 5 4 3 2 1

READING DIRECTIONS

This book reads from ***right to left***, Japanese style. If this is your first time reading manga, you start reading from the top right panel on each page and take it from there. If you get lost, just follow the numbered diagram here. It may seem backwards at first, but you'll get the hang of it! Have fun!!

1
2
3
4
5
6
7
8
9

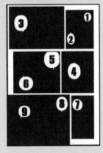